Changing [||||||] ns
for the K–12 Teacher
Workforce

Policies, Preservice Education, Professional Development, and the Workplace

Committee on Understanding the Changing Structure
of the K–12 Teacher Workforce

Robert Floden, Amy Stephens, Layne Scherer, *Editors*

Policy and Global Affairs

Board on Higher Education and Workforce

Division of Behavioral and Social Sciences and Education

Board on Science Education

A Consensus Study Report of

The National Academies of
SCIENCES · ENGINEERING · MEDICINE

THE NATIONAL ACADEMIES PRESS
Washington, DC
www.nap.edu

THE NATIONAL ACADEMIES PRESS   500 Fifth Street, NW   Washington, DC 20001

This activity was supported by contracts between the National Academy of Sciences and the William and Flora Hewlett Foundation (2018-7446). Any opinions, findings, conclusions, or recommendations expressed in this publication do not necessarily reflect the views of any organization or agency that provided support for the project.

International Standard Book Number-13:   978-0-309-49903-3
International Standard Book Number-10:   0-309-49903-8
Digital Object Identifier: https://doi.org/10.17226/25603
Library of Congress Control Number: 2020934597

Additional copies of this publication are available from the National Academies Press, 500 Fifth Street, NW, Keck 360, Washington, DC 20001; (800) 624-6242 or (202) 334-3313; http://www.nap.edu.

Printed in the United States of America

Suggested citation: National Academies of Sciences, Engineering, and Medicine. (2020). *Changing Expectations for the K–12 Teacher Workforce: Policies, Preservice Education, Professional Development, and the Workplace.* Washington, DC: The National Academies Press. https://doi.org/10.17226/25603.

The National Academies of
SCIENCES · ENGINEERING · MEDICINE

The **National Academy of Sciences** was established in 1863 by an Act of Congress, signed by President Lincoln, as a private, nongovernmental institution to advise the nation on issues related to science and technology. Members are elected by their peers for outstanding contributions to research. Dr. Marcia McNutt is president.

The **National Academy of Engineering** was established in 1964 under the charter of the National Academy of Sciences to bring the practices of engineering to advising the nation. Members are elected by their peers for extraordinary contributions to engineering. Dr. John L. Anderson is president.

The **National Academy of Medicine** (formerly the Institute of Medicine) was established in 1970 under the charter of the National Academy of Sciences to advise the nation on medical and health issues. Members are elected by their peers for distinguished contributions to medicine and health. Dr. Victor J. Dzau is president.

The three Academies work together as the **National Academies of Sciences, Engineering, and Medicine** to provide independent, objective analysis and advice to the nation and conduct other activities to solve complex problems and inform public policy decisions. The National Academies also encourage education and research, recognize outstanding contributions to knowledge, and increase public understanding in matters of science, engineering, and medicine.

Learn more about the National Academies of Sciences, Engineering, and Medicine at **www.nationalacademies.org**.

The National Academies of
SCIENCES · ENGINEERING · MEDICINE

Consensus Study Reports published by the National Academies of Sciences, Engineering, and Medicine document the evidence-based consensus on the study's statement of task by an authoring committee of experts. Reports typically include findings, conclusions, and recommendations based on information gathered by the committee and the committee's deliberations. Each report has been subjected to a rigorous and independent peer-review process and it represents the position of the National Academies on the statement of task.

Proceedings published by the National Academies of Sciences, Engineering, and Medicine chronicle the presentations and discussions at a workshop, symposium, or other event convened by the National Academies. The statements and opinions contained in proceedings are those of the participants and are not endorsed by other participants, the planning committee, or the National Academies.

For information about other products and activities of the National Academies, please visit www.nationalacademies.org/about/whatwedo.

Acknowledgments

This report would not have been possible without the many individuals who provided their expertise, including those who served on the committee as well as those who participated in discussions with the committee. We recognize their invaluable contributions to our work. The first thanks are to the committee members, for their passion, deep knowledge, and contributions to the study.

This report was made possible with support from the Hewlett Foundation. We particularly thank Kent McGuire (program director, Education) and Charmaine Mercer (program officer, Education).

Members of the committee benefited from discussion and presentation by many individuals who participated in our fact-finding meetings.

- At the first meeting, we had the opportunity to talk with our contacts at the Hewlett Foundation, Kent McGuire and Charmaine Mercer, to get further clarity on the statement of task. We also heard from Chad Alderman (Bellweather Education Partners), Heather Hill (Harvard Graduate School of Education), and Elena Silva (New America Foundation) who spoke to the varied perspectives on the K–12 teacher and school leader workforce.
- At the second meeting, the following topics were explored:
  - **Overview of the Landscape by States Focused on Licensure, Mobility, and Reciprocity.** Presenters included Stephanie Aragon (Education Commission of the States) and Elizabeth Ross (National Council on Teacher Quality).

      o   **Preparing Teachers in Light of Changing Expectations.** Present-
ers included Keffrelyn Brown (University of Texas at Austin),
Marybeth Gasman (University of Pennsylvania), and Cassandra
Herring (Branch Alliance for Educator Diversity).
      o   **Workforce Trends in the Professionalization of Teaching.** Pre-
senters included Mary Dilworth (Editor, *Millennial Teachers of
Color*) and James Wyckoff (University of Virginia).
- The third meeting included two panels:
      o   Panel 1 discussed **Innovation in Teacher Education,** including
Charles Hughes (University of Central Florida) and Elizabeth
van Es (University of California, Irvine).
      o   Panel 2 described **New Models and Evaluation.** Panelists in-
cluded Dan Coleman (Woodrow Wilson Academy of Teaching
and Learning) and Kevin Bastian (University of North Carolina
at Chapel Hill).
- At the last face-to-face meeting, the committee spoke with Marilyn
Cochran-Smith (Boston College) and Leslie Fenwick (Howard
University).

The committee is grateful for additional discussions with experts to include Richard Ingersoll (University of Pennsylvania), Lisa Dieker (University
of Central Florida), and Peter Laipson (Woodrow Wilson Graduate School
of Teaching & Learning). The committee is also appreciative of the efforts
of Rebecca Morgan, senior librarian for the Resource Center at the National Academies of Sciences, Engineering, and Medicine, who assisted the
committee in pulling together the relevant bodies of literature for review.

This Consensus Study Report was reviewed in draft form by individuals
chosen for their diverse perspectives and technical expertise. The purpose of
this independent review is to provide candid and critical comments that will
assist the National Academies in making each published report as sound as
possible and to ensure that it meets the institutional standards for quality,
objectivity, evidence, and responsiveness to the study charge. The review
comments and draft manuscript remain confidential to protect the integrity
of the deliberative process.

We thank the following individuals for their review of this report: Deborah
Lowenberg Ball, School of Education, University of Michigan; Robert Q.
Berry, Department of Mathematics, University of Virginia; Lisa Dieker,
TeachLivE™ and Lockheed Martin Mathematics and Science Academy/
University of Central Florida; Dessynie Edwards, Department of Educa-
tional Leadership, Curriculum and Instruction, Texas A&M University,
Corpus Christi; Michael J. Feuer, Graduate School of Education and Human
Development, The George Washington University; Susan Moore Johnson,
Graduate School of Education, Harvard University; Sarah S. Kavanagh,

Teaching, Learning, and Leadership Division, University of Pennsylvania; David Monk, College of Education, The Pennsylvania State University; and Kenneth Ziechner, Teacher Education (*emeritus*), University of Washington.

Although the reviewers listed above provided many constructive comments and suggestions, they were not asked to endorse the conclusions or recommendations of this report nor did they see the final draft before its release. The review of this report was overseen by Alan M. Lesgold, School of Education, University of Pittsburgh, and Bruce Alberts, Department of Biochemistry and Biophysics, University of California, San Francisco. They were responsible for making certain that an independent examination of this report was carried out in accordance with the standards of the National Academies and that all review comments were carefully considered. Responsibility for the final content of this report rests entirely with the authoring committee and the National Academies.

Thanks are also due to the project staff. Kenne Dibner, senior program officer, Board on Science Education (BOSE), provided expert guidance throughout the study. Alison Berger, senior program assistant, Board on Higher Education and Workforce (BHEW), managed the administrative tasks associated with getting the project started, as well as the first meeting's logistical and administrative needs. John Veras, senior program assistant with BHEW, managed the rest of the study's logistical and administrative needs, along with helping to see the report through publication. Tom Rudin, director, BHEW, and Heidi Schweingruber, director, BOSE, provided thoughtful advice and many helpful suggestions throughout the entire study.

Staff of the Division of Behavioral and Social Sciences and Education also provided help: Laura Elisabeth Yoder substantially improved the readability of the report; Kirsten Sampson Snyder expertly guided the report through the report review process; and Yvonne Wise masterfully guided the report through production.

Contents

xiii

Summary

The classroom teacher remains at the heart of American public schools and the success of schools hinges on the effectiveness of teachers in the classroom. Teaching involves connecting new learning experiences to the previous knowledge and experiences of the learner. Teachers need to understand who their students are, where they come from, and what previous ideas they are bringing into the classroom. Research over the past two decades confirms the critical role that teachers play in the success of their students both academically and with respect to longer term outcomes such as college attendance and lifetime income. Therefore, all teachers need to be prepared to recognize and leverage the various assets students bring into the classroom so that they can ensure the success of all students.

A number of shifts over the past two decades have impacted expectations for K–12 teachers. This report looks at three specific (although interrelated) aspects of K–12 that contribute to the demands on teachers: the policy context, an increasingly diverse student body, and the composition of the teacher workforce itself. First, the policy context has shifted such that teachers are increasingly required to attend to new curricular standards, participate in the selection and adaption of instructional materials while also being held accountable for student performance. Second, the diversity of the student population has rapidly changed such that a majority of students in U.S. K–12 schools identify as members of minoritized communities. As a result, teachers need to evaluate their teaching practices to ensure that they are creating classroom environments that are supportive for all learners. Finally, this report also examines the makeup of the teacher workforce itself. Together, these factors—to context and expectation alike—raise important questions about how teacher education—both preservice and inservice—may need to change to ensure teachers are able to meet new expectations and provide students with the kinds of classroom experiences that will put them on the path to future success.

At the request of the Hewlett Foundation, the Board on Higher Education and Workforce in collaboration with the Board on Science Education of the National Academies of Sciences, Engineering, and Medicine convened an expert committee to address these issues. The committee represented a diverse range of expertise and practice including a principal, state policy leaders, and researchers across academic disciplines (science, mathematics, and history) that explore issues related to preservice teacher preparation, inservice professional development, workforce conditions, and the analysis of teacher labor markets. The committee responded to questions grouped in three broad topics:

1. Impact of the changing landscape of K–12 education: How has the teacher workforce changed over the past 10–20 years? How have expectations of teachers changed over this same period? How might the teacher workforce change in the future?
2. Implications for preservice and inservice: What does the changing nature of the teacher workforce mean for the way higher education and other providers address K–12 teacher preservice and inservice education?
3. Taking preservice and inservice programs to scale: In light of the current and anticipated structural changes in the teacher workforce, how can effective models, programs, and practices for teacher education (including principles of deeper learning) be sustained and expanded?

In response to the charge, the committee explored the nature of the current teacher workforce and key changes in the landscape of K–12 education, examined models of preservice and inservice education, and identified factors involved in helping teachers become more effective.

TODAY'S CLASSROOMS AND EXPECTATIONS FOR TEACHERS

Overall, when examining the current composition of the national teacher workforce over the past 20 years, the committee did not find strong evidence of large changes despite national conversations that suggest a changing workforce. This difference in observed trends may be due in part to the shorter timeframe that the committee was charged to examine and the broader timeframes examined in the existing literature.

CONCLUSION 1: At the national level, the composition of the teacher workforce (e.g., distribution in gender, age, race and ethnicity, years of experience) has been relatively stable over the past 20 years.

Over the course of this study, the committee found, however, that what it means to be a teacher today—the expectations and demands placed upon teachers—has changed. This means that teachers must be adequately prepared to respond to these new demands and must experience workplace conditions and opportunities for professional development that are responsive to these changed expectations. The new demands include standards, learning approaches, student variability (including disability status), and equity.

The student population of America's public schools has grown substantially more diverse over the past two decades. This demographic change increases the demands on teachers as they strive to create supportive learning environments for children and youth from a broad range of backgrounds. Teachers are increasingly charged with ensuring that classrooms serve as equitable learning communities, fostering trusting and caring relationships among students and with teachers. They are also often called on to serve as a bridge between the school and families and communities.

In addition, the recent adoption of rigorous national content standards by many states raises the expectations for students' learning, which in turn raises expectations for instruction. These standards move from a focus on demonstrating understanding of concepts to asking students to demonstrate proficiency in disciplinary practices that require them to apply their knowledge to solve authentic problems. These increased expectations for learning, combined with the demand to create a responsive learning environment that supports the needs of diverse students, call for innovative approaches to instruction that may differ substantially from teachers' own experiences as students or their preservice education. The dual pressures of responding to new and more rigorous standards while working with a diverse student population are heightened by the accountability systems in place in many states. The committee concludes that:

CONCLUSION 2: There are more explicit demands placed upon K–12 teachers today. There continues to be an increase in the level of content and pedagogical knowledge expected of teachers to implement curriculum and instruction aligned to newer content standards and deeper learning goals. Teachers are called on to educate an increasingly diverse student body, to enact culturally responsive pedagogies, and to have a deeper understanding of their students' socioemotional growth. Integrating these various, layered expectations places substantially new demands on teachers.

CONCLUSION 3: The adoption of state standards and accountability systems has contributed to increased expectations for what teachers need to accomplish for all students in terms of achievement and content mastery.

THE TEACHER WORKFORCE

Teacher shortages, also described as staffing challenges, have been widely reported over the past few years. However, recent national-level data suggest declines in the number of individuals pursuing teaching degrees have slowed and, at least in some states, enrollment has begun to increase. More importantly, the long-term national trend (over the course of 30 years) is one of increased supply of potential teachers. In addition, although the overall national demographics of the teachers themselves has not changed substantially during this time, there have been some modest increases in the numbers of teachers of color entering the workforce.

However, the positive outlook conveyed in the national data may mask the dynamics of the labor markets at the state and local level. State policies determine teacher licensure, seniority, tenure, and pension rules, and these policies differ from one another in ways that can create barriers for cross-state teacher mobility. The strong state role in influencing teacher labor markets results in labor market conditions that vary from state to state and sometimes even from city to city. That said, a common finding across states is that staffing challenges are generally far greater for schools serving low-income students, low-achieving students, students of color, those geographically far from teacher education programs, and in high-needs areas, like science, technology, engineering, and mathematics subjects and special education. These are long-standing issues with the way the teacher labor market functions (or fails to function well) and merit greater attention.

The finding that labor market trends vary from state to state and even locally is also mirrored in teacher turnover. Turnover is substantially higher in the south than elsewhere, and turnover tends to be higher in cities than in suburbs or more rural areas. Moreover, teacher turnover is somewhat higher in schools where state tests scores are low and in schools that serve poverty-impacted communities and/or communities of color. These higher turnover rates have been attributed to lower-quality working conditions—such schools typically have less effective leaders, greater leadership churn, fewer resources, and less adequate facilities.

From these findings, the committee concludes that:

CONCLUSION 4: Teacher labor markets are quite localized. As a result, national statistics provide a limited understanding of the trends in the K–12 teacher workforce. Local labor markets are shaped by a

variety of factors including state rules and regulations regarding licensure, tenure, and pensions.

CONCLUSION 5: There is a mismatch between the areas of certification chosen by those preparing to be teachers and the areas in which schools and school systems struggle with teacher shortages. For example, there are often many more teacher candidates that are prepared with an elementary education credential than there are slots. At the same time, school systems often struggle to fill science, technology, engineering, and mathematics, and special education positions.

CONCLUSION 6: The current racial/ethnic composition of the teacher workforce does not mirror the racial/ethnic composition of students being served in schools today. The mismatch has grown larger over the past 20 years and is an artifact of both the rapidly changing student population and historical policy decisions connected to school desegregation efforts. There is good evidence that the discrepancy has negative consequences, particularly for underrepresented minority students who often lack teacher role models.

CONCLUSION 7: Students of color, students from low-income families, and students who are low-achieving more often are served by teachers who are less qualified. These inequities have been documented across states, districts, schools within districts, and even within schools.

TEACHER EDUCATION IN RESPONSE TO CHANGING EXPECTATIONS

Preservice and inservice education both play key roles in helping teachers respond to the changing conditions of K–12 education. Creating classroom learning experiences that respond to more rigorous content standards while promoting the success of all students regardless of background is no easy task. Responding to these dual demands is likely to require significant shifts in what teaching looks and sounds like in most U.S. classrooms. Moreover, given that teachers hone their instructional practices and develop their ways of relating to students and families in the context of daily work in schools, it is important to highlight that programs of teacher preparation and continuing professional development alone are insufficient to equip teachers to meet these expectations—teacher learning in the workplace is tantamount to teacher success.

Given the current evidence, it is difficult to identify specific program designs for preservice or inservice education that will definitively lead to changes in teachers' instructional practice or in students' learning. There is wide variation in preservice programs across the country, including online programs of teacher education. Over the past two decades, policy makers have supported new and flexible pathways into teaching while simultaneously moving to tighten the scrutiny of teacher education in institutions of higher education. And the overall data on preservice teacher education are limited. This presents a challenge for understanding the ways teachers are being prepared to meet the changes in the expectations of the classroom.

Similarly, inservice experiences for teachers vary widely, and there is disagreement in the research community about the strength of the evidence for effective design of professional development. Furthermore, the evidence suggests that inservice experiences alone are not sufficient for shaping teachers' instructional practice. Rather, what teachers do in their classrooms is shaped by the nature of the social relations, material resources, and organizational conditions of the schools and districts in which teachers work. To make substantial changes to current teachers' perspectives and practices will require significant and sustained opportunities for professional learning. Such opportunities encompass opportunities embedded in the school workplace as well as specially designed programs of professional development. A productive and large-scale response to new expectations for teaching and learning will likely depend on relationships established between external professional development providers and school leaders who are involved with overseeing local workplace conditions and learning opportunities. The committee concludes that:

> **CONCLUSION 8:** The current landscape of preservice teacher education in the United States exists as a large, varied array of programs and pathways. In this respect, it reflects the traditions of state and local control.

> **CONCLUSION 9:** There has been a significant growth over the past two decades in online teacher education and professional development, but very little is known about the efficacy of this increasingly prevalent mode of providing preservice and inservice education.

> **CONCLUSION 10:** The research base on preservice teacher preparation supplies little evidence about its impact on teacher candidates and their performance once they are in the classroom. Preservice programs in many states assess the performance of teacher candidates for purposes of licensure, but few states have developed data systems that link information about individual teacher's preservice experiences with other data about those teachers or their performance. Overall, it is difficult to assess the causal impact of teacher preparation programs.

CONCLUSION 11: Features of the school and district context in which teachers do their work matter greatly for teacher retention, for teachers' attitudes about their work, and for how teachers' preservice and inservice experiences translate into effective classroom instruction. Characteristics of the workplace matter for ensuring that teachers are equipped to respond to the changing expectations.

CONCLUSION 12: Induction supports for newly credentialed teachers are associated with reduced odds that teachers (a) leave the profession or (b) move schools within the first 5 years of teaching. Providing multiple supports increases the retention of teachers in the profession and reduces teacher migration in the first 5 years.

CONCLUSION 13: Based on nationally representative surveys, teachers report that they receive minimal opportunities to engage in professional development that are explicitly focused on supporting a broad and diverse student population (e.g., English learners, students who receive special education supports). Moreover, teachers report that when they do receive professional development focused on supporting specific student populations, it tends to be disconnected from the subject matter they teach.

CONCLUSION 14: There is mixed evidence about the impact of professional development on student outcomes. There is better evidence that inservice, content-specific professional development programs with the following characteristics can have a positive impact on student learning:

- work on instructional strategies is specific to the content area;
- professional development is organized around the actual instructional material teachers use;
- teachers participate with colleagues from their own school; and
- opportunities are built into the professional development sessions to discuss how to adapt the focus to teachers' local needs.

The amount and frequency of professional development are not necessarily related to student learning outcomes; the impact depends on the quality of the professional development.

Although reports from the National Academies often provide explicit recommendations to the field, the committee notes that due to a number of different concerns, it declines to prescribe specific actions for education stakeholders to pursue. However, the committee feels strongly that there are areas that require immediate attention if the U.S. teacher workforce is to meet changing expectations. The committee identifies four high-priority issues:

1. preparing teachers to meet changing expectations;
2. diversifying the teacher workforce;
3. ensuring the equitable distribution of teachers; and
4. mapping teacher preparation to teacher and student outcomes.

Within each of these issues, the committee offers a set of considerations that policy makers and others should attend to in order to make decisions for their specific contexts. The report also concludes with a research agenda for the scholarly community to pursue.

1

Introduction

The American public continues to rely on classroom teachers to perform the work of educating youth. Indeed, the function and success of American schools hinge on the effectiveness of the teachers in its classrooms. But what precisely is the work of teachers supposed to accomplish? Debates about the goals of public schooling have raged since the advent of compulsory education, and embedded in those conflicts are a series of unresolved assumptions about how to effectively prepare teachers to do their jobs. At a high level, there is agreement that teachers ought to help students in knowledge acquisition, and most would likely agree they should also help with broader civic and social goals, such as preparing students for empathic and engaged civic participation in a diverse democracy. But how, precisely, these types of outcomes should be measured is a topic that often gives rise to disagreement. Further, given the realities that the population of public school students continues to become increasingly diverse, and given that expectations surrounding what those students should be able to do upon leaving school have changed, another set of fundamental questions remain: Has the teaching workforce kept up with these changes? What do these changing student demographics and expectations mean for the substance of teachers' work?

Concurrently, the policy context in which teachers do their work has shifted dramatically in the past several decades. Teachers are increasingly thrust into a complicated policy matrix that includes new curricular standards, protocols for instructional materials selection, and increased accountability for student performance. Teachers are expected to demonstrate student achievement at the levels mandated by standards regardless of the level of funding and resources at their disposal.

Given this increasingly complicated policy and practice landscape, what can be done to support and prepare teachers in their complex and critical work? What are the best ways to grow and retain a dynamic and responsive teacher workforce that is capable of meeting society's demands for the future? Sponsored by the Hewlett Foundation, this report directly addresses these questions in order to shine a light on a pathway toward developing a teacher workforce that meets the needs of American public schools. This report investigates the tensions inherent in contemporary expectations for teachers and highlights promising practices and pedagogies for supporting teachers across their professional lifespan.

CHARGE TO THE COMMITTEE

The Board on Higher Education and Workforce of the National Academies of Sciences, Engineering, and Medicine, in collaboration with the Board on Science Education, convened an expert committee to examine the K–12 teacher workforce over the past 10 to 20 years and to identify emerging trends that will continue to shift the preservice and inservice needs and experiences of the teacher workforce in the next 10 to 20 years (see Box 1-1). The committee members represented a diverse range of expertise and practice including a principal, state policy leaders, and researchers across academic disciplines (science, mathematics, and history) who explore issues related to preservice teacher preparation, inservice professional development, and teacher labor markets.

STUDY APPROACH

The committee met five times over an 8-month period in 2018 and 2019 to gather information about a number of issues that have affected and defined the landscape of the teacher workforce over the past 20 years, including changing expectations for teaching and learning. The committee also considered the implications of such changes for teacher education including preservice experiences, induction, and inservice professional learning opportunities. In doing its work, the committee reviewed the published literature pertaining to its charge and engaged with many experts.

Study Process

The committee spent a great deal of time discussing the charge and the best ways to respond to it. Evidence was gathered from presentations

BOX 1-1
Statement of Task

An ad hoc committee under the auspices of the Board on Higher Education and Workforce and the Board on Science Education will conduct a 15-month fast-track study of the changing structure of the K–12 teacher workforce and the implications of such change for teacher preservice and inservice education. The study will examine a number of issues within three research questions:

1. The Landscape of K–12 Education: How have the demographics of the K–12 teacher workforce changed over the past 10 to 20 years? How have the expectations of K–12 education shifted, in terms of the knowledge and skills students are expected to develop, and how are those changes reflected in the expectations of teachers? What do the current workforce demographics and expectations of the teacher workforce suggest about how the future workforce will change?
2. The Implications of the Changing Landscape for Preservice and In-Service Teacher Education: What does the changing nature of the teacher workforce mean for the way higher education and other providers address K–12 teacher preservice and inservice education? These changes may include the effects of requirements and credentials for teachers, teacher evaluation, incentive and salary structures, teacher mobility, teacher career structures, demographic composition, recruitment and retention, and the effect of education standards.
3. Taking Teacher Education Programs and Practices to Scale: In light of the current and anticipated structural changes in the teacher workforce, how can effective models, programs, and practices for teacher education (including principles from deeper learning) be sustained and expanded?

and a review of the existing literature (including peer-reviewed materials, book chapters, reports, working papers, government documents, white papers and evaluations, and editorials) over the past 20 years. This material also included previous reports by the National Academies (see Box 1-2). The committee was charged with considering the past 20 years. In some instances, however, it was necessary to consider a longer time period in order to understand a particular workforce trend. In such cases, the committee then specified a modified period of interest and a rationale for the decision.

The committee searched for information on the teacher workforce as related to shifts (changes, innovations, or trends) in teacher performance outcomes (expectations, skills, or knowledge) that occur during preservice teacher education or inservice professional development. As part of the search, the committee examined interventions related to a number of

---

BOX 1-2
Previous Relevant Reports by the National Academies of Sciences, Engineering, and Medicine

Previous consensus studies and other activities by the National Academies have addressed similar issues since 2010, when the National Research Council (NRC) report *Preparing Teachers: Building Evidence for Sound Policy* was published. This report recommended the development of a national education data network that would integrate existing information on and expand new data in light of limited data on K–12 teacher preparation. *Monitoring Progress Toward Successful K–12 STEM Education: A Nation Advancing?* (NRC, 2013) described 14 indicators—including students' access to quality learning, educator's capacity, and policy and funding initiatives—to track progress in K–12 science, technology, engineering, and mathematics (STEM) education.

A number of reports in the past 5 years have focused more explicitly on the needs and roles of the teacher, in particular in the STEM fields. For example, in June 2014, the NRC hosted a convocation that focused on empowering teachers to play greater leadership roles in education policy and decision making in STEM education at the national, state, and local levels (see *Exploring Opportunities for STEM Teacher Leadership: Summary of a Convocation* [NRC, 2014]). *Science Teachers' Learning: Enhancing Opportunities, Creating Supportive Contexts* (NRC, 2015) noted that teachers have the responsibility of applying the standards in the classroom and as such there was a need for strengthening K–12 science teachers' professional learning to support the implementation of rigorous content standards. This was further articulated in the report *Science and Engineering for Grades 6–12: Investigation and Design at the Center* (National Academies of Sciences, Engineering, and Education [NASEM], 2019). Recent reports have also focused on pedagogical shifts in response to changing student demographics (*English Learners in STEM Subjects: Transforming Classrooms, Schools, and Lives* [NASEM, 2018a]) and an increased recognition of the role of culture in shaping how people learn (*How People Learn II: Learners, Contexts, and Cultures* [NASEM, 2018b]).

---

different labor market factors including requirements, credentials, incentives, salaries, mobility, recruitment, retention, or standards. In reviewing the evidence, many different types of studies were included: meta-analyses and reviews, qualitative case studies, ethnographic and field studies, interview studies, and a few large-scale studies.

Throughout the study, members of the committee benefited from discussion and presentations by a number of individuals who participated in the fact-finding meetings. At the first meeting, the committee had an opportunity to speak with the sponsors to ask questions and get clarity on the statement of task. In particular, the committee wanted to better understand the sponsor's stance on deeper learning and changes in the expectations of teachers (see Chapter 3). It was through this dialogue that the committee was able to begin to develop a common language for what was meant by deeper learning (see Chapter 3 for a discussion of the term). The committee also had the opportunity to hear more about different perspectives on the K–12 teacher workforce from various experts in the field.

During the second meeting, the presentations addressed the first question in the statement of task by providing an overview of the national landscape. In particular, speakers focused on the variability of state-level issues including licensure, mobility, and reciprocity; the preparation of teachers for the changing expectations in K–12 education; and issues surrounding workforce trends in the professionalization of teaching.

During the third meeting, the committee focused on innovations in teacher education and new models and evaluation in teacher education. At the fourth meeting, the committee heard about new graduate schools of education and the historical context that in part led to shortages in teachers of color within the teacher workforce. In between meetings, the committee also had in-depth conversations with leading experts in the field to ensure that as much available evidence as possible was considered as it relates to the statement of work.

At the fifth meeting, the committee reviewed the current draft of the report to ensure that there was sufficient evidence for the claims being made. As appropriate, throughout the report, the type of research reviewed and the strength of that evidence is clearly articulated. The majority of this meeting was devoted to discussing the conclusions, recommendations, and research agenda to reach consensus. During these discussions, the committee was careful to qualify and temper the conclusions and subsequent recommendations (or lack thereof), given the type and strength of the evidence presented.

Assumptions, Key Concepts, and Challenges

The committee faced a number of challenges throughout the study. They grappled particularly with a number of terms and assumptions they viewed as implicit in the statement of task. For example, the third question begins with the phrase, "in light of the current and anticipated changes in the teacher workforce . . . ." The committee interpreted this as an implicit assumption that there have been changes to the teacher workforce, and that these changes necessitate a corresponding shift in what preservice teacher preparation programs should provide. Over the course of the study, it became clear that there have been changes in the demographics of students in the demands placed upon teachers. However, at a national level, the makeup of the teacher workforce has remained relatively stable. This is in contrast to the underlying assumption within the charge and has consequences for the conclusions the committee was able to reach.

The committee also grappled with some key terms and ways in which to conceptualize teacher education. For example, the degree to which teacher education can be described in stages (i.e., preservice, early careers, and experienced) is complicated by the reality that there is no clear demarcation. And unpacking what happens at each of these different stages adds to the complexity. That is, there is a large and varied array of programs and pathways into teaching as well as variability in the inservice education that teachers receive.

The committee also considered the definition of deeper learning and its emerging role in K–12 education. As discussed in Chapter 3, greater attention has been placed on deeper learning. That is, over the past decade much attention has been paid to "21st century skills"—those skills that have been identified to contribute to success—and to "deeper learning" as a mechanism by which these skills and deep conceptual understanding are achieved. The ways deeper learning has been conceptualized and framed in new content standards is articulated in that chapter.

The committee noted that while it is commonplace to distinguish between "traditional" and "alternative" programs and pathways it is a distinction that defies precise definition. The 2010 National Research Council (NRC) report *Preparing Teachers* concluded that the variations within and across the two categories rendered the labels too complex to be useful (see p. 13). For the purposes of the present report, what constitutes as "alternative route" is defined by each state (U.S. Department of Education, 2019), which includes college- and university-based teacher education programs (see Chapter 4 for more discussion).

The committee recognized the importance of the teacher educator workforce and looked for evidence related to the makeup of this workforce. That is, the committee looked for what pipelines exist for teacher educators, how they are prepared, how they are supported, and their access to curricular resources. The committee noted that the most recent data on teacher educators were collected and disseminated by the American Association of Colleges for Teacher Education in 2018. However, the data dealt with faculty in colleges of education, not specifically teacher educators; as such, the committee was unable to address questions related to this important piece of the teacher education workforce.

Lastly, the committee also considered what it would mean to take programs and practices to scale. The committee examined the current state of the evidence for teacher education and concluded that the evidence is relatively limited for preservice teacher education programs (see Chapter 5) and is more robust for inservice professional development (PD), but remains mixed (see Chapter 6 as it relates to PD that occurs outside of the workplace and Chapter 7 for job-embedded PD). Moreover, the committee investigated trends in the national labor market and observed that aggregated national statistics mask what is happening regionally. This gave rise to the conclusion that there is no national teacher labor market. Chapter 4 makes a strong case for this claim through the examination of policies and practices that give rise to what is happening in schools, districts, and states. Furthermore, with the changes in expectations for K–12 teachers (see Chapter 3), the committee found that there was disagreement on what kinds of outcomes should matter and how these are linked with policy and programming in teacher education and programming. Taken together, the committee found it challenging to specify a uniform course of action for taking programs and practices to scale. Instead the committee chose to identify areas of additional research that could get the field closer to understanding how to take programs to scale.

Major Data Sources

To study how the state of education in the United States has changed, data from several large national databases as well as the extant literature was examined. The major sources of data are listed below.

Schools and Staffing Survey[1]

The Schools and Staffing Survey (SASS) was conducted by the National Center for Education Statistics (NCES) seven times between 1987 through 2011. SASS was designed to provide descriptive data regarding the context of elementary and secondary education by investigating public and private school districts, schools, principals, and teachers. As a large and comprehensive source of data, SASS covered a wide range of areas including teacher demand, teacher and principal characteristics, general conditions in schools, principals' and teachers' perceptions of school climate and problems in their schools, teacher compensation, district hiring and retention practices, and basic characteristics of the student population.

National Teacher and Principal Survey[2]

After 2010–2011, NCES redesigned SASS and termed it the National Teacher and Principal Survey (NTPS) to reflect the tool's new emphasis on the teacher and principal labor market as well as on the state of K–12

---

[1] For additional information, see https://nces.ed.gov/surveys/sass.
[2] For additional information, see https://nces.ed.gov/surveys/ntps.

school staff. NTPS, which was first conducted by NCES in 2015 to 2016, is a system of related questionnaires that provide descriptive data on the context of public elementary and secondary education while also providing policy makers with a variety of statistics on the condition of education in the United States. By focusing on flexibility, timeliness, and integration with other education data, the NTPS system allows for the characteristics of principals, teachers, and students to be analyzed in detail.

However, there are a number of limitations to this data source including: (1) reporting standards are not met for many of the demographic variables in various data collection years; (2) there are no school-level data listed for teachers from Hawaiian/Pacific Islander or American Indian/Alaska Native backgrounds, and there are between 8 and 11 school-level characteristics missing for teachers from Latino, Black, Asian, and White backgrounds, per racial/ethnic group; (3) only a few teachers are sampled in any school; (4) professional development items have been dropped from the survey; and (5) classroom process variables are not connected to student achievement and/or attainment variables.

Civil Rights Data Collection, Office of Special Education Programs (OSEP) Annual Report to Congress, and Common Core of Data[3]

Because national data on the extent to which individual students' teachers are fully certified (and the characteristics of those students) are not currently available in comparable specifications or across all states, school-level data from the Civil Rights Data Collection (CRDC) and the NCES Common Core of Data (CCD) were used to determine the degree to which schools with high proportions of certain types of students and schools located in rural and urban areas have teachers who are not fully certified. More specifically, CRDC data were used for the 2011–2012 and 2013–2014 school years to determine the number of teachers overall and the numbers of teachers who are not certified, total student enrollment, student enrollment by race and ethnicity, and enrollment of English learners (ELs). The characteristics of students with disabilities were available in the 2018 OSEP Annual Report to Congress. The committee combined these data with CCD data for the same year on numbers of students eligible for free or reduced-price lunch and enrollment in rural and urban schools.

The quality of the data depends on accurate collection and reporting by participating districts via district superintendents, or the superintendents' designees, who certify the CRDC submissions, inconsistencies may exist in

---

[3]For additional information, see https://ocrdata.ed.gov.

the data file. That is, outliers (as well as null or missing data) in the dataset may be a function of districts misreporting data.

REPORT ORGANIZATION

The committee was charged with describing the changing landscape of K–12 education, exploring the implications of such changes for preservice and inservice teacher education, and providing guidance on how to take programs to scale. Chapter 2 gives an overview of the broader landscape, first sketching the current demographics of teachers and then exploring other facets of K–12 education: the importance of a diverse teacher workforce, increasing diversity in the student population, how federal policies have contributed to an emphasis on accountability and student achievement, and changes to national content areas standards.

Chapter 3 focuses on many of the questions within the first bullet of the charge. It provides a closer look at how deeper learning has been articulated within disciplinary guidance documents and standards. It also examines changing expectations for teachers in light of changing expectation for student learning and ensuring teachers are equipped to teach in an increasingly diverse classroom.

Chapter 4 delves into the trends observed in the teacher labor market. The chapter begins with a presentation of the current state of the labor market, including teacher supply and demand, the long-standing labor market misalignment, pathways into the profession, and localness of teacher labor markets. It then describes other factors that have implications for the workforce, including teacher mobility, the equitable distribution of teachers, working conditions, teacher evaluation, pay, constraints, and desirability of the teaching profession.

Chapters 5, 6, and 7 address the remaining aspects of the charge. Chapter 5 describes the landscape of preservice teacher education, highlighting the variety of preparation programs and illustrating the varied ways in which teacher candidates are prepared to teach to meet the changing expectations of the K–12 classroom. Chapter 6 describes the landscape of inservice professional development, including the proliferation of professional development programs and providers, emerging forms of professional development, and how these experiences contribute to teacher learning and student outcomes. Chapter 7 describes the ways in which workplace conditions, including job-embedded professional learning opportunities that have implications for the support and retention of teachers.

Chapter 8 presents the consensus conclusions and high-priority issues for action that are derived from the evidence provided in the earlier chapters, and articulates an agenda for future research.

REFERENCES

National Academies of Science, Engineering, and Medicine. (NASEM). (2018a). *English Learners in STEM Subjects: Transforming Classrooms, Schools, and Lives.* Washington, DC: The National Academies Press.

_____. (2018b). *How People Learn II: Learners, Contexts, and Cultures.* Washington, DC: The National Academies Press.

_____. (2019). *Science and Engineering for Grades 6–12: Investigation and Design at the Center.* Washington, DC: The National Academies Press.

National Research Council. (NRC). (2010). *Preparing Teachers: Building Evidence for Sound Policy.* Washington, DC: The National Academies Press.

_____. (2013). *Monitoring Progress Toward Successful K–12 STEM Education: A Nation Advancing?* Washington, DC: The National Academies Press.

_____. (2014). *Exploring Opportunities for STEM Teacher Leadership: Summary of a Convocation.* Washington, DC: The National Academies Press.

_____. (2015). *Science Teachers' Learning: Enhancing Opportunities, Creating Supportive Contexts.* Washington, DC: The National Academies Press.

U.S. Department of Education. (2019) *Title II Tips for Reporting.* Available: https://title2.ed.gov/public/TA/FAQ.pdf.

2

Contextual Factors That Shape the Current Teacher Workforce

Changes to the national landscape of K–12 education over the past 20 years have shaped both the needs and dynamic nature of the current teacher workforce. Chief among these changes are revisions to federal policy, new rigorous national content standards, and an increasingly diverse student population (including, e.g., race and ethnicity, culture, spoken language, disability). In this chapter, the committee provides an overview of these key changes and lays the groundwork for the next chapter's closer look at how these changes in policy, standards, and increasing emphasis on classroom inclusion give rise to changes in expectations for teaching. The chapter begins by giving a clear picture of the current demographics of the teacher workforce. This discussion of teacher demographics is followed by an exploration of the makeup of the student population, including students who vary with respect to the home language and cultures they represent, their linguistic proficiency, socioeconomic status, and disability status. The increasing diversity of the classroom in terms of student demographics has outpaced the changes in the demographics of teachers, resulting in a deepening mismatch between the makeup of the teacher workforce and the student population in public schools. The chapter concludes with a discussion of changes in federal legislation related to elementary and secondary education since 2000. We explain how the recent (voluntary) adoption and implementation of more rigorous national content standards by some states has increased the expectations for both students and teachers.

DEMOGRAPHICS OF THE TEACHER WORKFORCE

Before looking at factors that impact the work teachers do in the classroom, it is important to understand the current demographics of the teacher workforce. In this section, the committee presents demographic data on the current teacher workforce and discusses the relationship between these demographic characteristics and those of the population of K–12 public school students.[1] We draw on the latest available nationally representative data on the trends in the K–12 teaching profession: the 2011–2012 Schools and Staffing Survey (SASS) and the 2015–2016 National Teacher and Principal Survey (NTPS).[2]

In fall 2017, there were approximately 3.8 million full-time-equivalent public school elementary and secondary teachers in the country (McFarland et al., 2019). The majority of these K–12 teachers were White (80.1%), and the majority were women (76.6% of K–12 teachers in 2015). To contextualize the low proportion of Black teachers in the workforce, Box 2-1 unpacks the notable historical context including school desegregation. Moreover, it should be noted that the committee was unable to find data related to the number of teachers with disabilities; that is, there are no data systems at the local, state, or national level that provide the number of teachers who identify themselves as having a disability.

Changes Over Time

Notably, the demographic makeup of the teacher workforce has undergone relatively small changes over the past 20 years (see Table 2-1). For example, as will be described in the subsequent section, the percentage of White teachers in 2003 was roughly 83 percent and fell to 80 percent by 2016. This is somewhat contrary to other notable claims in the field that have suggested bigger changes in the workforce (e.g., Ingersoll et al., 2018). However, the changes are more pronounced going back 30 years to 1987 where White teachers comprised 88 percent of the total workforce.

Race and Ethnicity[3]

Data in Table 2-1 show that the number of Black teachers has remained relatively steady over the past 20 years, whereas there has been an

---

[1] All demographic data about the U.S. teacher workforce population cited in this chapter are from Goldring et al. (2013) and Taie and Goldring (2017), unless otherwise noted.

[2] The 2015–2016 NTPS is a redesign and replacement of the SASS, which has served as one of the key sources of nationally representative data on a range of important education topics since the 1987–1988 school year.

[3] When reporting the race and ethnicity demographics, the committee uses the nomenclature from the studies described throughout the report and recognizes that this leads to inconsistencies in reporting.

BOX 2-1
Impact of School Desegregation for Black Teachers

The low proportion of Black teachers in the workforce is a cause of concern, and there are several factors that may be contributing to this trend. One potential cause is the long-term impact of school desegregation in the 1960s and 1970s, following the landmark case Brown v. Board of Education in 1954, passage of the Civil Rights Acts (CRA) in 1964, and the federal desegregation guidelines of 1966. Notably, while the Brown decision and subsequent legislation and regulations sought to protect Black students, there were no provisions to prevent the displacement of Black educators.

A small number of studies take an empirical look at the impact of desegregation on employment of Black teachers. In general, they find that the impact of desegregation varied by region. In the South, the number of Black teachers dropped significantly, whereas in the non-South, employment of Black teachers increased slightly.

In a study focused on staffing of elementary schools over the period from 1970 to 2000, Oakley et al. (2009) examined mandated desegregation in metropolitan areas across the country. They looked separately at trends from 1970 to 1990 and from 1990 to 2000. Results looking at metropolitan areas across the country overall show that greater segregation of White and Black students was associated with larger proportions of Black teachers. The authors suggest this is likely due to employment of Black teachers in schools with large populations of Black students. Further, mandated desegregation has a small, positive correlation with decreases in the proportion of Black teachers. The trends from 1990 to 2000 look different, whereas increases in the number of Black students overall are significantly related to the proportion of Black teachers; patterns of segregation or desegregation are not related to changes in the Black teaching force.

These overall results mask important regional trends. In the South from 1970 to 1990, there was a significant relationship between court-mandated desegregation and decreases in the number of Black teachers. In the non-South, in contrast, mandated desegregation appears to be linked to an increase in the proportion of Black teachers.

Another study, focused only on the South, documented similar trends (Thompson, 2019). The study drew on archival data from 781 southern school districts between 1964 and 1972 as well as data from the 1960 and 1970 Decennial Censuses. The author found that the desegregation process following the CRA led to reductions in the employment of Black teachers in the south and that southern school districts both increased recruitment of white teachers following the loss of Black teachers, or reduced the number of teachers employed overall. Furthermore, approximately one-half of the Black teachers who left teaching jobs entered other, lower skilled professions in the South. The other half migrated out of the region to continue or to pursue teaching. The author stresses that these impacts on Black teachers were the result of how desegregation was implemented in these districts. These results suggest that, as for many aspects of the teacher workforce, the impact of desegregation varies by region.

That said, the causes of the current lack of Black teachers are complex and likely not solely due to the historical impact of desegregation. Other factors may include increased access to other career opportunities, biases in the competency testing used for certification, and dissatisfaction with the teaching profession.

TABLE 2-1 Teacher Workforce Demographics from 1987 to 2016 in Percentages of Total Workforce, by Demographic Characteristic

	1987–1988	2003–2004	2011–2012	2015–2016
Male	29.3	25.0	23.7	23.4
Female	70.2	75.0	76.3	76.6
American Indian/Native American	1.1	0.5	0.5	0.4
Asian/Pacific Islander	0.9	1.5	1.9	2.5
Black	8.2	7.9	6.8	6.7
White	88.3	83.1	81.9	80.1
Multiple Races	n/a	0.7	1.0	1.4
Hispanic	2.9	6.2	7.6	8.8
Average Age	—	42.5	42.4	41.4
Less Than 30	13.4	16.6	15.3	15.0
30–49	67.4	50.4	54.0	55.9
50 or More	17.9	33.0	30.7	29.0

NOTE: The data do not have equal spacing due to the reporting years available.
SOURCE: U.S. Department of Education, NCES 2018-070. Available: https://nces.ed.gov/programs/digest/d17/tables/dt17_209.10.asp?referrer=report.

increase of roughly 2.5 percent in the number of Hispanic teachers over the same time period. As Figure 2-1 demonstrates, in the past decade, Latinx teachers have supplanted Black teachers as the most represented teachers of color: in 2015, 8.8 percent of teachers were Latinx, whereas Black teachers made up only 6.7 percent of the workforce. The issue of

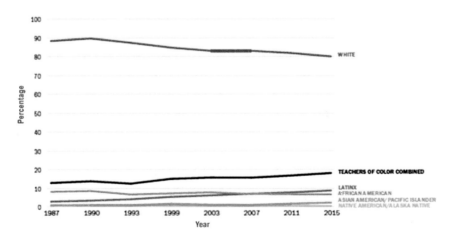

FIGURE 2-1 The percentage of teachers of color in the teacher workforce, 1987–2015.
SOURCE: Carver-Thomas (2018). Available: https://learningpolicyinstitute.org/sites/default/files/product-files/Diversifying_Teaching_Profession_REPORT_0.pdf.

TABLE 2-2 Science and Math Teacher Demographics, by Teacher Characteristics (in percentage)

	Science			Math		
	Elementary	Middle	High	Elementary	Middle	High
Sex						
Female	94	71	57	94	70	60
Male	6	28	43	6	30	40
Race						
White	88	91	91	89	89	91
Hispanic	9	7	6	10	8	7
Black or African American	8	8	5	7	8	5
Asian	2	2	5	3	3	4
American Indian or Alaskan Native	1	2	2	1	1	2
Native Hawaiian or Other Pacific Islander	1	0	0	0	1	1

SOURCE: Banilower et al. (2018).

teacher demographics as it relates to the labor market is discussed in detail in Chapter 4.

The issue of underrepresentation of teachers of color occurs across grade bands and content areas. In a 2018 survey of teachers in science, technology, engineering, and mathematics (STEM) content areas, Banilower and colleagues disaggregated teachers by grade range (i.e., elementary, middle, and high school) and by subject taught to demonstrate that the percentage of teachers of color is even less prevalent in the STEM fields than it appears to be in the population of teachers at large (see Table 2-2). Among high school science and math teachers, 91 percent of teachers identify as White (Banilower et al., 2018). In addition, teachers of color are highly concentrated in certain geographical areas: in 2011 an estimated 40 percent of schools had no teachers of color, meaning students of color in those schools might never experience a teacher of their own race or ethnicity (Bireda and Chait, 2011).

Gender and Age

The teacher workforce has also remained relatively stable with respect to gender and age.[4] There has been little change in the percentages

---

[4] It should be noted that during the reporting period the survey instruments did not offer respondents an opportunity to identify as any gender other than male or female. Therefore, there are likely a population of non-binary teachers that are not represented in the data.

of men and women in the teaching workforce since the early 2000s. The proportion of female teachers in public schools across the country was 75 percent in 2003–2004 and 76.6 percent in 2015–2016, while the percentage of male teachers was 25 percent in 2003–2004 and 23.4 percent in 2015–2016. Whereas women make up the majority of the teaching staff at schools throughout the United States, the proportion of male teachers increases as grade level increases. This remains particularly true in the STEM content areas, with men making up 40 percent of high school math teachers and 43 percent of high school science teachers, as compared to 36 percent of high school teachers generally (Banilower et al., 2018; Taie and Goldring, 2017).

The average age of teachers has also remained consistent over time. In 2016, the average age of K–12 public school teachers was 41.4 years old, whereas in 2003–2004 that average was 42.5 years old. However, there were slight changes in the distribution of teachers' ages from 1987 to 2015. There was a decrease in the percentage of teachers ages 30–49 and an increase in the percentage of teachers ages 50 and older (refer to Table 2-1). These changes in the ages over the broader timeframe is more consistent with data reported by Ingersoll and colleagues (2018). Similarly, teacher experience has also remained relatively consistent: in 2003–2004, 17.8 percent of all public school teachers reported less than 3 years of full-time teaching experience, while that number dropped to 15 percent in 2016.

The Importance of a Diverse Teacher Workforce

As highlighted by a recent National Academies of Sciences, Engineering, and Medicine report, *Monitoring Educational Equity* (NASEM, 2019), "there is growing and compelling evidence that teacher-student racial match has important effects on student outcomes" (p. 87). Not only do these effects appear for both short-term outcomes, such as student test scores and academic attitudes (Dee, 2004; Egalite and Kisida, 2018; Egalite, Kisida, and Winters, 2015; Goldhaber and Hansen 2010) but also they are observed for long-term outcomes, such as dropping out of high school (Gershenson, Jacknowitz, and Brannegan, 2017).

For example, Gershenson and colleagues (2018) conducted a longitudinal study in North Carolina and found that Black students who were assigned to a class with a Black teacher at least once in 3rd, 4th, or 5th grade were less likely to drop out of high school and more likely to aspire to go to college. Black boys that had at least one Black teacher during grades 3–5 were more likely to stay in school as evidenced by the high school dropout rate cut in half. Although less pronounced, the same holds true for Black boys from low-income families who were 39 percent less likely to drop out of high school than those who had never had a Black teacher (for more discussion, see Carver-Thomas, 2018). In other words, the benefit of having a Black teacher for just 1 year in elementary school can persist over several years, especially for Black students from low-income families (Carver-Thomas, 2018).

In addition to academic benefits, students of color can experience social and emotional benefits from having teachers of color. A study using longitudinal data for North Carolina K–5 students and teachers between 2006 and 2010 found that students with teachers of another race had more unexcused absences and an increased likelihood of being chronically absent than students with race-matched teachers (Lindsay and Hart, 2017). In particular, boys of color taught by White teachers were more likely to be chronically absent and to have more suspensions than did other students. Thus, it is increasingly clear that students of color benefit from having teachers of color. While the mechanisms that lead to these positive impacts are not fully understood, the committee notes that the underrepresentation of teachers of color in the workforce is particularly troubling.

Although one option for trying to create more purposeful role models for students of color would be to place more teachers of color in schools serving high concentrations of students of color, the committee argues that it is important that *all* teachers are able to recognize and leverage the various assets students are bringing into the classroom, and receive some preparation to respond to the shifting population of students (the ways in which the makeup of the student population has changed will be described in the next section). Central to the work of teachers is for them to be aware of when teachers and their students do not share similar backgrounds and experiences, as teachers need to develop an understanding of their students' incoming knowledge and experience. Additionally, as Chapter 4 will articulate, there are substantial local differences in the distribution of teachers—inherent inequity exists when a school system has students from one race but lacks many teachers of that race. Lastly, as articulated above, students can benefit from having teachers from the same background in terms of motivation and having visible role models. Through the use of inclusive pedagogies, discussed in Chapter 3, teachers can equip themselves with a better understanding of their students and position them as capable learners and contributors in the classroom.

STUDENT DIVERSITY IN THE CLASSROOM

There have been substantial changes to the student population over the past 20 years. These shifts in student population and new understandings of the role of culture in learning (see Chapter 3) have also given rise to changing expectation for teachers. We outline these changes in student demographics below.

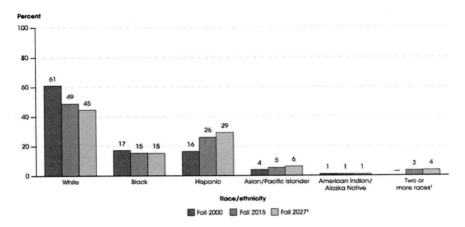

FIGURE 2-2 Percentage distribution of all public school students enrolled in preK–12, by race and ethnicity: fall 2000, fall 2015, and fall 2027 (projected).
SOURCE: de Brey et al. (2019).

Race and Ethnicity

One of the major changes in student demographics over the period from 2000 to 2015 is the decline in the percentage of White students in the K–12 public school population from 61 percent to 49 percent.[5] In 2015, 50 percent of the students enrolled in public schools were students of color (i.e., Black, Hispanic, Asian/Pacific Islander, American Indian/Alaska Native, and two or more races[6]), reflecting an ongoing increase in the racial/ethnic diversity of students in U.S. public schools (de Brey et al., 2019; see Figure 2-2). The fastest growing group are Hispanic students; between fall 2000 and fall 2015, the proportion of Hispanic students increased from 16 percent to 26 percent. Over the same period, the percentage of Black students dropped slightly from 17 percent to 15 percent. The percentage of Asian students stayed almost the same moving from 4 percent to 5 percent.

Native Language and Country of Origin

Coupled with the increase in the racial/ethnic diversity of U.S. public school, the linguistic diversity within the student population has also

---

[5] Note that the percentage of White students is 49 percent, whereas the percentage of White teachers is 80 percent. For that same time, Hispanic students were 26 percent of the population and Hispanic teachers were only 8.8 percent. This difference is less striking for the relationship between Black students (15%) and Black teachers (6.7%)

[6] Students self-identifying as two or more races were first reported in the 2008–2009 school year.

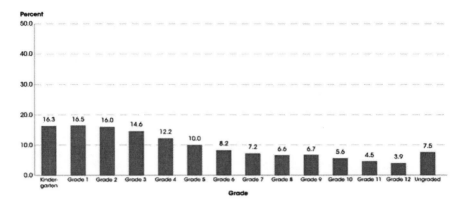

FIGURE 2-3 Percentage distribution of EL students in public schools by grade level: fall 2015
SOURCE: McFarland et al. (2018).

increased (see NASEM, 2018). Students enrolled in U.S. schools come with
a variety of linguistic resources. For many students, English is not spoken
in the home, or is not the only language spoken in the home. One way that
research instruments have attempted to capture information about linguistic
diversity is by classifying students as English learners (ELs). While the practices that districts and researchers have used to make these classifications are
fraught, looking across data on students that have been classified as ELs does
reveal important trends.

ELs constitute a sizable and fast-growing segment of the K–12 student
population in the United States: nearly 5 million students are classified
as ELs in K–12 public schools, making up about 10 percent of total students enrolled (McFarland et al., 2018). Although ELs are found across
all grades in K–12 public schools, there are higher percentages of ELs in
the elementary grades (see Figure 2-3; McFarland et al., 2018). ELs are
enrolled in every state and the District of Columbia, and a significant
proportion of EL students (nearly 54.6%) reside in California, Texas, and
Nevada. Following California, Texas, and Nevada, New Mexico (15.7%)
and Colorado (11.6%) reported the next highest percentages of ELs.
Additionally, ELs are more concentrated in urban and suburban areas
(McFarland et al., 2018).

There has also been a rise in the number of immigrant students in U.S.
elementary and secondary schools, reflected in the increase in the population
overall.[7] The proportion of U.S. children, ages 0–17, growing up in immigrant

---

[7] All data were accessed from the Migration Policy Institute's Data Hub, see https://www.
migrationpolicy.org/programs/data-hub/state-immigration-data-profiles.

families[8] is approximately 26 percent. Currently, the overwhelming majority of all children in immigrant families (88%) were born in the United States. However, within the group of children and youth born outside of the country, there has been an increase in the number of unaccompanied minors, growing from 13,625 in 2012 to 57,496 in 2014. The majority (approximately 75%) of these children are ages 14–18 and they are entering U.S. schools without the support of adult family members.

Socioeconomic Status

"Among all children under age 18 in the United States, 41 percent are low-income children and 19 percent—approximately one in five—are poor" (Jiang and Koball, 2018). The low-income category includes individuals who would qualify as poor (defined as below 100% of the federal poverty threshold [FPT]) and near poor (defined as between 100% to 199% of the FPT).[9] Deep poverty is defined as less than 50 percent of the FPT. Younger children (birth to age 11) were more likely to be in either low-income or poor families compared to older children (ages 12–17) (Jiang and Koball, 2018).

As shown in Figure 2-4, Black, American Indian, and Hispanic children are disproportionately low income and poor, and Hispanics comprise the largest share of all low-income children and poor children (Jiang and Koball, 2018). The number of children living in low-income families varies by region with 4.1 million (35%) children in the Northeast, 5.8 million (39%) in the Midwest, 7.2 million (41%) in the West, and 12.5 million (45%) in the South.

Jiang and Koball also show that children living in low-income families are 50 percent more likely to have less residential stability. However, research conducted by Aratani (2009) shows that stable housing is important for healthy child development. Overall, research points to links between educational outcomes and family incomes; that is, the incidence, depth, duration, and timing of poverty all influence a child's educational attainment (Ferguson, Bovaird, and Mueller, 2007; OECD, 2018).

---

[8]The term "immigrants" refers to people residing in the United States who were not U.S. citizens at birth. This population includes naturalized citizens, lawful permanent residents, certain legal nonimmigrants (e.g., persons on student or work visas), those admitted under refugee or asylee status, and persons illegally residing in the United States. The term "immigrant family" refers to children under age 18 with at least one immigrant parent.

[9]The 2016 FPT is equivalent to $24,339 for a family of four with two children; $19,318 for a family of three with one child; and $16,543 for a family of two with one child. See http://www.nccp.org/publications/pub_1194.html for additional information.

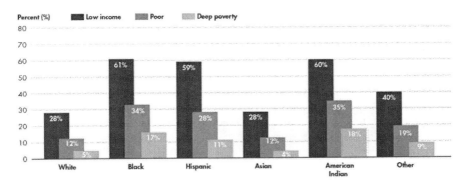

FIGURE 2-4 Percentage of children under age 18 in families classified as low income, poor, or deep poverty by race and ethnicity in 2016.
SOURCE: Jiang and Koball (2018).

Individuals with Disabilities

In 2016, the number of children and youth ages 3–21 receiving special education services was roughly 6 million, or about 9 percent of all public school students (Office of Special Education and Rehabilitative Services, 2018). Among students receiving special education services, the most prevalent disability category is *specific learning disabilities* in which 38.6 percent of students receive services (Office of Special Education and Rehabilitative Services, 2018). The number of students with Individual Education Plans, which are required for special education students, has remained relatively stable, with minor fluctuations from 1998 to 2017.

However, compared to a decade ago, students identified as needing special services are slightly more likely to be educated inside a regular education classroom than pulled out and served through a designated special education classroom. In 2008, 58.5 percent of students needing special services received 80 percent or more of their instruction in a regular classroom compared to 63 percent in 2016.[10] Close to one-half of students categorized with multiple disabilities or intellectual disabilities received their education inside a regular classroom less than 40 percent of the time (Office of Special Education and Rehabilitative Services, 2018).

Another shifting trend associated with students receiving special education services is the number of students who may be categorized with health impairments. Special education eligibility classifications have fluctuated

---

[10] This includes students who are classified under the speech or language impairment, visual impairment, specific learning disability, developmental delay, or other health impairment categories.

over the past 20 years, due in part to new disability classifications. For example, traumatic brain injury (TBI) and autism were first reported as unique disability categories in 1991–1992. Students with TBI and autism (0.9%) have always existed within special education populations; however, prior to 1991 they were identified as eligible for Individuals with Disabilities Education Act services by meeting other category criteria such as mental retardation or speech impairment (Brock, 2006). New classification structures allow students to receive the individual services they need to be successful. However, this can place additional demands on classroom teachers who may not be adequately prepared to meet the unique needs of students who require differentiated supports.

Summary

Overall, students in today's classrooms are racially and ethnically diverse, more likely to speak a language other than English at home, and students in these classrooms have a higher percentage of immigrants. Special education students are more likely to receive instruction in the general education classroom than in specialized settings. These shifting demographics indicate that teachers today need the knowledge and skills to successfully understand the diversity of their students. This also calls for positive beliefs and attitudes about the changing demographics. There have been changes not only in the student population, but also in the views about schools' responsibilities to students with varying needs. That is, teachers are being asked to further differentiate instruction, connect learning experiences to the interests and identities of their students, and set up inclusive and welcoming learning environments (for a deeper discussion of these expectations, see Chapter 3).

FEDERAL EDUCATION POLICY

Changes in federal education policy over the period from 2000 to 2019 led to substantial policy changes at the state, district, and school level that had consequences for teachers' work. Some of these changes in policy are in response to comparisons made globally to determine how the "nation's students are prepared to compete with their counterparts in a globalizing economy" (Singer, Braun, and Chudowsky, 2018, p. vii). In the following section we briefly describe three pieces of legislation that had significant effects on districts and schools: the No Child Left Behind Act (NCLB), the Race to the Top (RTTT) Program, and the Every Student Succeeds Act (ESSA). (Note that NCLB and ESSA are reauthorizations of the Elementary and Secondary Education Act).

No Child Left Behind Act

The passage of NCLB in 2001[11] marked a number of critical changes in the federal education policy landscape and significantly increased the federal role in holding schools responsible for the academic progress of all students. NCLB required states and local districts to (1) have academic standards, (2) make annual progress toward having every student achieve those standards and closing gaps between all students and certain groups of students, (3) test students to see whether they are learning, and (4) collect and report data on how students are doing. Specifically, the law required that all U.S. public schools test and report student achievement in mathematics and English language arts (and eventually science) annually in grades 3–8 and once in high school. Schools were required to report the results, for both the student population as a whole and for particular subgroups of students, including English learners, students in special education, students from low-income families, and students from racial/ethnic minoritized groups.

The NCLB legislation also required that every classroom be staffed by a "highly qualified" teacher and that "highly qualified" teachers were evenly distributed among schools with high concentrations of poverty and wealthier schools. Highly qualified here meant holding a bachelor's degree, having state licensure or certification, and demonstrating knowledge of the subject they teach. This gave states latitude in determining how subject knowledge would be measured. As a result, states varied in the tests they used and even when they used the same tests, they might set different passing scores (RAND Corporation, 2007).

Under the law, schools and districts became responsible for demonstrating that *all* their students not only were making adequate yearly progress in their achievement in different subjects, but also had access to highly qualified teachers to support this progress. And, for the first time in history, states, districts, and schools were required to report achievement data that was disaggregated by race, class, sex, ability, language, and other characteristics. When schools failed to demonstrate adequate yearly progress, they entered into a sequence of sanctions that included requirements around the provision of supplemental education services, loss of funds, loss of local control, and the provision of pathways for students to transfer out of low-performing schools.

Starting in 2011, the Obama administration allowed states to apply for waivers that would give them flexibility from key mandates of the law, such as the target that all students would be proficient by the 2013–2014 school year. However, to receive a waiver, states had to agree to other provisions. For example, states were required to agree to set standards aimed at preparing students for higher education and the workforce. States could either

---

[11] See No Child Left Behind Act of 2001, Pub. L. 107–110.

choose the Common Core State Standards (CCSS) or have their own state's standards approved by local higher education institutions. States then had to put in place assessments aligned to those standards, and they had to institute teacher-evaluation systems that took into account student progress on state standardized tests. By 2015, more than 40 states had been granted waivers.

In the years following the passage of the law and as states were granted waivers, states obtained control over the content of their assessments, when and how assessments were performed, and how achievement results were to be interpreted. This state-level control resulted in wildly divergent state accountability systems across the country, and the level of rigor associated with state performance standards varied considerably from state to state (Phillips, 2014).

Although there have been a number of criticisms of NCLB, implementation of the law shed light on student populations that had historically been underperforming and underserved: states, schools, and districts were tasked with attending to the underperformance of any group of students, regardless of how well the school was performing overall. ELs and students with disabilities are examples of subgroups who were identified and whose progress was then monitored through state accountability systems, with specific consequences for how educators work with these subgroup populations. The law also highlighted the chronic underperformance of schools serving larger numbers of students of color and students living in poverty (Milner and Williams, 2008). As states implemented new school accountability models, designed to increase achievement for all students, school administrators and classroom teachers began to examine and implement tiered interventions and differentiated instructional supports to better meet the diverse needs of all students being served.

Taken together, the provisions of NCLB raised the stakes for teachers and schools. Student performance on annual assessments that were tied to content standards had direct implications for schools, placing pressure on teachers to ensure that students scored well. In addition, the disaggregation of scores meant that teachers were also held responsible for promoting the success of a diverse range of students.

Race to the Top Program

The Department of Education's RTTT Program, a part of the America Recovery and Reinvestment Act of 2009, provided funding for competitive grants to states to encourage education innovation and reform in four areas: (1) enhancing standards and assessments, (2) improving collection and use of data, (3) increasing teacher effectiveness and achieving equity in teacher distribution, and (4) turning around low-achieving schools. The program rolled out in three phases; by the end of Phase 3 in December 2011, 18 states and the District of Columbia had received awards.

RTTT went beyond teacher quality as defined in NCLB to include a focus on teacher effectiveness. It did this by giving higher scores to proposals that included teacher performance evaluations based on student achievement. States responded by creating educator evaluation systems that considered student achievement data alongside teacher observations and other sources of evidence of student learning. These teacher evaluation systems had direct consequences for teachers.

Every Student Succeeds Act

In 2015, the passage of ESSA revised the previous policies outlined in NCLB to provide states more discretion in the use of federal funds and in implementation and revision of accountability measures. ESSA[12] reframed conversations about how federal funding and accountability could be leveraged to promote more equitable systems of education for all students. Under ESSA, states had flexibility to develop their own long-term and short-term goals, though they were required to address proficiency on tests, English language proficiency, and graduation rates. Furthermore, the goals had to set an expectation that gaps in achievement and graduation rates between all students and students in particular groups would become smaller over time. Additionally, under ESSA, states were not required to evaluate teachers through student outcomes and the "highly qualified teacher" requirement was relaxed.

ESSA ushered in a focus on a "well-rounded education for all students" with an emphasis on schools utilizing Title IV, Part A funding to ensure all students have access to courses such as social studies and fine arts and that all students be provided a safe and healthy school environment. As states began to submit their state ESSA plans, equity became a central theme in several initiatives, including new accountability models and plans that emphasized and provided recognition for growth among subgroups of students within a population.

Though the passage of ESSA has eased some of the high stakes associated with NCLB's accountability requirements and RTTT's educator evaluation systems, the increased focus on student performance and achievement ushered in at the beginning of the 21st century has fundamentally altered the work of educators (for more on this, see Chapter 3).

CONTENT AREA STANDARDS

The standards-based reform movement developed in response to *A Nation at Risk* (National Commission on Excellence in Education, 1983) was driven by the idea that standards could catalyze improvements in the

---

[12] Every Student Succeeds Act of 2015, Pub. L. 114–95.

American education system and ensure the nation's economic competitiveness. In 1994 the reauthorization of the Elementary and Secondary Education Act made standards-based reform the official national approach to public schooling by requiring states to set challenging standards aligned to assessments and accountability measures (Massell, 2008). The testing requirements imposed by NCLB built on the commitment to standards and assessments linked to them.

Standards for students learning in the content areas have been in use at the state level since the early 1990s. By the early 2000s, every state had developed and adopted its own learning standards that specify what students in grades 3–8 and high school should be able to do. However, standards varied across states and each state had its own definition of proficiency. Concern about the lack of consistency across state standards led to the development of the CCSS in mathematics and English language arts (ELA) in 2009 (National Governors Association Center for Best Practices and Council of Chief State School Officers, 2010). These standards are intended to ensure that all students leave high school ready to enter college or start a career; they are more rigorous than many previous state standards. In 2010, 45 states initially adopted the CCSS in mathematics and ELA, though since that time 8 of the 45 states are no longer part of the consortium. Similarly, the *Next Generation Science Standards: For States, By States* (NGSS; NGSS Lead States, 2013) were developed to provide guidance for K–12 science education. The NGSS are also more challenging than many previous state standards in science. As of 2019, 44 states have adopted the NGSS or standards that are based on them. These more rigorous standards, coupled with the increased accountability demands placed by NCLB, raise the expectations for teachers, which are discussed in detail in Chapter 3.

SUMMARY

Teachers work within a larger, ever-expanding and shifting education system, characterized by ongoing federal reform efforts. The demographics of the teacher workforce have remained relatively stable, but the expectations placed on teachers have changed enormously. The 2001 federal law, No Child Left Behind, established accountability standards for all U.S. public schools by requiring that all students in grades 3–8, and once in high school, be tested in mathematics and ELA, and eventually science. The relatively recent adoption and implementation of rigorous national content standards in some states has raised the expectations for students' learning, which in turn raised the expectations for instruction (see Chapter 3 for a deeper discussion of the shifts of standards across content areas). It is this broader policy landscape that provides part of the context for what is expected of K–12 teachers.

Another important change in the education system is the increasing diversity of the student population; that is, there are more students in the classroom who vary with respect to their cultural backgrounds, the language that they speak, their proficiency with English, as well as students who qualify for disability status. As articulated above (see section on The Importance of a Diverse Teacher Workforce) and developed more in Chapter 3, emerging research suggests that it can be beneficial for students to have teachers from similar backgrounds at some point in their educational experience. Given the emerging research that shows benefits to students when they have role models, the lack of diversity (including teachers with disabilities) in the teacher workforce is concerning.

Overall, it is clear that the work of teachers today is impacted by increased and explicit demands placed on them, demands that stem in part from accountability legislation, shifts in rigorous content standards, and the increasing diversity of students in the classroom. Each of these factors are compounded by and responsive to the others. In the following two chapters, the committee explores both the changing expectations for teachers (Chapter 3) and the dynamics of the teacher workforce (Chapter 4) in greater detail.

REFERENCES

Aratani, Y. (2009). *Homeless Children and Youth: Causes and Consequences.* New York: National Center for Children in Poverty, Columbia University, Mailman School of Public Health. Available: http://www.nccp.org/publications/pdf/text_888.pdf.

Banilower, E.R., Smith, P.S., Malzahn, K.A., Plumley, C.L., Gordon, E.M., and Hayes, M.L. (2018). *Report of the 2018 NSSME+.* Chapel Hill, NC: Horizon Research, Inc.

Bireda, S., and Chait, R. (2011). *Increasing Teacher Diversity: Strategies to Improve the Teacher Workforce.* Washington, DC: Center for American Progress.

Brock, S.E. (2006). An examination of the changing rates of autism in special education. *The California School Psychologist, 11,* 31–40. Available: https://files.eric.ed.gov/fulltext/EJ902516.pdf.

Carver-Thomas, D. (2018). *Diversifying the Teaching Profession: How to Recruit and Retain Teachers of Color.* Palo Alto, CA: Learning Policy Institute.

de Brey, C., Musu, L., McFarland, J., Wilkinson-Flicker, S., Diliberti, M., Zhang, A., Branstetter, C., and Wang, X. (2019). *Status and Trends in the Education of Racial and Ethnic Groups 2018* (NCES 2019-038). U.S. Department of Education. Washington, DC: National Center for Education Statistics. Available: https://nces.ed.gov/pubs2019/2019038.pdf.

Dee, T.S. (2004). Teachers, race, and student achievement in a randomized experiment. *Review of Economics and Statistics, 86*(1), 195–210.

Egalite, A.J., and Kisida, B. (2018). The effects of teacher match on students' academic perceptions and attitudes. *Educational Evaluation and Policy Analysis, 40*(1), 59–81.

Egalite, A.J., Kisida, B., and Winters, M.A. (2015). Representation in the classroom: The effect of own-race teachers on student achievement. *Economics of Education Review, 45,* 44–52.

Ferguson, H.B., Bovaird, S., and Mueller, M.P. (2007). The impact of poverty on educational outcomes for children. *Paediatrics Child Health, 12*(8), 701–706.

Fontenot, K., Semega, J., and Kollar, M. (2018). *Income and Poverty in the United States: 2017.* Washington, DC: U.S. Government Publishing Office.

Gershenson, S., Jacknowitz, A., and Brannegan, A. (2017). Are student absences worth the worry in U.S. primary schools? *Education Finance and Policy, 12*(2), 137–165.

Gershenson, S., Hart, C.M.D., Hyman, J., Lindsay, C., and Papageorge, N.W. (2018). *The Long-Run Impacts of Same-Race Teachers.* NBER Working Paper No. 25254. Available: https://www.nber.org/papers/w25254.pdf.

Goldhaber, D., and Hansen, M. (2010). Using performance on the job to inform teacher tenure decisions. *American Economic Review, 100*(2), 250–255.

Goldring, R., Taie, S., Rizzo, L., Colby, D., and Fraser, A. (2013). *User's Manual for the 2011–12 Schools and Staffing Survey Volumes 1–6.* (NCES 2013-330 through 2013-335). U.S. Department of Education. Washington, DC: National Center for Education Statistics.

Ingersoll, R.M., Merrill, E., Stuckey, D., and Collins, G. (2018). *Seven Trends: The Transformation of the Teacher Force—Updated October 2018.* CPRE Research Reports. Available: https://repository.upenn.edu/cpre_researchreports/108.

Jiang, Y., and Koball, H. (2018). *Basic Facts about Low-Income Children: Children under 18 Years, 2016.* New York: National Center for Children in Poverty, Columbia University Mailman School of Public Health. Available: http://www.nccp.org/publications/pdf/text_1194.pdf.

Lindsay, C.A., and Hart, C.M. (2017). Teacher race and school discipline. *Education Next, 17*(1). Available: https://www.educationnext.org/teacher-race-and-school-discipline-suspensions-research.

Massell, D. (2008). *The Current Status and Role of Standards-Based Reform in the United States.* Paper prepared for the National Research Council Workshop on Assessing the Role of K–12 Academic Standards in States, January 17–18, Washington, DC.

McFarland, J., Hussar, B., Wang, X., Zhang, J., Wang, K., Rathbun, A., Barmer, A., Forrest Cataldi, E., and Bullock Mann, F. (2018). *The Condition of Education 2018* (NCES 2018-144). U.S. Department of Education. Washington, DC: National Center for Education Statistics.

McFarland, J., Hussar, B., Zhang, J., Wang, X., Wang, K., Hein, S., Diliberti, M., Forrest Cataldi, E., Bullock Mann, F., and Barmer, A. (2019). *The Condition of Education 2019* (NCES 2019-144). U.S. Department of Education. Washington, DC: National Center for Education Statistics.

Milner IV, H.R., and Williams, S.M. (2008). Analyzing education policy and reform with attention to race and socio-economic status. *Journal of Public Management & Social Policy, 14*(2).

National Academies of Sciences, Engineering, and Medicine (NASEM). (2018). *English Learners in STEM Subjects: Transforming Classrooms, Schools, and Lives.* Washington, DC: The National Academies Press.

———. (2019). *Monitoring Educational Equity.* Washington, DC: The National Academies Press.

National Governors Association Center for Best Practices and Council of Chief State School Officers. (2010). *Common Core State Standards.* Washington, DC: Author.

NGSS Lead States. (2013). *Next Generation Science Standards: For States, By States.* Washington, DC: The National Academies Press.

Oakley, D., Stowell, J., and Logan, J.R. (2009). The impact of desegregation on black teachers in the metropolis, 1970–2000. *Ethnic and Racial Studies, 39*(9), 1576–1598.

OECD. (2018). *Equity in Education: Breaking Down Barriers to Social Mobility.* Paris: OECD Publishing.

Office of Special Education and Rehabilitative Services. (2018). *40th Annual Report to Congress on the Implementation of the Individuals with Disabilities Education Act.* Washington, DC: U.S. Department of Education. Available: https://www2.ed.gov/about/reports/annual/osep/2018/parts-b-c/40th-arc-for-idea.pdf.

Phillips, G.W. (2014). *International Benchmarking: State and National Education Performance Standards.* Available: https://www.air.org/sites/default/files/downloads/report/AIR_International%20Benchmarking-State%20and%20National%20Ed%20Performance%20Standards_Sept2014.pdf.

RAND Corporation. (2007). *Evaluating Teacher Quality Under No Child Left Behind.* Research Brief. Available: https://www.rand.org/pubs/research_briefs/RB9287/index1.html.

Singer, J.D., Braun, H.I., and Chudowsky, N. (2018). *International Education Assessments: Cautions, Conundrums, and Common Sense.* Washington, DC: National Academy of Education.

Taie, S., and Goldring, R. (2017). *Characteristics of Public Elementary and Secondary School Principals in the United States: Results from the 2015–16 National Teacher and Principal Survey First Look* (NCES 2017-070). U.S. Department of Education. Washington, DC: National Center for Education Statistics.

Thompson, O. (2019). *School Desegregation and Black Teacher Employment.* NBER Working Paper No. 25990. Available: https://www.nber.org/papers/w25990.pdf.

3

Changing Expectations for
Teaching and Learning

Every day, millions of American students rely on teachers to provide them with robust and engaging learning experiences that support them in developing and pursuing their dreams. Teachers are expected to enter the classroom with both strong content knowledge (a body of conceptual and factual knowledge) and pedagogical content knowledge (understanding of how learners acquire knowledge in a given subject) (National Research Council [NRC], 2010b). And their work involves connecting new learning experiences to the previous knowledge and experiences of the learner. Therefore, teachers need to understand who their students are, where they come from, and the ideas and experiences they bring into the classroom. Whereas this has been a long-standing expectation for the teaching profession, many other aspects of that profession have shifted dramatically over the past 20 years. Chapter 2 examined key factors contributing to this changing landscape and concurrent shifts in expectations for teaching and learning: federal legislation, national standards, and changing student demographics. This chapter looks at some aspects of those areas in further detail, elaborating on content area standards, especially their promotion of deeper learning; examining the increasing emphasis on the role of culture in learning; and considering ways in which technological advances have changed expectations about how teachers communicate with students and families.

Since the early standards-based reform effort of various states and professional organizations during the 1980s and 1990s, teachers in the United States have seen numerous cycles of federal initiatives to revise and further standardize content standards indicating what students should know and be able to do (see Chapter 2). As standards change (with variations noted across states), so do curriculum, assessments, instruction, and support services. And, so too does the work of the teacher in the classroom. The first section in this chapter looks closely at pedagogies for deeper learning as recommended by recent standards (both general and discipline-specific). Through this analysis the committee highlights the shift from an emphasis on simply acquiring knowledge to engaging in disciplinary practices that require learners to use knowledge in the context of discipline-specific activities and tasks (National Academies of Sciences, Engineering, and Medicine [NASEM], 2018b). This shift requires a corresponding change in the role of the teacher from one who transmits knowledge to one who helps students build deep understanding.

The second section examines the role of culture in learning and teaching. With the expansion of the types of support services provided to students (i.e., special education services, English learner supports, and social and emotional supports), classroom teachers are being asked to change the way they support learning for all students in their classrooms. As highlighted in Chapter 2 and discussed throughout this report, central to the work of teachers is an appreciation for what their students know. Experiential differences (e.g., race, ethnicity, home language, culture, disability) between teachers and students may have implications for teachers use of pedagogical approaches when implementing new standards.

Finally, this chapter discusses advancements in technology from the perspective of expectations for teachers. Such advancements present a steady wave of changes for classroom teachers as they incorporate new educational technologies for instruction and engage in new ways of communicating assignments, grades, and other classroom activities to students and families. The use of new technologies may increase the amount of time teachers need to spend communicating with both students and families.

In each of these sections, this chapter views changing expectations for teachers through the lens of changing expectations for students learning, considering the ways new standards and tools for learning require new ways of teaching.

INCREASING EMPHASIS ON DEEPER LEARNING

Well into the first quarter of the 21st century, there continues to be much thought and discussion as to what skills individuals will need to possess to actively engage in their communities and be successful in the workforce. NRC's 2010 report *Exploring the Intersection of Science Edu-*

cation and 21st Century Skills identified five skill sets important to the success of individuals of the present: (1) adaptability, (2) complex communications, (3) nonroutine problem solving, (4) self-management, and (5) systems thinking.

In 2016, the American Institutes for Research report *Does Deeper Learning Improve Student Outcomes* suggested that these 21st century skills were achieved through "deeper learning" (Bitter and Loney, 2015). That report characterized deeper learning as including a deeper understanding of core academic content; the ability to apply that understanding to novel problems and situations; and the development of a range of competencies, including people skills and self-control. The same report identified six dimensions of deeper learning that, collectively, have become the focus of national initiatives to promote deeper learning in K–12 schools: (1) mastery of core academic content; (2) critical thinking and problem solving; (3) effective communication; (4) ability to work collaboratively; (5) learning how to learn; and (6) academic mindsets.

Table 3-1 below showcases the differences between deeper learning classroom practices and traditional classroom practices. As briefly described above, the shift to student-centered approaches requires teachers to optimize learning environments to achieve the goals of deeper learning. To ensure that students with disabilities have access to these optimized learning experiences, teachers may need additional guidance on accommodations and assistive technologies, strategies for differentiating instruction and

TABLE 3-1 Deeper Learning Versus Traditional Classroom Practices

Role of Learner in Deeper Learning	Role of Learner in Traditional Classroom Practices
Connect new ideas and concepts to previous knowledge and experience.	Course material treated as disconnected from what already know.
Integrate knowledge into interrelated conceptual systems.	Course material treated as disconnected bits of knowledge.
Look for patterns and underlying principles.	Memorize facts and carry out procedures without understanding how or why.
Evaluate new ideas and relate them to conclusions.	Difficulty in making sense of new ideas that differ from what is in the textbook.
Understand process of dialogue and examine the logic of an argument critically.	Facts and procedures treated as static knowledge, handed down from an all-knowing authority.
Reflect on own understanding and process of learning.	Memorize without reflecting on purpose or own learning strategies.

SOURCE: Adapted from Sawyer (2006).

classroom management, as well as procedures for ensuring students have the appropriate Individualized Education Program.[1]

High school graduates today require a deep conceptual understanding of complex concepts, and the ability to work with them creatively to generate new ideas, new theories, new products, and new knowledge. However, many schools today continue to design learning around acquisition of compartmentalized and decontextualized facts. As evidence continues to emerge demonstrating that effective classroom instruction incorporates the deeper learning practices articulated in Table 3-1 (Sawyer, 2006) and as American businesses, industries, and policy makers continue to demand a comprehensive education system that prepares students for the 21st century workforce needs (Burrus et al., 2013), the urgency for schools and teachers to provide learning experiences that meet these needs will continue to grow. Below, the committee analyzes the changing demands on teachers, who are increasingly asked to provide deeper learning experiences and environments that function differently from traditional classrooms.

The report *A Nation at Risk* (National Commission on Excellence in Education, 1983) inspired a new emphasis on standards-based educational reform. This era of standards reform included the development of several national reform documents (described below) that identified broad goals for mathematics, science, English language arts (ELA), and social studies education; some states have begun to adopt (or adapt) these content standards and are in varying phases of implementation (see Chapter 2). Because some states are still in the process of implementation, it is challenging to assess how well schools can demonstrate that all students are well served by instruction that is geared to deeper learning.

More recently, guiding documents for various standards-based reform efforts emphasize engagement in disciplinary practices or activities similar to those undertaken by people doing that work in a professional capacity as a way to promote deeper learning (Moje, 2015; Shanahan and Shanahan, 2008).[2] The following sections explore the shifts in teaching and learning of individual disciplines over the past 20 years toward approaches that incorporate disciplinary practices.

---

[1] The IRIS Center, supported by the U.S. Department of Education's Office of Special Education Programs, develops and disseminates online resources to support the education of all students, particularly struggling learners with disabilities. More information and access to resources are available at https://iris.peabody.vanderbilt.edu.

[2] The August 2018 volume of *Science and Children* published by the National Science Teachers Association was devoted to focusing on the practices of the Next Generation Science Standards.

Progression of Science Practices

During the 1990s and 2000s, several key national documents identified goals for science teaching and learning that were eventually used by states to develop state standards that would guide instruction, curriculum and assessment decisions. NRC's *National Science Education Standards* (NSES) focused on science literacy for all students and proposed standards for high school students designed to help them develop (1) abilities necessary to do scientific inquiry and (2) understanding about scientific inquiry (NRC, 1996, p. 173). The standards also conveyed that high school students "must actively participate in scientific investigations," emphasizing that students should engage in using evidence, applying logic, and constructing arguments and explanations for observations made during investigations. The NSES recommendations described an approach to laboratory investigations that centered on student engagement in practices mirroring what scientists do as they investigate and explain events in the natural world, rather than investigations built on a set of prescribed steps to be followed to achieve an expected outcome.

Taking Science to School (NRC, 2007) later continued to examine how students learn science and provided recommendations for how science should be taught in K–8 classrooms, declaring that students who are proficient in science (1) know, use, and interpret scientific explanations of the natural world; (2) generate and evaluate scientific evidence and explanations; (3) understand the nature and development of scientific knowledge; and (4) participate productively in scientific practices and discourse. While the four proficiency strands were informed by scientific practices found in previous national science education documents, they also represented a departure from previous recommendations in that they indicated that the practices of science were inextricably linked to content knowledge.

In 2012, NRC published *A Framework for K–12 Science Education* (the *Framework*), intended as a framework of unifying guidance for K–12 science education, which articulated three dimensions for science teaching and learning: (1) Disciplinary Core Ideas (big ideas in science); (2) Science and Engineering Practices (what scientists and engineers do); and (3) Crosscutting Concepts (how scientists and engineers think). The *Framework* states a need for all three dimensions to be integrated in standards, curricula, instruction, and assessment to support science learning for all students. There are eight disciplinary practices: (1) asking questions and defining problems; (2) developing and using models; (3) planning and carrying out investigations; (4) analyzing and interpreting data; (5) using mathematics and computational thinking; (6) constructing explanations and designing solutions; (7) engaging in argument from evidence; and (8) obtaining, evaluating, and communicating information (NRC, 2012).

The *Framework* provided the basis for the *Next Generation Science Standards* (NGSS), which has been adopted by 20 states as of 2019 and informed the development of science standards in 24 other states. A recent study of teachers who were implementing instruction aligned to the NGSS found shifts from "simply presenting information to supporting students building explanations of phenomena and proposing

---

BOX 3-1
What Can Deeper Learning in Science Look Like?

In 2012, the National Research Council released *A Framework for K–12 Science Education* (the *Framework*), an evidence-based report that lays out scientific concepts that students should learn before graduating from high school. The report includes information on practices to learning and conceptual development consistent with how scientists and engineers work. Based on the *Framework*, participating states, alongside Achieve, American Association for the Advancement of Science, the National Academies, National Science Teachers Association, and other partners developed the *Next Generation Science Standards* (NGSS) to align with the *Framework*. The NGSS are framed around performance expectations that describe how students should be able to use their knowledge. An example of a performance expectation from the NGSS is below.

3-LS4-4 Make a claim about the merit of a solution to a problem caused when the environment changes and the types of plants and animals that live there may change.

The snapshot pictured here is an example from California of a lesson that moves students toward this performance expectation. It is drawn from the 2016 Science Framework for California Public Schools: Kindergarten Through Grade Twelve. The Anchoring Phenomenon identifies an event or situation that students likely have observed or could observe. The rest of the snapshot details where the NGSS dimensions appear in the situation, such as a Science and Engineering Practice, are highlighted in blue and Cross-Cutting Concepts appear in green.

Illustrated in the above example are the ways in which the teacher supported the students in using the eight disciplinary practices associated with the three dimensions of the *Framework*. That is, she helped students to make sense of the Anchoring Phenomenon through facilitating the students in developing and using meaningful, relevant questions. She guided the students in gathering and analyzing data and information while allowing students to develop arguments for how their evidence supports explanations. This reflects the shift to a more student-centered approach being called for in science education (NASEM, 2019).

SOURCE: Based on the California Department of Education (2016) California Science Framework.

solutions to problems" to requiring students to "develop explanatory models, show chains of reasoning that provide explanations, and use evidence to justify their" ideas (Krajcik et al., 2014, p. 173). An example of a three-dimensional performance expectation and students engaging in instruction aligned to the performance expectation can be found in Box 3-1.

Grade Three Snapshot 4.4: Living Things in Changing Environments

Anchoring Phenomenon: Some places on the schoolyard have lots of plants and animals while other places have fewer.

Ms. J introduced her students to the idea of environmental changes (EP&C II) by taking her class on a field trip to visit the campus, surrounding neighborhood, and a local park. In preparation for this activity, Ms. J identified three areas near the school where her students could see plants and animals, and observe the effects of human activities; she also enlisted a parent volunteer to go along. Before going outside, Ms. J explained to the students that they would be going on a local field trip to make observations and collect evidence about environmental changes on campus and in the local neighborhood. She told them to bring pencils and their science journal so that they could make notes about their observations.

While walking around campus, the students observed and **asked questions [SEP-1]** about why there were very few plants and animals on the school grounds. Ms. J had them make notes about their observations and record any questions in their science notebooks during their **investigation [SEP-3]** of environmental changes in the local area. The class walked down the street, making observations and taking notes as they went by houses and apartment buildings in the neighborhood. They observed that some areas had green spaces with different kinds of plants and animals, and saw many birds sitting on the branches of the bushes and squirrels running through the yards. Finally, Ms. J took them to visit a local park where they saw even more plants and animals. As they walked back to the school, Ms. J kicked off a discussion by asking students if they observed any **patterns [CCC-1]** regarding the variety and numbers of plants and animals they observed in the three different areas.

Back in their classroom, Ms. J guided a student discussion of similarities and differences among the areas they visited during their field trip. She made a four-column list on the board labeled "Place," "Description of Area," "Plants We Saw," and "Animals We Saw." With their data recorded, Ms. J asked the students to contribute to a list of the differences in plants and animals among the three habitats: campus, neighborhood, and park. The class then began a discussion to **analyze and interpret [SEP-4]** the data they collected and began thinking about the **causes [CCC-2]** of these differences. Students identified several human activities, such as removing trees, making streets, paving the campus, and building houses. Once they completed their list, Ms. J asked students to identify the evidence they saw during their field trip that supports the **argument [SEP 7]** that changes in habitats affect the organisms living there. Some organisms can survive well, some survive less well, and some cannot survive at all. Ms. J recorded the students' evidence on the board.

Progression of Mathematical Practices

The National Council of Teachers of Mathematics (NCTM) was the first North American professional association to publish a set of research-based principles and standards for student learning and for the teaching of mathematics. Published first in 1989 and then revised in 2000, the *Principles and Standards for School Mathematics* included two kinds of standards: *content* standards in a number of mathematical domains (i.e., what students should learn) and *process* standards (i.e., how students should be supported to learn mathematics with understanding).

Historically, mathematics had been treated in schools as a set of discrete ideas. Students were asked to memorize procedures for solving predictable sets of problems, often without attention to understanding *why* procedures work, or *when* it makes sense to apply one procedure over another (Stigler and Hiebert, 1999). In contrast, the NCTM *Standards* suggested that students should develop understandings and capabilities much more akin to those of mathematicians, for example, posing and solving novel problems, engaging flexibly with numbers, making sense of why procedures work, and treating mathematics as a set of connected ideas. As such, the learning goals and vision of high-quality instruction represented in the 2000 *Standards* (and more currently, the 2014 *Principles to Actions*) marked a significant shift from typical expectations in math classrooms.

In addition to the *Standards*, another important foundational text for teaching and learning of mathematics is NRC's 2001 report on the state of U.S. math education, *Adding It Up*. Drawing on contemporary research, the report identified five strands that together comprise mathematical proficiency:

1. Conceptual understanding: comprehension of mathematical concepts, operations, and relations
2. Procedural fluency: skill in carrying out procedures flexibly, accurately, efficiently, and appropriately
3. Strategic competence: ability to formulate, represent, and solve mathematical problems
4. Adaptive reasoning: capacity for logical thought, reflection, explanation, and justification
5. Productive disposition: habitual inclination to see mathematics as sensible, useful, and worthwhile, coupled with a belief in diligence and one's own efficacy (NRC, 2001, p. 5)

In the first decade of the 21st century, these seminal documents informed state and districts' development of standards, curriculum, instruction, as well as of classroom-, district-, and state-level assessment tools.

However, there was still variation from state to state. The *Common Core State Standards for Mathematics* (CCSS-M) released in 2010 began a national initiative to make math education standards across various states more uniform with the CCSS-M. The *Standards* were the result of a collaboration between the National Governors Association (NGA) and the Council of Chief State School Officers (CSSO). Like the *Standards*, CCSS-M included *content* standards in core mathematical domains and *process* standards, referred to as the Standards for Mathematical Practice (SMP). CCSS-M content standards recommended that teachers focus on fewer topics in order to have time for students to develop proficiency—that is, to build stronger and deeper foundations in the underlying concepts of mathematics. In doing so, CCSS-M stressed *coherence* within and across grade levels through *learning progressions* with an emphasis on rigor.[3]

Supporting these shifts in math instruction relies on the integration of the content and process standards. The practices highlight the importance of making sense of and being able to explain why a particular strategy makes sense, and the ability to use various representations to support reasoning; they suggest that learning and doing mathematics is fundamentally a sense-making enterprise. While the ideas behind the SMP are not new, requiring them as standards to be taught and assessed was (Mateas, 2016). The role of the teacher is to create a learning environment that is conducive to allowing students to engage in meaningful discourse. An example of students engaging in the practices of mathematics as a means to deeper understanding of mathematical concepts can be found in Box 3-2.

Progression of Literacy Practices

In the 1990s, states were writing their own standards for literacy; in 1996, the National Council for Teachers of English and the International Reading Association produced content standards for English language arts. In 2010, the Common Core State Standards for English Language Arts and Literacy in History/Social Studies, Science, and Technical Subjects (CCSS-ELA) were published. As in mathematics, they were developed through a collaboration between the NGA and the CSSO. Like other standards, they are not curriculum; they describe grade-level expectations in the areas of reading, writing, speaking, and listening. They are grounded in research, built on the strengths of several state standards published at the time,

---

[3] Rigor does not refer to making math harder; rather, it refers to deep, authentic understanding of mathematical concepts. For more information on Key Shifts in Mathematics, see http://www.corestandards.org/other-resources/key-shifts-in-mathematics.

BOX 3-2
What Can Deeper Learning Look Like in Mathematics?

As teachers build lessons that meet new standards, students may have different reactions, responses, and questions as they attempt to develop deeper conceptual understanding. The fictional dialogue below provides an example of what questions middle school students might consider as they work through a problem. The dialogue among Sam, Dana, and Anita provides teachers with the opportunity to meet new goals for math education that emphasize conceptual understanding, making sense of problems, constructing viable arguments and reasoning with others, and prompting deeper learning opportunities for students than traditional instructional approaches to math learning, which may have focused more on procedural fluency.

(1) Sam: How do you do 2/5 + 1/2?

(2) Dana: It's just 3/7, isn't it?

(3) Anita: But 3/7 is less than 1/2 , so it can't be that!

(4) Sam: So . . . how do you do it?

(5) Dana: But we're just adding: 2 + 1 is 3, and 5 + 2 is 7, so it *should* be 3/7.

(6) Anita: We already know that 2 fifths plus 1 fifth is 3 fifths [writes 2/5 + 1/5 = 3/5]. It's not 3 tenths. You can't just add everything you see.

(7) Sam: So...how *do* you do it?

(8) Dana: [To Anita] Oh, right, I get it. It's like when we were saying, "2 cats plus 1 cat, 2 grapes plus 1 grape, 2 fifths plus 1 fifth."

(9) Sam: Yeah, I get it, *too*, but how do we do 2 *fifths* plus 1 *half*?! It's not just 3 of something, but what *is* it? We're adding two different things. Like 2 cats and 1 grape; 2 feet and 1 inch. Or, maybe like 2 thousand and 1 hundred. We *can* add them, but they're not 3 of something.

Note: The conversation is not meant to be an accurate illustration of how typical middle school students talk but does accurately illustrate the type of thinking that typical middle school students can use. This conversation comes from PD materials (see http://www.mathpractices.edc.org) that have been reviewed by teachers, teacher educators, and mathematicians.

SOURCE: Based on Mateas (2016).

internationally benchmarked, based on rigorous content, and they entail higher-order thinking skills (NGA and CCSSO, 2010).

The CCSS-ELA changed the landscape of ELA curriculum across many states across the country. In particular, they include a wider range of literacy practices, such as digital literacies, attention to cultural influences on all literacy practices, and disciplinary literacy in history/social studies and science. They describe what it means to be "a literate person in the 21st century:"

> Students who meet the Standards readily undertake the close, attentive reading that is at the heart of understanding and enjoying complex works of literature. They habitually perform the critical reading necessary to pick carefully through the staggering amount of information available today in print and digitally. They actively seek the wide, deep, and thoughtful engagement with high-quality literary and informational texts that builds knowledge, enlarges experience, and broadens worldviews. They reflexively demonstrate the cogent reasoning and use of evidence that is essential to both private deliberation and responsible citizenship in a democratic republic. (NGA and CCSSO, 2010, p. 3)

The CCSS-ELA emphasize three major areas: regular practice with complex texts and their academic language; reading, writing, and speaking grounded in evidence from texts, both literary and informational; and building knowledge through content-rich nonfiction.[4] This last practice indicates an increased attention to informational text—nonfiction text that provides information about the natural and social world (Duke and Bennett-Armistead, 2003). These shifts in standards for reading, writing, speaking, and listening require changes in instruction for all students, including English learners.[5]

Figure 3-1 shows the practices of the *CCSS-M and CCSS-ELA* and the science and engineering practices from the NGSS. There are strong similarities between the disciplinary practices in Figure 3-1 and five skill sets important to the success of individuals in the 21st century (NRC, 2010) and the deeper learning practices (Sawyer, 2006).

---

[4] For more information for shifts, see https://achievethecore.org/page/2727/college-and-career-ready-shifts-in-ela-literacy.

[5] For more information on language development in English learners within content instruction, see the recent NASEM (2018a) report, *Supporting English learners in STEM Subjects: Transforming Classrooms, Schools, and Lives.* The report identifies promising practices for facilitating content learning and content development (Chapter 4).

Practices in Mathematics, Science, and English Language Arts		
Math	**Science**	**English Language Arts**
M1. Make sense of problems and persevere in solving them.	**S1.** Asking questions (for science) and defining problems (for engineering).	**E1.** They demonstrate independence.
M2. Reason abstractly and quantitatively.	**S2.** Developing and using models.	**E2.** They build strong content knowledge.
M3. Construct viable arguments and critique the reasoning of others.	**S3.** Planning and carrying out investigations.	**E3.** They respond to the varying demands of audience, task, purpose,
M4. Model with mathematics.	**S4.** Analyzing and interpreting data.	and discipline.
M5. Use appropriate tools strategically.	**S5.** Using mathematics, information and computer technology, and computational thinking.	**E4.** They comprehend as well as critique.
M6. Attend to precision.	**S6.** Constructing explanations (for science) and designing solutions (for engineering).	**E5.** They value evidence.
M7. Look for and make use of structure.		**E6.** They use technology and digital media strategically and capably.
M8. Look for and express regularity in repeated reasoning.	**S7.** Engaging in argument from evidence.	**E7.** They come to understanding other
	S8. Obtaining, evaluating, and communicating information.	perspectives and cultures.

FIGURE 3-1 Common Core State Standards practices for Mathematics and English Language Arts and science and engineering practices for the Next Generation Science Standards.
SOURCE: NGA and CCSSO (2010) and NGSS Lead States (2013).

Progression of Social Studies Practices

Recommendations for effective social studies teaching and learning, along with the development of social studies standards, occurred roughly concurrently with reforms developed within the other three major academic subject areas. Social studies comprises a broad range of disciplines; the four major ones are economics, geography, history, and political science (known as civics and government in K–12 settings). Throughout the 1990s, experts from organizations representing these four disciplines produced voluntary content standards (see Center for Civic Education, 1994; National Center for History in the Schools, 1996; National Council for Geographic Education, 1994; National Council on Economic Education, 1997).

In 1994, the National Council for the Social Studies (NCSS), the leading national organization for social studies education, published its *Curriculum Standards for Social Studies*, which it revised slightly in 2010. The standards are based on NCSS's "Ten Themes of Social Studies:" (1) culture; (2) time, continuity, and change; (3) people, places, and environment; (4) individual development and identity; (5) individuals, groups, and institutions; (6) power, authority, and governance; (7) production, distribution, and consumption; (8) science, technology, and society; (9) global connections;

and (10) civic ideals and practices. The Ten Themes served as a framework for curriculum and instruction design with broader goals for how students should interact meaningfully with state-identified disciplinary standards for civics and government, economics, geography, and history.

States then began developing their own standards, based in part on the NCSS standards and the voluntary disciplinary content standards. There were some commonalities across states; for example, most elementary grades used the "expanding communities" framework to organize standards (Halvorsen, 2013) and most standards were organized around the four major disciplines: civics and government, economics, geography, and history. However, in important ways, the standards varied widely state by state, and as states revised them in the next decade, such variations persisted.

In 2013, NCSS published the *College, Career & Civic Life: C3 Framework for Social Studies Standards* (the *C3 Framework*). As with previous guidance documents for state social studies standards, the *C3 Framework* focused on broader concepts that underlie a rich program for social studies education, but did not include recommendations for specific content to be covered, leaving those decisions to states as they develop standards. However, the *C3 Framework* outlines four dimensions of learning that together represent an informed and greatly expanded view of the ways students should engage with social studies content. The four dimensions comprise an *Inquiry Arc* whereby students: (1) develop questions and plan inquiries; (2) apply disciplinary concepts and tools; (3) evaluate sources and use evidence; and (4) communicate conclusions and take informed action (NCSS, 2013, p. x). See Table 3-2 below.

In the past 20 years, expectations for social studies learning have increased in intellectual rigor. Standards now emphasize skills such as developing questions, conducting inquiry, evaluating both primary and secondary sources, and communicating conclusions. (See Box 3-3 for differences in the

TABLE 3-2 C3 Framework Organization

DIMENSION 1: Developing Questions and Planning Inquiries	DIMENSION 2: Applying Disciplinary Tools and Concepts	DIMENSION 3: Evaluating Sources and Using Evidence	DIMENSION 4: Communicating Conclusions and Taking Informed Action
• Developing Questions and Planning Inquiries	• Civics • Economics • Geography • History	• Gathering and Evaluating Sources • Developing Claims and Using Evidence	• Communicating and Critiquing Conclusions • Taking Informed Action

SOURCE: Recreated from NCSS (2013, p. x).

BOX 3-3
Incorporation of the *C3 Framework* into State Standards

The *C3 Framework* is organized around an "inquiry arc" comprising four dimensions representing the disciplinary practices for social studies: (1) developing questions and planning inquiries: (2) applying disciplinary concepts and tools; (3) evaluating sources and using evidence; and (4) communicating conclusions and taking informed action (NCSS, 2013). States have already begun to incorporate these practices into standards documents. Recently, for example, Oklahoma adopted new social studies standards that include five practices for social studies: (1) engage in democratic processes; (2) analyze and address authentic civic issues; (3) acquire, apply, and evaluate evidence; (3) read critically and interpret information; and (5) engage in evidence-based writing. The standards document makes it clear that the practices are meant to be integrated with the instruction of content standards for social studies (Oklahoma State Department of Education, 2019). New York's social studies state standards include the following social studies practices: gathering, interpreting, and using evidence; chronological reasoning and causation; comparison and contextualization; geographic reasoning; economics and economic systems; and civic participation (New York State Education Department, 2014).

---

ways that states have incorporated these practices into standards documents.) Simultaneously, expectations for social studies teaching have increased: teachers are expected to be able to integrate social studies with other subject areas (namely language arts), to move beyond lecture and rote learning and instead conduct collaborative activities and to help students engage in deeper learning.

Shifting instruction to meet the demands of deeper learning and 21st century skills called for in current standards requires shifts in instruction, curriculum, and assessment. For some teachers these shifts may be slight, whereas for others they may be considerable if their instruction emphasis is on telling and explaining concepts to students. Moreover, these shifts and practices for students with disabilities and English learners have not kept up; the research in these areas is limited and outdated practices may still be in use. Chapters 5 and 6 will further explore the changes needed in preservice and inservice teacher preparation to meet the shifting expectations for teaching and learning called for in recent disciplinary standards.

Lack of Aligned Instructional Materials for Deeper Learning

As teachers make changes in instructional approach and pedagogical goals, they can be supported through the provision of standards-aligned instructional materials. However, a *lack* of standards-aligned instructional materials and limited instructional time are perceived by many teachers to be significant barriers to the implementation of new standards (Trygstad et al., 2013). Some of this lack is due to states' and districts' decisions about curricular materials, which may or may not be aligned with new standards; when the existing purchased materials are not aligned, teachers are then left to modify these materials so as to align them with new standards.

Research has shown the lack of standards-aligned instructional materials extend across disciplines. According to a recent RAND report on math education, "Most of the materials that teachers reported using regularly for their instruction during the 2015–2016 school year were not highly aligned with Common Core" (Opfer et al., 2018, p. 1). Only "16 percent of elementary mathematics teachers and 5 percent of secondary teachers reporting regularly using material with a high degree of alignment" (p. 2). The report also revealed that "teachers using at least one aligned main material more frequently reported their students engaging 'to a great extent' in standards-aligned practices than teacher not using at least one aligned main material" (Opfer et al., 2018, p. 3). This finding suggests that well-aligned instructional materials play a critical role in providing students with opportunities to engage in the disciplinary practices for mathematics that correlate with deeper learning.

Lack of well-aligned instructional materials remains a challenge for science teachers across the nation as well. Recently, EdReports,[6] an independent nonprofit organization that conducts standards-based reviews of curriculum, published reviews of six middle school science curricula, deeming only one as meeting the expectations for alignment to the GSS. Successful implementation of the vision of the *Framework* and NGSS often requires making substantive shifts in school curriculum to support teachers as they work to implement the new standards (NRC, 2012).

In the absence of well-aligned instructional materials teachers are left to adapt existing materials or develop or download materials. For example, since the adoption of CCSS-M by several states, 97 percent of elementary and 98 percent of secondary mathematics teachers reported that they use materials that they developed or selected themselves (Opfer et al., 2018). Eighty-two percent of elementary and 91 percent of secondary teachers reported using the materials they developed or selected themselves at least once a month (Opfer et al., 2018). Researchers have also looked in more detail at where teachers are finding materials online. The most common sources (Opfer et al., 2018) were Google (elementary 94%; secondary 95%), Pinterest (elementary 87%; secondary 62%) and Teacherspayteachers.com (elementary 87%; secondary 51%). The availability of instructional materials accessible online for free has especially

---

[6]For more information and access to reviews, see https://www.edreports.org.

changed the mechanism by which teachers gain instructional resources and, in many ways, has shifted the expectation for instructional material acquisition or development to the classroom teacher, rather than the school or district.

In addition to spending time seeking out instructional materials, teachers are also spending time modifying materials to align with state standards. Which is to say, although teachers have increased access to online materials, not all of these materials have been rigorously aligned with state standards. Creating well-aligned materials, even ones based on online resources, demands *time*. On average, teachers are spending 12 hours a week creating instructional materials that align with the standards they teach (Goldberg, 2016). Without concentrated efforts to support teachers with high-quality, well-aligned instructional materials, teachers will continue to utilize valuable planning time to search for lessons or units, which may lead to inconsistencies in the quality of materials and impact student performance (Opfer et al., 2018). This could lead to less time analyzing student learning to inform instruction or considering how to differentiate instruction to meet the needs of an increasingly diverse population of students. They will also continue to spend time outside of school developing curricula, thereby reducing time they might otherwise spend on self-care or with their families (McCarthy et al., 2016).

INCREASING EMPHASIS ON THE ROLE OF CULTURE IN LEARNING

Research on student learning has shown that students' unique lived experiences and communities are inextricably linked to learning and intellectual development and growth. The recent National Academies report *How People Learn II* (2018b) concluded that "each learner develops a unique array of knowledge and cognitive resources in the course of life that are molded by the interplay of that learner's cultural, social, cognitive, and biological contexts" (p. 3). That report points out that understanding the culture of learners is central to understanding how they learn (NASEM, 2018b). It also characterizes learning as the product of a dynamic system of social activities; from this perspective, learning happens through practices that cultural communities develop, enact, and refine, and that serve contemporary and historical purposes valued by the community (Lave and Wenger, 1991; NASEM, 2018a; NRC, 2012; Rogoff, 2003, 2016).

This deeper understanding of the role of culture in student learning changes expectations for teachers. Paris and Alim (2017) argue that "we can no longer assume that the White, middle-class linguistic, literate, and cultural skills and ways of being that were considered the sole gatekeepers to the opportunity structure in the past will remain so as our society changes" (p. 89). The student population is growing increasingly diverse and the demographics in the United States are moving, in general, toward a majority multilingual, multicultural society of color; this is in contrast to the teaching population, which has remained relatively consistent in terms of racial and linguistic backgrounds (see Chapter 2). As teachers embark on instruction based on changing standards, they must also consider how they will foster instruction that is responsive to the multicultural and multilingual diversity represented in their classrooms and look for opportunities to center cultural knowledge, practices, and worldviews in ways that address inequities in the classroom.

Research from the broader field of inclusive education[7] may offer insights into the variety of approaches that can successfully involve students from a wide range of diverse backgrounds and abilities learning alongside their peers in school settings. Adoption of these approaches can help teachers to better meet the needs of all students (Loreman, 1999). These inclusive pedagogies recognize culture, identity, language, literacy, and community as valuable assets in the classroom that can be aligned to standards-based instruction to make it more culturally and socially relevant. There are a variety of ways of thinking about inclusive pedagogies; though they are distinctive, they share a framing in their potential to make teaching and learning more inclusive to all students (NASEM, 2019).

Descriptive studies documenting the ways culture influences how people learn have given rise to efforts to promote pedagogies that embrace cultural differences in an effort to promote equity. *Culturally responsive pedagogy* is an approach whereby teaching is made relevant to the languages, literacies, and cultural practices of students leading with the goal of promoting academic success, cultural competency, and critical consciousness that understands and challenges the status quo (Gay, 2010; Ladson-Billings, 1995). However, as suggested by Paris (2012), although CRP-based approaches made progress against deficit approaches that drove teaching and learning prior to the 1990s, it did not go far enough toward ensuring that a multiethnic and multilingual society was encouraged and valued. *Culturally sustaining pedagogy* highlights the value of supporting "young people in sustaining the cultural and linguistic competence of their communities while simultaneously offering access to dominant cultural competence" (Paris, 2012, p. 95). It extends the frame of culturally responsive pedagogy by replacing previous educational goals of creating a monocultural

---

[7]Mensah and Larson (2017) define inclusive education as "a broad field [that] involves students from a wide range of diverse backgrounds and abilities learning with their peers in schools settings that have adapted and changed the way they work in order to meet the needs of all students" (Loreman, 1999).

and monolingual society, to instead "perpetuate and foster—to sustain—linguistic, literate and cultural pluralism as part of the democratic project of schooling" (Paris, 2012, p. 93). Working toward cultural pluralism via culturally sustaining pedagogy involves: (1) acknowledging the historically rooted power dynamics between particular cultural worldviews (e.g., Western academic knowledge vs. Indigenous knowledge); (2) working to revitalize the cultural knowledge systems of non-dominant communities (e.g., promoting Indigenous resurgence in the face of colonialism); and (3) attending to community-based accountability (e.g., enacting responsibilities such as supporting the teaching of Indigenous knowledge) (Lee and McCarty, 2017).

Contemporary views on teaching and learning in mathematics, science, ELA, and social studies support more expansive ways of knowing by engaging students in a variety of sense-making opportunities and encourage teachers to allow students to exhibit their sense-making in diverse ways (i.e., discourse, writing, drawing). In many ways, current standards and disciplinary practices support culturally sustaining pedagogies. However, together the practices and pedagogies alone are not enough to ensure classrooms are responsive to the learning of individual students. Teachers must also ensure that classrooms serve as equitable learning communities, fostering trusting and caring relationships among students, teachers, and the community at large (Antrop-Gonzalez and DeJesus, 2006; Bang et al., 2017; Garza, 2009; Khalil and Kier, 2018; Yeager et al., 2017). Developing and sustaining equitable communities of learning involves (1) disrupting adverse stereotypes, storylines, and practices; (2) engaging in classroom talk that frames the diverse communicative resources of learners as assets; and (3) engaging in ongoing instructional feedback to expand understanding of students (Morrison and Bell, 2018).

Creating classrooms and school environments that prompt and allow all students to feel safe, express their feelings, learn to communicate respectfully, learn to set boundaries and be guided by boundaries, as well as learn and grow socioemotionally and academically adds to the challenge of being a teacher (Hamilton, Doss, and Steiner, 2019). However, this challenge is made more difficult by the lack of diversity in the teacher workforce. While teachers from a particular race or ethnicity should not be presumed to represent or understand an entire culture, teachers from a particular race/ethnicity are more likely to be familiar with the culture of students who share a similar background. Embracing cultural pluralism and cultural equity should extend beyond the students but to include the teachers and administrators who shape the goals and environments of today's schools.

Preservice and inservice teachers may require training that facilitates the acquisition of expertise with instructional practices that are inclusive of and responsive to all students and the development of a classroom environment that supports culturally sustaining pedagogies (see Chapters 5 through 7 for further discussion). As teachers gain the skills and knowledge necessary to incorporate culturally responsive and sustaining pedagogies into instruction, they also need sufficient planning and preparation time to frame curriculum and instruction around the interests and identities of their students.

ADVANCES IN TECHNOLOGY AND FAMILY COMMUNICATION

Alongside changes in expectations for teaching precipitated by emphases on deeper learning and culturally responsive pedagogies, changes in technology are shaping the work of teachers and expectations about what happens in and outside of the classroom. Across schools, districts, and states, disparities and inequities related to learning technologies can take different forms; two important ones include access (learning technologies available to some schools and their students, but not others), and teachers' abilities or capacity to use the available technologies efficiently. More specifically, with the exponential rise of technology, teachers are tasked both with using technology as a tool for teaching and *also* developing students' technological literacy (Uerz, Volman, and Kral, 2018). However, the use of technology in the classroom varies widely within and between schools and its use overall is lagging (Tondeur et al., 2013); as such, there is limited research on implementation and promising strategies for use.

Communication between teachers and the families of their students is an essential component for providing a well-rounded, successful education for all students (Jerome, 2006; Kilgore, 2010; Oostdam and Hooge, 2013). Technology has evolved dramatically over the past 20 years, better facilitating communication and enhancing relationships between teachers and their students' families (Barrera and Warner, 2006; Flowers, 2015; Kraft and Rogers, 2015). Advance in technology allow families and teachers to connect instantly through a variety of digital applications allowing teachers to post daily homework, upcoming events, and due dates for projects, and to request meetings through school-based digital platforms. Technology also allows families to easily access information from their child's teacher using their phone, tablet, or computer. All of these applications have features that allow students and their families to respond or ask questions at a time that is convenient for them; such features also allow for immediate responses or feedback from teachers. However, it should be noted that not all families have access to or are comfortable with the use of technology as a communication tool. As a result, teachers need to understand not only how to manage expectations and how to use technology for communications with families, but also the economic, experiential, and cultural factors that make any particular communications approach work better for some families than for others (Gilgore, 2015; Olmstead, 2013).

Digital communication can be an effective tool when used appropriately to communicate with families, but they can also increase expectations for teachers and add to the demands on them. Many teachers today are expected to post assignments and grades online and respond to digital communication with families and students. The mode of communication also creates expectations about the speed and frequency of response. A recent study of parent-teacher communication revealed an increase in parents' preference for frequent email, text messages, and messages via social media (Thomas, Mazer, and Grady, 2015). An expectation of frequent communication includes an expectation of immediate feedback, which can make teachers feel like they are working 24 hours a day (Thomas, Mazer, and Grady, 2015). Like many people, teachers feel guilty if they have to wait to respond to an e-mail sent to them (Myres, 2006). Teachers may need support from schools and districts in the form of professional development on using digital communication, creating boundaries, and managing expectations of families regarding communication response time. Additional studies on expectations and pressures felt by teachers in an era of technology-rich communication would benefit policy makers and school leaders in understanding changing expectations of teachers.

SUMMARY

A number of significant changes in U.S. education policies and practices, student demographics, and technologies have led to changing expectations for instruction and curriculum that have translated into changing expectations for teachers. Some of these changes in education are aimed at engaging students in deeper learning. Teachers have seen recommendations for teaching and learning shift as cognitive and learning scientists learn more about how students learn. They have also seen changes in the standards whereby disciplinary practices are given equal weight to disciplinary content knowledge, with a strengthened emphasis on the integration of content standards and disciplinary practices. For some teachers, these shifts may be slight; for teachers whose instructional approach is telling and explaining concepts to students, these shifts may be considerable. Often, instructional resources needed to support these changing expectations are absent or unavailable to teachers, requiring many to search for or develop the instructional materials on their own; this adds to the already-increasing expectations being placed on teachers.

Differentiating instruction and connecting instruction to student interests and identities are essential aspects of instructional preparation and implementation required for *all* students to have access to deeper learning experiences. As student populations are becoming increasingly diverse while the teacher workforce remains relatively consistent in terms of racial and linguistic backgrounds, there are growing expectations for teachers to learn about and utilize culturally sustaining pedagogies to promote equity across racial and ethnic communities. In addition to changing expectations for teaching and learning, advances in technology may introduce pressure for teachers to spend more time communicating with their students' families.

This and the previous chapter have focused on changes to the education landscape at large that have resulted in changing expectations for teachers in particular. Chapters 5, 6, and 7 examine some ways that preservice education (Chapter 5), inservice professional development (Chapter 6), and the workplace (Chapter 7) might support teachers as they navigate this changing landscape and find ways to best teach all students.

REFERENCES

Antrop-Gonzalez, R., and De Jesus, A. (2006). Toward a theory of critical care in urban small school reform: Examining structures and pedagogies of caring in two Latino community-based schools. *International Journal of Qualitative Studies in Education (QSE)*, *19*(4), 409–443.

Bang, M., Brown, B., Calabrese-Barton, A., Roseberry, A., and Wareen, B. (2017). Toward more equitable learning in science. In *Helping Students Make Sense of the World Using the Next Generation Science and Engineering Practices*. Arlington, VA: NSTA Press.

Barrera, J.M., and Warner, L. (2006). Involving families in school events. *Kappa Delta Pi Record*, *42*(2), 72–75.

Bitter, C., and Loney, E. (2015). *Deeper Learning: Improving Students Outcomes for College, Career, and Civic Life*. Policy Brief. Washington, DC: Education Policy Center at American Institutes for Research.

Burrus, J., Jackson, T., Xi, N., and Steinberg, J. (2013). *Identifying the Most Important 21st Century Workforce Competencies: An Analysis of the Occupational Information Network (O*NET)*. Available: https://www.ets.org/Media/Research/pdf/RR-13-21.pdf.

California Department of Education. (2016). *California Science Framework*. Available: https://www.cde.ca.gov/ci/sc/cf/cascienceframework2016.asp.

Center for Civic Education. (1994). *National Standards for Civics and Government*. Calabasas, CA: Author.

Duke, N.K., and Bennett-Armistead, V.S. (2003). *Reading and Writing Informational Text in the Primary Grades: Research-Based Practices*. New York: Scholastic.

Flowers, T.M. (2015). *Examining the Relationship Between Parental Involvement and Mobile Technology Use*. (Order No. 3670518). Available: http://pearl.stkate.edu/login?url=http://search.proquest.com.pearl.stkate.edu/docview/1650707837?accountid=26879.

Garza, R. (2009), Latino and white high school students' perceptions of caring behaviors: Are we culturally responsive to our students? *Urban Education*, *44*(3), 297–321.

Gay, G. (2010). *Culturally Responsive Teaching: Theory, Research, and Practice*. (Second Ed.). New York: Teachers College.

Gilgore, S. (2015). Probing the impact of parent-teacher digital communication. *Education Week*. Available: https://www.edweek.org/ew/articles/2015/09/16/probing-the-impact-of-parent-teacher-digital-communication.html.

Goldberg, M. (2016). *Classroom Trends: Teachers as Buyers of Instructional Materials and Users of Technology.* MDR Reports. Available: https://mdreducation.com/reports/classroom-trends-teachers-buyers-instructional-materials-users-technology.

Halvorsen, A. (2013). *A History of Elementary Social Studies: Romance and Reality.* New York: Peter Lang.

Hamilton, L.S., Doss, C.J., and Steiner, E.D. (2019). *Support for Social and Emotional Learning Is Widespread: Principals and Teachers Give Insight into How They Value, Address, and Measure It, and Which Supports They Need.* Available: https://www.rand.org/pubs/research_briefs/RB10064.html.

Jerome, B.P. (2006). *The Relationship of Parent Involvement on Student Achievement.* (Order No.3239158). Available: http://pearl.stkate.edu/login?url=http://search.proquest.com.pearl.stkate.edu/docview/305 311900?accountid=26879.

Khalil, D., and Kier, M. (2018). Critical race design: Designing a community of practice for urban middle school students through a critical race perspective. In E. Mendoza, B. Kirshner, and K. Gutiérrez (Eds.), *Designing for Equity: Bridging Learning and Critical Theories in Learning Ecologies for Youth.* Charlotte, NC: Information Age Press.

Kilgore, A.J. (2010). *Teachers' Perspectives on Using E-mail to Communicate with Parents.* (Order No. 3418344). Available: http://pearl.stkate.edu/login?url=http://search.proquest.com.pearl.stkate.edu/docview/753939594?accountid=26879.

Kraft, M.A., and Rogers, T. (2015). The underutilized potential of teacher-to-parent communication: Evidence from a field experiment. *Economics of Education Review, 47,* 49–63.

Krajcik, J., Codere, S., Dahsah, C., Bayer, R., and Mun, K. (2014). Planning instruction to meet the intent of the Next Generation Science Standards. *Journal of Science Teacher Education, 25*(2), 157–175.

Ladson-Billings, G. (1995). Toward a theory of culturally relevant pedagogy. *American Educational Research Journal, 32*(3), 465–491.

Lave, J., and Wenger, E. (1991). *Situated Learning: Legitimate Peripheral Participation.* Cambridge: Cambridge University Press.

Lee, T.S., and McCarty, T.L. (2017). Upholding indigenous education sovereignty through critical culturally sustaining/revitalizing pedagogy. In *Culturally Sustaining Pedagogies: Teaching and Learning for Justice in a Changing World.* New York: Teachers College Press.

Loreman, T. (1999). Integration: Coming from the outside. *Interaction, 13*(1), 21–23.

Mateas, V. (2016). Debunking myths about the Standards for Mathematical Practice. *Mathematics Teaching in the Middle School, 22*(2), 9–99.

McCarthy, C.J., Lambert, R.G., Lineback, S., Fitchett, P., and Baddouh, P.G. (2016). Assessing teacher appraisals and stress in the classroom: review of the classroom appraisal of resources and demands. *Educational Psychology Review, 28,* 577–603.

Mensah, F.M., and Larson, K. (2017). *A Summary of Inclusive Pedagogies for Science Education.* Paper commissioned for the National Academies of Sciences, Engineering, and Medicine's Committee on Science Investigations and Engineering Design Experiences in Grades 6–12.

Moje, E.B. (2015). Doing and teaching disciplinary literacy with adolescent learners: A social and cultural enterprise. *Harvard Educational Review, 85*(2), 254–278.

Morrison, D., and Bell, P. (2018). *How to Build an Equitable Community in Your Science Classroom.* STEM Teaching Tools Initiative, Institute for Science + Math Education. Seattle: University of Washington. Available: http://stemteachingtools.org/brief/15.

Myres, K. (2006). Communicate, communicate, communicate. *Franchising World, 38*(11), 80–82.

National Academies of Sciences, Engineering, and Medicine (NASEM). (2018a). *English Learners in STEM Subjects: Transforming Classrooms, Schools, and Lives.* Washington, DC: The National Academies Press.

———. (2018b). *How People Learn II: Learners, Contexts, and Cultures.* Washington, DC: The National Academies Press.

———. (2019). *Science and Engineering for Grades 6–12: Investigation and Design at the Center.* Washington, DC: The National Academies Press.

National Center for History in the Schools. (1996), *National Standards for History, Basic Education.* Los Angeles: University of California.

National Commission on Excellence in Education. (1983). A Nation At Risk: The Imperative for Educational Reform. *The Elementary School Journal, 84*(2), 113–130.

National Council for Geographic Education. (1994). *Geography for Life: National Geography Standards.* Washington, DC: Author.

National Council for Teachers of English and the International Reading Association. (1996). *The Standards for the English Language Arts.* Available: http://www.ncte.org/standards/ncte-ira.

National Council for the Social Studies. (NCSS). (1994). *Curriculum Standards for Social Studies: Expectations of Excellence.* Silver Spring, MD: Author.

———. (2010). *National Curriculum Standards for Social Studies: A Framework for Teaching, Learning, and Assessment.* Silver Spring, MD: Author.

———. (2013). *The College, Career, and Civic Life (C3) Framework for Social Studies State Standards: Guidance for Enhancing the Rigor of K–12 Civics, Economics, Geography, and History.* Silver Spring, MD: Author.

———. (2016). A vision of powerful teaching and learning in the social studies: A position statement of the National Council for the Social Studies. *Social Education, 80*(3), 180–182.

National Council of Teachers of Mathematics. (NCTM). (2000). *Principles and Standards for School Mathematics.* Reston, VA: Author.

———. (2014). *Principles to Actions: Ensuring Mathematical Success for All.* Reston, VA: Author.

National Council on Economic Education. (1997). *Voluntary National Content Standards in Economics.* New York, NY: Author.

National Governors Association Center for Best Practices and Council of Chief State School Officers. (2010). *Common Core State Standards for English Language Arts and Literacy in History/Social Studies, Science, and Technical Subjects.* Washington DC: Author.

National Governors Association Center for Best Practices and Council of Chief State School Officers. (2019). *Key Shifts in English Language Arts.* Available: http://www.corestandards.org/other-resources/key-shifts-in-english-language-arts.

National Research Council. (NRC). (1996). *National Science Education Standards.* Washington, DC: National Academy Press.

———. (2001). *Adding It Up: Helping Children Learn Mathematics.* Washington, DC: National Academy Press.

———. (2007). *Taking Science to School: Learning and Teaching Science in Grades K–8.* Washington, DC: The National Academies Press.

———. (2010). *Exploring the Intersection of Science Education and 21st Century Skills.* Washington, DC: The National Academies Press.

———. (2012). *A Framework for K–12 Science Education: Practices, Crosscutting Concepts, and Core Ideas.* Washington, DC: The National Academies Press.

———. (2015). *Guide to Implementing the Next Generation Science Standards.* Washington, DC: The National Academies Press.

New York State Department of Education. (2014). *New York State Department of Education Social Studies Framework.* Available: http://www.nysed.gov/curriculum-instruction/K–12-social-studies-framework.

NGSS Lead States. (2013). *Next Generation Science Standards: For States, By States.* Washington, DC: The National Academies Press.

Oklahoma State Department of Education. (2019). *Oklahoma Academic Standards for Social Studies.* Oklahoma City: Author.

Olmstead, C. (2013). Using technology to increase parent involvement in schools. *TechTrends, 57*(6), 28–37.

Oostdam, R., and Hooge, E. (2013). Making the difference with active parenting; Forming educational partnerships between parents and schools. *European Journal of Psychology of Education, 28*(2), 337–351.

Opfer, D.V., Kaufman, J.H., Pane, J.D., and Thompson, L.E. (2018). *Aligned Curricula and Implementation of Common Core State Mathematics Standards: Findings from the American Teacher Panel.* Santa Monica, CA: RAND Corporation.

Paris, D. (2012). Culturally sustaining pedagogy: A needed change in stance, terminology, and practice. *Educational Researcher, 41*(3), 93–97.

Paris, D., and Alim, H.S. (2017). *Culturally Sustaining Pedagogies: Teaching and Learning for Justice in a Changing World.* New York: Teachers College Press.

Rogoff, B. (2003). *The Cultural Nature of Human Development.* New York: Oxford University Press.

Rogoff, B. (2016). Culture and participation: A paradigm shift. *Current Opinion in Psychology, 8,* 182–189.

Sawyer, K.R. (2006). Introduction: The new science of learning. In K.R. Sawyer (Ed.), *The Cambridge Handbook of the Learning Sciences* (Ch. 1). New York: Cambridge University Press.

Shanahan, T., and Shanahan, C. (2008). Teaching disciplinary literacy to adolescents: Rethinking content-area literacy. *Harvard Educational Review, 78*(1), 40–59.

Stigler, J.W., and Hiebert, J. (1999). *The teaching gap: Best ideas from the world's teachers for improving education in the classroom.* New York: Summit Books.

Thomas, B.C., Mazer, J.P., and Grady, E.F. (2015). The changing nature of parent-teacher communication: Mode selection in the smartphone ear. *Communication Education, 64*(2), 187–207.

Tondeur, J., Pareja Roblin, N., van Braak, J., Fisser, P., and Voogt, J. (2013). Technological pedagogical content knowledge in teacher education: In search of a new curriculum. *Educational Studies, 39*(2), 239–243.

Trygstad, P., Smith, P., Banilower, E., and Nelson, M. (2013). *The Status of Elementary Science Education: Are We Ready for the Next Generation Science Standards?* Chapel Hill, NC: Horizon Research. Available: https://files.eric.ed.gov/fulltext/ED548249.pdf.

Uerz, D., Volman, M., and Kral, M. (2018). Teacher educators' competences in fostering student teachers' proficiency in teaching and learning with technology: An overview of relevant research literature. *Teaching and Teacher Education, 70,* 12–23.

Yeager, D.S., Purdie-Vaughns, V., Hooper, S.Y. and Cohen, G.L. (2017). Loss of institutional trust among racial and ethnic minority adolescents: A consequence of procedural injustices and a cause of life-span outcomes. *Child Development, 88*(2), 658–676.

4

Trends and Developments in the Teacher Labor Market

In this chapter, the committee provides an overview of the trends in the teacher labor market, highlighting some of the issues that arise from staffing different types of classrooms and subject areas for schools in different labor markets and serving students from diverse backgrounds with varying educational needs. These include issues related to the nature of teacher labor markets and the impacts this has on teacher supply and demand, teacher turnover, and equity of teacher distribution. This chapter also considers the perceived desirability of the teaching profession.

It is important to recognize that descriptions at the national level ignore how states and local entities have control over many factors in the teacher labor market. This holds true for policies (e.g., licensure, salary, tenure, and pensions) and other measures of interest in the labor market (e.g., turnover and exit rates, including retention of teachers of color). Which individuals staff the nation's classrooms is determined by several different processes that interact with one another and are governed by various state systems. States regulate who is eligible to teach through traditional and alternative licensure policies, but school systems run job searches, evaluate applicants, and make hiring decisions. The fact that individuals are eligible does not mean they *will* be offered jobs (for recent evidence on teacher hiring and its connection to effectiveness, performance, and retention, see Bruno and

Strunk, 2019; Goldhaber, Grout, and Holden, 2017a,b; Jacob et al., 2018; and Sajjadiani et al., 2019).[1]

Even though trends may hold true across states, such as the relative decline in teacher salary or increase in the rate of teachers leaving, the degree of change can vary from the state down to the school level. Each additional layer of policy, from the national to the state to the district, creates a more complex matrix of variables. And although data about teachers have improved significantly over the past two decades (Figlio et al., 2016), there is no national annual dataset that includes information about all teachers, how they entered the profession, what credentials they hold, where they teach, or their disability status. Given this, while the committee generally focuses on trends over the past two decades, there may not be data dating that far back in all instances. Additionally, for some aspects of the teacher labor market, when the data are available, earlier datasets are drawn upon if they help to describe important long-term trends.

It is challenging to say definitively how changes to state regulations for who is eligible to teach would affect the teacher workforce in general, or in particular school systems (Boyd et al., 2007). In fact, even at a national level, accurately gauging how many teachers are coming into the profession through different routes is difficult due to the fact that each state defines for itself what constitutes a traditional or alternative route (U.S. Department of Education, 2019).[2]

There is little doubt, however, that there are public concerns about the desirability of the teaching profession and how that desirability impacts the quality of the teacher workforce. During 2019, there was, for instance, widespread coverage of teacher strikes over compensation and workplace conditions (e.g., Wolf, 2019) as well as stories about declining enrollments in teacher preparation programs since the Great Recession (e.g., Higgins, 2019). Yet disentangling the factors influencing who opts into, or stays, in teaching is complicated given that individuals will be influenced by salary and other workplace conditions as well as perceptions of the prestige of the teaching profession (Martin and Mulvihill, 2016). Some of these factors, such as salary, are often determined at the

---

[1] The committee uses the term "effectiveness" to refer to estimates of a teacher's contribution to student learning on standardized tests (also referred to sometimes as "value added"). The committee uses the term "performance" to refer to documented teacher performance evaluations. The means by which these are derived can differ by state and locality, but almost always include a classroom observation of teaching practices as a component of the evaluation.

[2] See Q100 and answer under Alternative Routes to Teacher Certification of Licensure in Title II Tips for Reporting Frequently Asked Questions. See https://title2.ed.gov/public/TA/FAQ.pdf.

district level, but some states regulate aspects of teacher salaries, and all states (and some counties as well) affect compensation more generally through pension and retirement health care. And the overall prestige of the teaching profession will be influenced by broader societal factors, such as media portrayals of teaching.

Finally, given that the committee is focused on the choices that teachers and their employers are jointly making (Boyd et al., 2013) while operating under state regulations, we are cautious about interpreting the findings we describe below as causal. To put this more simply, when making job choices people are faced with a lot of options and considerations, and there are rarely, if ever, randomized control trials/experiments in the teacher labor market to help in identifying how particular factors influence those choices.

TEACHER SUPPLY AND DEMAND AND LONG-STANDING LABOR MARKET MISALIGNMENT

Reports of teacher shortages, also characterized in the broader literature as staffing challenges, have been widely reported in recent years (Dee and Goldhaber, 2017). There are various theories as to the causes of the increased difficulties schools and school systems face in finding qualified teachers to staff the nation's classrooms. For instance, some suggest that labor market fluctuations have contributed to greater difficulties with finding individuals who are willing to teach, even during the tightening labor market in the past decade since the Great Recession (Blom et al., 2015; Khalil and Chao, forthcoming; Khalil and Griffen, 2012; Nagler et al., forthcoming). Others point to the long-term decline in teacher salaries relative to salaries in other occupations (Allegretto and Mishel, 2018; Hanushek and Pace, 1995), or to the possibility that recent school or teacher accountability policies make teaching a less desirable profession (Kraft et al., 2018). These factors that play a key role in shaping the teacher workforce are discussed in more detail in the section below on the desirability of pursuing a teaching career. However, the committee first turns to a deeper discussion of the changes to the prospective teacher labor supply over time.

Evidence of Changes to Prospective Teacher Labor Supply Over Time

One possible reason for recent staffing challenges may be due to the downturn over the past decade in the number of students enrolled in and graduating with a teaching credential from traditional college- and university-based teacher education programs, and reports of a declining interest among young people in pursuing a teaching career (Aragon,

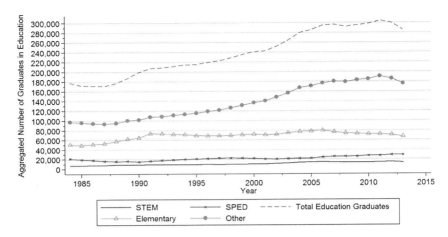

FIGURE 4-1 Aggregated number of degrees in education, 1984–2013.
NOTE: As described in Cowan et al. (2016), "the aggregated number of degrees issued in education fields . . . may not represent the true number of newly credentialed teachers because alternatively-certified teachers are not included, individuals who graduate but do not complete the requirements to receive a teaching credential are included, and teachers who receive a Bachelor's and higher degree in education may be double-counted" (p. 462).
SOURCE: Cowan et al. (2016).

2016; King and Hampel, 2018).[3] More recent data, however, suggest that this decline has slowed or even recently reversed (Alderman, 2019; also see Figure 1 in a recent report from the Center for American Progress; Partelow, 2019). Moreover, particularly for some states, there is potential for a longer-term trend of increasing supply of potential new teachers (Partelow, 2019). However, there is limited evidence that points to specific changes (e.g., active recruitment, modernization of programs) that has led to these trends.

Whereas the total number of education degrees granted in 2013 was down slightly from the 2011 peak of slightly more than 300,000, it was far higher than the production of teaching credentials in any year from 1985 to 2005 (see Figure 4-1).[4] And the number of credentials granted far exceeds the number of newly hired teachers, typically by 100,000 or more in any year (Cowan et al., 2016).

---

[3] A survey of college of education deans showed enrollment was reported to have declined in 82 percent of the institutions, and deans cited "perceptions of teaching as an undesirable career as the number-one reason for the enrollment drop" (King and Hampel, 2018, p. 63).

[4] Though as we elaborate below, it is probably misleading to look exclusively at national figures because the regulation of teacher labor markets is a state function and there are considerable barriers to cross-state teacher mobility.

There is good evidence that in the past decades (from the 1960s to late 1990s), college graduates with high standardized test scores were less likely to become teachers. Some of this trend could be attributed to the increasing labor market opportunities—due to reductions in structural barriers to participating in different labor markets—for women and people of color beginning in the 1960s (Corcoran et al., 2004). Importantly, the disproportionately low number of teachers of high academic caliber (as measured by college entrance exams) of teachers has not persisted in more recent decades (Goldhaber and Walch, 2014; Lankford et al., 2014).[5]

Factors That Contribute to Staffing Challenges

Regional heterogeneity in staffing challenges underscores that there is no national labor market for teachers. The national picture painted by aggregate figures masks the fact that there are more acute teacher shortage issues for particular states, "hard-to-staff" schools serving traditionally disadvantaged students (Dee and Goldhaber, 2017; Ingersoll, 2003; Sutcher et al., 2016; Will, 2016), and rural schools that are geographically far from teacher education systems (Goldhaber et al., 2018). In a study of Chicago schools (Engel et al., 2014), for instance, the number of applicants per school in a year ranged from more than 300 to fewer than 5, and schools serving more advantaged student populations were far more likely to have multiple applications per open teaching slot. The committee will look at the specific issue of staffing challenges for schools serving students from traditionally disadvantaged backgrounds in more detail below when describing inequities in the distribution of teacher quality across students.

Staffing challenges arise in part because heterogeneous state regulations make it more difficult for teachers to cross state borders. As noted above, states regulate teacher labor markets through licensure, seniority, tenure, and pensions in ways that create barriers to cross-state teacher mobility (Dee and Goldhaber, 2017). Several studies focusing on the interstate mobility of teachers find it to be far lower than within-state mobility, even for teachers who are working on a state border, such that an employment move from one state to another would not necessitate a residential move (Goldhaber et al., 2015a; Kim et al., 2016; Podgursky et al., 2016). Goldhaber and colleagues (2015a), for instance, examined the Oregon–Washington cross-state mobility of teachers and found that even in the Portland–Vancouver

---

[5]There is disagreement about whether the long-term decline in the academic caliber is more closely connected to the average salaries in other occupations (Corcoran et al., 2004) or the compression of pay inside the teaching profession at the same time that salaries in the private sector have trended toward greater rewards to strong academic skills (Hoxby and Leigh, 2004).

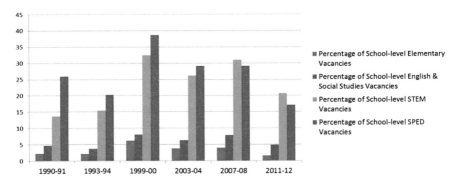

FIGURE 4-2 Percentage of schools reporting difficulty filling vacancies within specific disciplines.
SOURCE: Cowan et al. (2016).

metropolitan area that straddles the border, within-state moves are eight times more likely among teachers than moves to a school in the other state.

Although staffing challenges vary by state, they tend to be more acute in "hard-to-staff" specific subject areas; in particular, there are long-standing staffing challenges in mathematics (Liu et al., 2008) and science (commonly referred to as "STEM"), as well as in special education. Cowan and colleagues (2016) show that in every year that school systems have been surveyed about the difficulty of filling open teaching slots, STEM and special education are consistently cited as the hardest subjects to fill (see Figure 4-2). Buttressing this reporting, Goldhaber and colleagues (2014) found that the probability that a student teacher employed in a public school in Washington (the same state in which their student teaching was observed) after receiving a teaching credential is more than 10 percentage points higher for student teachers who receive an endorsement in a STEM or special education area relative to elementary education. Despite these consistent patterns, the teacher labor market does not appear to be very responsive to challenges in staffing particular subject areas in terms of the training of new teachers (Goldhaber et al., 2015b). Goldhaber and colleagues found that over a 30-year period within Washington State, production of new teachers with elementary endorsements far exceeded the number of estimated openings in that area, while the in-state production of new teachers in STEM and special education was consistently less than the number of openings.

The long-standing misalignment of teacher supply and demand across subject areas and school types (e.g., private, public, charter) might be considered a feature of the teacher labor market. Why the labor market does not adjust to supply and demand conditions is a matter of much speculation (Goldhaber et al., 2011). The mechanism through which we would expect adjustments in the private sector—wages—is less readily adjustable in public schools because teacher salaries are subject to a public policy-making process. Also, as just described, state-specific licensure, tenure, and pension policies likely constrain labor market mobility, making it more difficult for schools to hire qualified teachers from other states when vacancies arise.

Finally, there is significant misalignment between the race and ethnicity of students and teachers (discussed in Chapter 2); there may also be misalignment with respect to disability status, but there are limited data to address this question. This misalignment, particularly for categories of race and ethnicity, exists despite some increases in the diversity of the teacher workforce over the past 30 years (e.g., Ingersoll et al., 2017).[6] Villegas et al. (2012), for instance, finds that the share of teachers of color increased from 13 percent to 17 percent from 1987 to 2007; by 2016, the share had increased to about 20 percent (Hansen and Quintero, 2019). As such, the relative changes in the labor market are less pronounced when looking back over the past 10 to 20 years—which was the charge given to the committee—than what is observed in comparisons with a wider timeframe. Yet despite these small increases in teacher diversity, the "diversity gap"— measured by the percentage point differential between teachers and students of color—has increased because the racial/ethnic diversity of the student body has risen more quickly than the diversity of the teacher workforce.

PATHWAYS INTO THE PROFESSION AND THE LOCALNESS OF TEACHER LABOR MARKETS

The difficulty of filling some teaching specialties or staffing schools that have been considered traditionally disadvantaged may be an important impetus for the creation of specific pathways into the profession or programs designed to address the misalignment issues we described above. Some programs targeting areas of need operate as part of traditional college- and university-based education. The UTeach program, for example, focuses on encouraging and training students to teach in math and science. It was originally created in 1997 at the University of Texas at Austin, but there are now UTeach programs in more than 20 states (Backes et al., 2018).

Programs such as UTeach, Teach For America, The New Teacher Project (TNTP), and Teach.com, illustrate the complex and sprawling landscape of teacher recruitment, preparation, and placement. These are

---

[6] Over the longer term, dating back to the 1960s and 1970s, there likely has been a drop in the overall racial/ethnic diversity in the teacher workforce, particularly in the South, where Black teachers and leaders lost their jobs in large numbers, often to less qualified White teachers and leaders (Fenwick, 2019, personal communication), as a result of school desegregation efforts. While many of them moved to a teaching job in the North, many others never returned to the teacher labor market (Thompson, 2019).

all programs that have emerged since the mid-1990s and play interrelated, and sometimes overlapping roles in drawing new people into teaching, preparing them, and addressing the difficulties that hard-to-staff schools face in recruiting new teachers. But it is difficult to definitively categorize these types of programs given that the role they play may vary from state to state depending on a state's licensure policies. As noted above, the definition of what constitutes an alternative program is left up to states. Thus, in some states, Teach For America, for example, would be considered an alternative route (or alternative licensure) program, commonly thought of as one in which teachers can be the teacher of record while not having completed all of the traditional preservice licensure requirements.[7] But in other states, Teach For America corps members are required to satisfy the same preservice requirements as individuals obtaining traditional teacher licenses. In short, university, non-university, and online programs can all be either alternative or traditional (and institutions, like universities, can house both alternative and traditional programs), and as a result the traditional/alternative nomenclature will often be insufficient for program categorization.

Teacher Supply and Traditional and Alternative Routes

As noted above, it is difficult to accurately gauge how many teachers come into the profession through alternative routes because what constitutes an alternative route is defined by each state and, moreover, college- and university-based teacher education programs can operate alternative route programs (U.S. Department of Education, 2019). Consequently, some disagreement exists about the extent to which alternative route programs play a role in supplying new teachers. Still, a striking change to the structure of the teacher labor market over the past 35 years is the increased proportion of teachers who are entering the profession through alternative routes. In the mid-1980s, fewer than a dozen states had any type of alternative route programs, but by 2000 the great majority did (Editorial Projects in Education Research Center, 2004).[8] Data available in recent years suggest that over the past decade the growth in individuals with alternative credentials as a share of people preparing to teach has declined. For

---

[7] Specifically, Title II of the Higher Education Act defines alternative route programs as "preparation programs [that] typically serve candidates whom states permit to be the teachers of record in a classroom while working toward obtaining an initial teaching credential" and notes that "for purposes of *HEA Title II* reporting, each state determines which teacher preparation programs are classified as alternative programs) (U.S. Department of Education, 2016, p. 7).

[8] See the National Council on Teacher Quality site, which allows for the interrogation of routes for all states at https://www.nctq.org/yearbook/home.

example, the share of alternative program completers was about 20 percent in 2007–2008 versus 15 percent in 2012–2013; in each year about one-half of the alternative program completers were from a college- or university-based alternative program.[9]

What is clearer is that the use of alternative routes varies considerably by state. A recent report issued by the Southern Regional Education Board (SREB) shows that the percentage of teacher candidates enrolled in alternative programs was 0 percent in West Virginia but greater than 70 percent in Texas (SREB, 2018).

It also appears that alternative routes are more likely to bring teachers of color into the profession (Kabaker, 2012, U.S. Department of Education, 2016). However, nontraditional teacher education providers are small enough as a fraction of the overall supply of new teachers that observers question whether the efforts of these programs can constitute more than a small component of an overall strategy to diversify the teacher workforce (Putman et al., 2016). Historically black colleges and universities (HBCUs) and other minority-serving institutions are another important source of teachers of color (for additional information, see Chapter 5). As of 2012–2013, for example, HBCUs enrolled 2 percent of candidates in institutes of higher education–based teacher preparation programs, but 16 percent of all such candidates who identified as Black.

Another trend in alternative teacher training is the increasing number of new teachers being prepared through online programs, many of which are at for-profit institutions (Sawchuk, 2013). Here too, however, the exact numbers are murky because they depend on how one defines online preparation. In a survey conducted by the American Association of Colleges for Teacher Education of its member schools, 70 percent of respondents claimed to offer distance-education courses; moreover, the U.S. Department of Education reported that the four largest education schools in 2011 were online programs (Liu, 2013).

The Localness of Teacher Labor Markets

One consistent feature of the pathway a teacher candidate takes into the profession—whether traditional or alternative—is that it tends to be localized; teachers tend to work close to where they did their training and/or went to high school (Khalil and Chao, forthcoming). Boyd and colleagues (2005a) finds "teacher labor markets to be geographically very small. Teachers express preferences to teach close to where they grew up

---

[9]These figures are based on authors' calculations from Title II reports. See Figure 2.4 at https://title2.ed.gov/Public/TitleIIReport16.pdf.

and, controlling for proximity, they prefer areas with characteristics similar to their hometown."[10] The localness of labor markets arises in different contexts (e.g., Krieg et al., 2016) and is also found in national data, which show that teacher labor markets appear to be more localized than other occupations (Reininger, 2012). And while proximity to teacher education programs predicts first jobs, the location of student teaching is even more predictive.[11] Thus, where student teaching occurs might be a policy lever for addressing teacher shortages or the equity of teacher quality distribution (discussed below).

It is not clear precisely why teacher labor markets are so localized, because it is difficult to distinguish between the preferences of hiring officials from those of teacher candidates.[12] Nevertheless, this strong connection between specific teacher education programs and schools has important equity implications (Goldhaber, 2018). Teachers tend to grow up and go to college in more advantaged areas (Engel and Cannata, 2015), and student teaching tends to occur in more advantaged schools (Krieg et al., 2016).

Some of the localness of teacher labor markets results from the aforementioned state-specific licensure, tenure, and pensions. Again, while there is relatively little evidence on the between-state mobility of teachers, the evidence that does exist shows that very few teachers with inservice experience in one state show up in another state's public school workforce. This finding is not surprising given that teachers who move from one state to another have to navigate different state licensure rules, often will take a hit on pension wealth, and may lose tenure protections (Goldhaber, Grout, and Holden, 2017a,b). In addition to the localness promoted by state borders, the degree of localness may be related to the institutional structures of teacher preparation and K–12 schooling (e.g., the number and size of teacher education programs and school districts). These structures can be quite different across states. For example, in Florida, research by Mihaly et al. (2013) finds that more than 50 percent of schools employed teachers from a single teacher education program. By contrast, in Washington State, less than 20 percent of schools are found to employ teachers from just a single program (Goldhaber et al., 2014).

---

[10] Boyd et al. (2005a) report that nearly 70 percent of new teachers in New York find a job within 40 miles of where they obtained their teaching credential. Krieg et al. (2016) find over half of first jobs are within 25 miles of home and about two-thirds are within 50 miles. And, using data from online applications to school systems in Vermont, Killeen et al. (2015) also find that over half of first jobs are within 25 miles of where teachers grew up.

[11] Krieg et al. (2016) report that 15 percent of teacher candidates are hired into the very same school in which they completed their student teaching.

[12] Evidence on this issue is mixed; see Boyd et al. (2013) and Hinrichs (2014).

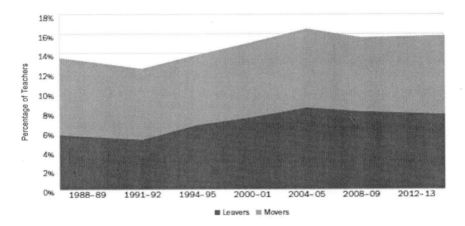

FIGURE 4-3 Rate of learning teaching has increased.
SOURCE: Carver-Thomas and Darling-Hammond (2017).

TEACHER TURNOVER

Teaching is marked by substantial turnover. According to estimates from the 2011–2012 Schools and Staffing Survey (SASS) and 2012–2013 Teacher Follow-up Survey (TFS), the annual turnover rate for U.S. public school teachers is 16 percent (Goldring, Taie, and Riddles, 2014). This turnover rate—where *turnover* is defined as any case in which a teacher in year t is no longer teaching in the same school in year $t + 1$—is split evenly between teachers who move to other schools but remain in teaching (8%) and teachers who exit the teaching profession (8%).[13] The turnover rate is just down from a peak of 16.5 percent in 2004–2005 (with an 8.4% exit rate) but higher than rates reported in earlier SASS waves; the annual turnover rate was just 12.4 percent as recently as 1991–1992, a year when just 5.1 percent of teachers exited (see Figure 4-3). There is mixed evidence about whether we should consider teacher turnover to be high relative to turnover in other occupations. For instance, according to Ingersoll, Merrill, and Stuckey (2014), exit rates from teaching are higher than those for nurses (and much higher than professionals in the fields of law, engineering, architecture, and academia), but Harris and Adams (2007) find little difference in turnover across competing occupations after adjusting for demographics.

---

[13]The largest category of leavers is retirees (Goldring, Taie, and Riddles, 2014). About 30 percent of teachers classified as exiters in fact remain in K–12 education but not as a regular classroom teacher. Also, nearly 60 percent of teachers who change schools move within the same district rather than to another school district.

Average national turnover rates mask significant differences among geographical areas. Turnover is substantially higher in the South (16.7% according to the 2012–2013 TFS) than elsewhere; the turnover rate in the Northeast Census region is only 10.3 percent (Carver-Thomas and Darling-Hammond, 2017). Turnover also tends to be higher in cities than in suburbs or more rural areas, though research also demonstrates that turnover rates can vary widely even among urban districts (Papay et al., 2017).

Variation in Teacher Turnover by School Type

A large body of research demonstrates that teachers are much less likely to stay in some kinds of schools than others (see Box 4-1). In particular, turnover is substantially more common in schools with larger numbers of students of color and students living in poverty (Borman and Dowling, 2008; Boyd et al., 2005b; Guarino, Santibañez, and Daley, 2006; Hanushek, Kain, and Rivkin, 2004; Ingersoll, 2001; Ladd, 2011; Lankford, Loeb, and Wyckoff, 2002). Higher turnover rates in such schools often are attributed to lower-quality working conditions and are correlated with factors such as less effective leaders, greater leadership churn, fewer resources, and less adequate facilities (Bartanen, Grissom, and Rogers, 2019; Grissom, 2011; Grissom, Viano, and Selin, 2015; Johnson, Kraft, and Papay, 2012; Ladd, 2011; Loeb, Darling-Hammond, and Luczak, 2005).

Variation in Teacher Turnover by Teacher Characteristics

Average rates also mask differences in turnover rates among teachers with different characteristics. These include level of experience, subject taught, and race and ethnicity of the teacher. For example, turnover is highest among beginning teachers, though exit rates among new teachers are substantially lower than once believed; according to estimates from the Beginning Teacher Longitudinal Study, 17 percent of new teachers in 2007–2008 were no longer teaching as of 2011–2012 (Gray and Taie, 2015). These high rates of attrition for novice teachers have been linked to low pay for new teachers under fixed salary schedules, a "sink or swim" mentality in which new teachers are thrown into isolated classrooms with little support, and new teachers' low initial investment in the profession as they go through a "trying on" phase with teaching (Grissom, Viano, and Selin, 2015; Johnson and Birkeland, 2003; Peske et al., 2001). Turnover rates and exit rates are also substantially higher for teachers of some subjects, with particularly high turnover rates for mathematics, science, special education, and English language development teachers as compared to general elementary teachers (Carver-Thomas and Darling-Hammond, 2017).

BOX 4-1
The School Workplace and Retention of Teachers of Color

Workplace conditions matter especially in the retention of teachers of color (Ingersoll, May, and Collins, 2019). Based on an analysis of the 2003–2004 Schools and Staffing Survey (SASS) and its longitudinal supplement, the 2004–2005 Teacher Follow-up Survey (TFS), Ingersoll, May, and Collins (2019) found that both teachers of color and teachers from non-minoritized groups who self-report that they either migrate to different schools or leave the profession because of job dissatisfaction indicate they do so for similar reasons: "the way their school is administered, . . . how student assessments and school accountability affected teaching, . . . student discipline problems, and . . . a lack of input into decisions and lack of classroom autonomy over their teaching" (p. 20). However, for teachers of color, unlike teachers from non-minoritized groups, Ingersoll, May, and Collins (2019) found that school characteristics were *not* statistically significant predictors of attrition. Instead, the leading statistically significant predictors of teachers' of color attrition was "higher levels of schoolwide faculty decision-making influence" and "classroom autonomy" (pp. 25–26). This suggests that "retaining and sustaining" (Mosely, 2018) teachers of color requires specific attention to the organizational conditions of schools.

Studies of the experiences of Black male teachers are directly relevant, given the greater propensity of these teachers to leave teaching than other "minority" populations (Ingersoll, May, and Collins, 2019). Based on a study of 86 Black male teachers' responses to the Black Male Teacher Environment Survey in an urban district, Bristol (2018) found that teachers' experiences varied in relation to the "number of Black men on the faculty" (p. 334). Teachers of color, in general, tend to teach in schools with predominantly non-minoritized teaching staff. Bristol found that in schools in which there was only one Black male on the faculty, Black male teachers "reported that their White colleagues had greater influence on school policy than teachers of color, believed that being Black caused people to fear them in their schools, and reported having a greater desire to leave their schools than [schools in which there were four or more Black males on the faculty]" (p. 334). On the whole, the work of Bristol and his colleagues suggests that "decreasing the isolation of staff of color in their schools could be an important lever for improving the retention of staff of color" (Bristol and Shirrell, 2019, p. 890).

Research conflicts on how race/ethnicity correlates with turnover, with some studies finding higher turnover rates among White teachers and others finding slightly higher turnover rates among teachers of color, depending on what other factors are adjusted for (e.g., Achinstein et al., 2010; Borman and Dowling, 2008; Carver-Thomas and Darling-Hammond, 2017; Guarino, Santibañez, and Daley, 2006). However, more research is still needed to further interrogate which factors are essential in giving rise to these observed differences in turnover rates with respect to race and ethnicity. Whereas earlier studies had not found important differences (Grissom, 2008), in more recent years teachers entering through alternate routes are more likely to turn over than traditionally certified teachers, even conditioning on characteristics of their schools and other factors (Redding and Smith, 2016).

Research also is not conclusive about whether more effective teachers are more likely to stay in their schools.[14] Some studies find that more effective teachers are more likely to stay in teaching or in the same school (Feng and Sass, 2011; Goldhaber, Gross, and Player, 2011; Krieg, 2006; West and Chingos, 2009). Others find that more effective teachers are more likely to leave teaching, especially early in their careers (Clotfelter, Ladd, and Vigdor, 2007; Wiswall, 2013). Still others find evidence that whether effectiveness positively predicts turnover depends on school level (Harris and Sass, 2011). Higher rates among ineffective teachers may be due to nontrivial rates of involuntary staffing action, such as contract nonrenewal, particularly among novice teachers (Gray and Taie, 2015), while higher rates among effective teachers may reflect higher returns to job skills in nonteaching professions (Chingos and West, 2012).

Effective teachers may be especially more likely to transfer from less to more advantaged schools (Boyd et al., 2005b; Feng and Sass, 2011; West and Chingos, 2009). Sorting of teachers toward more advantaged schools—as measured by student characteristics—across their careers is a well-documented pattern (Lankford, Loeb, and Wyckoff, 2002). This sorting typically occurs within districts; nearly 60 percent of teachers who change schools move within the same district rather than to another school district (Goldring, Taie, and Riddles, 2014). Across-district sorting is especially uncommon across state lines. State-specific licensing requirements, seniority rules, and the lack of portability for teachers' defined benefit pensions appear to constrain teacher labor markets to be local and segmented (Dee and Goldhaber, 2017). For instance, studies find that the interstate mobility of teachers, even those residing near state borders, is substantially below levels that would be expected in light of levels of within-state mobility (e.g., Goldhaber et al., 2015a; Podgursky et al., 2016).

EQUITY OF TEACHER DISTRIBUTION

Given the aforementioned staffing challenges and trends in teacher mobility, it is all but a forgone conclusion that there is inequity in the distribution of teachers across students. Importantly, there is no uniformly agreed upon means of determining the "quality" of teachers, but there is long-standing evidence from a variety of settings that teacher *qualifications* are inequitably distributed with students of color and students living in poverty tending to be assigned to less experienced and less credentialed teachers

---

[14]By "effective," we mean teachers who have higher value added, a statistical measure of how much teachers are contributing to the test score growth of the students in their classrooms.

(e.g., Betts et al., 2003; Clotfelter, Ladd, and Vigdor, 2005; Goldhaber, Lavery, and Theobald, 2015; Kalogrides and Loeb, 2013; Lankford, Loeb, and Wyckoff, 2002).

A newer body of evidence also shows inequity in the distribution of teacher effectiveness (as measured by their value added) (Goldhaber et al., 2015a; Isenberg et al., 2016; Mansfield, 2015; Sass et al., 2010) and documented performance (Cowan et al., 2017).[15] There is some disagreement about the magnitude or import of teacher quality gaps (TQGs), but these gaps are another clear feature of the teacher labor market. They also are not new. Goldhaber and colleagues (2017) investigated the distribution of teacher quality over several decades in North Carolina and Washington State and found that "TQGs exist in every year in each state, and for all measures [of quality]" (abstract). In other words, the available evidence suggests that inequity in the distribution of teacher quality, however it is measured, is a consistent feature of the teacher labor market.

THE DESIRABILITY OF THE TEACHING PROFESSION

There is a significant amount of research that touches on issues of the desirability of the teaching profession. Discussions of desirability can be organized around two topics: compensation and working conditions.

Compensation

According to the Digest of Education Statistics, teachers' annual salaries averaged $58,950 in 2016–2017. In constant dollars, average salaries are considerably higher than in 1970 ($55,411) or 1980 ($49,917), but in fact lower than in 1990 ($59,944) or 2000 ($59,924). This 1.6 percent decline in average salary nationally from 2000 to 2017 (see Figure 4-4) is small relative to the declines in some states (e.g., 15.7% in Indiana, 15.0% in Colorado).[16] These declines matter because the best available evidence suggests that lower pay increases teacher turnover (Hendricks, 2014); approximately a fifth of exiting teachers report financial reasons as being "very important" in their decision to leave teaching (Carver-Thomas and Darling-Hammond, 2017). Indeed, many teachers report moonlighting (having second jobs) to make ends meet (Blair, 2018; Startz, 2018).

---

[15] Again, value added is a statistical means of assessing teacher contributions to student test score gains, and document performance refers to the performance evaluations that teachers receive from their districts of employment (and the way these are determined can vary across districts and states).

[16] Some states have also increased teacher pay substantially over this time period, including North Dakota (20.6%) and Wyoming (19.9%).

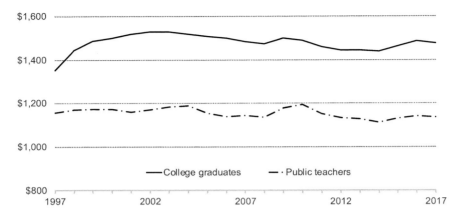

FIGURE 4-4 Average weekly wages of public school teachers and other college graduates, 1997–2017 (2017 dollars).
NOTE: Teachers are elementary, middle, and secondary public school teachers. "College graduates" excludes public school teachers.
SOURCE: Adapted from Allegretto and Mishel (2018). Data from the Current Population Survey Outgoing Rotation Group.

This percentage varies by gender (males are more likely) and school level (secondary are more likely). The variation in the percentage is due to how one defines a second job. The ratio of teachers engaging in the practice of working outside their contractual arrangement varies from 15 percent to 71 percent (Blair, 2018, p. 2). Lower salaries may also attract fewer high-quality teachers into the workforce (Ballou and Podgursky, 1995; Martin and Mulvihill, 2016).

Teachers in the United States typically are paid according to a single salary schedule that sets compensation levels by experience and degree attainment. In recent years, school districts increasingly have experimented with alternative compensation schemes, including pay-for-performance and retention bonuses for teachers in hard-to-staff schools or subjects. Effects of such programs on outcomes such as teacher performance and retention, however, have been mixed (e.g., Hill and Jones, 2018; Podgursky and Springer, 2007; Springer et al., 2012; Springer, Swain, and Rodriguez, 2016; Yuan et al., 2013).

Beyond take-home pay, benefits represent a substantial expenditure on teacher compensation for states and school districts. Among these benefits, researchers have raised substantial concern about states' investments in teacher pensions. Defined-benefit pension systems for public employees are collectively underfunded by potentially several trillion dollars (Novy-Marx and Rauh, 2011), and liabilities for teachers' pensions are a large portion of this total. As a consequence, a significant portion of current educational expenditures are going to fund prior pension promises. Backes et al. (2016) estimate that, on average, states set aside more than 10 percent of current teachers' earnings to pay for pension liabilities already accrued.

The substantial costs of pensions are particularly concerning given that they do not appear to have much influence on making teaching a desirable profession (Goldhaber and Grout, 2016; Holden, 2018). In particular, young and mid-career teachers do not seem to value highly the amount invested in what they perhaps regard as a distant retirement benefit; consequently, Fitzpatrick (2015) estimates that investment in retirement plans is unlikely to yield high returns in attracting employees. Studies have also found little evidence that defined benefit plans are preferred to defined contribution plans by more effective teachers (Chingos and West, 2015; Goldhaber and Grout, 2016), nor that defined benefit plans produce lower teacher turnover than other plans (Goldhaber, Grout, and Holden, 2017a,b). However, given the incentives they create, pension plans can distort the work behavior of late-career teachers. In particular, they push out teachers when their accrued pension wealth peaks, including teachers who might have otherwise preferred to remain in teaching (Koedel, Podgursky, and Shi, 2013; Koedel and Xiang, 2017). That said, much is not known about alternatives to traditional defined pension plans in education because defined benefit plans are so prevalent, thus it is important not to jump to strong conclusions about the potential efficacy of alternative types of pension arrangements for teachers.

Working Conditions

Research on teacher working conditions often focuses on factors that predict teacher turnover, as discussed previously. Factors associated with more positive teacher working conditions include high-quality school leadership (Grissom, 2011; Ladd, 2011), better school facilities (Buckley, Schneider, and Shang, 2005; Loeb, Darling-Hammond, and Luczak, 2005), more robust teacher support systems (Borman and Dowling, 2008; Ladd, 2011), more positive teacher relationships (Kraft, Marinell, and Yee, 2016), and greater autonomy and input into school decisions (Guarino, Santibañez, and Daley, 2006; Ingersoll, 2001; Ingersoll and May, 2012). Although we have less evidence about working conditions and entrants to the teaching profession, it is likely that more positive working conditions allow for attracting a higher-quality teacher workforce by raising the overall desirability of teaching.

The recent accountability, teacher evaluation, and tenure reform movements have generated substantial discussion about whether these changes to the education policy environment have impacted the desirability of teaching. However, the evidence with respect to these questions is limited. Some research suggests that, counter to conventional wisdom, No Child

Left Behind (NCLB) alone may not have led to substantial impacts on the desirability of the teaching profession. That is, NCLB had minimal impact on the job attitudes of teachers or their turnover rates (Grissom, Nicholson-Crotty, and Harrington, 2014; Sun, Saultz, and Ye, 2017). Moreover, the research also suggests that more academically capable people are entering teaching in the era since NCLB's enactment (Goldhaber and Walch, 2014; Lankford et al., 2014).

Multiple-measure teacher evaluation systems—that is, those that pair rubric-based classroom observations with measures of student achievement and/or growth—have become near-universal in the post-Race to the Top era (Steinberg and Donaldson, 2016). Research suggests that teachers increase productivity (as measured by increases in their students' test scores) in response to evaluation (Taylor and Tyler, 2012). Some evidence suggests that implementation of evaluation reforms resulted in declines in the supply of new teachers (Kraft et al., 2018). However, a study of evaluation implementation in Chicago Public Schools found no effect on teacher turnover for the average teacher but higher turnover among low-rated teachers, suggesting that schools used evaluation information to make staffing decisions (Sartain and Steinberg, 2016). Evidence consistent with schools' use of evaluation information to retain high-performing teachers and remove low-performing ones has been found elsewhere (Dee and Wyckoff, 2015; Grissom and Bartanen, 2019).

More generally, emerging evidence suggests that the availability of multiple measures of teacher performance, including standardized, rubric-based measures of teacher instructional strengths and weaknesses of the kind that have become widespread in the post-Race to the Top era, might be leveraged to facilitate teacher improvement. Principals report using teacher evaluation information for feedback and teacher support strategies (Kraft and Gilmour, 2016; Neumerski et al., 2018). Experimental evidence suggests that classroom observation information can be used to increase teacher performance by pairing teachers with areas of weakness with other teachers in their school with a complementary strength to work together for improvement (Papay et al., 2016).

SUMMARY

There are competing views about how to address staffing challenges related to certain subjects and how to address the inequitable distribution of teachers. But as emphasized throughout the chapter, it is important to recognize that descriptions at the national level ignore how states and local entities have control over many factors in the teacher labor market. This holds true for policies (e.g., licensure, salary, tenure, and pensions) and other measures of interest in the labor market (e.g., turnover and exit rates, including retention of teachers of color). Each layer of policy from the national to the state to the district creates a more complex matrix of variables. Even though some trends may hold true across states, such as the relative decline in teacher salary or increase in teacher leave rate, the degree of change can vary from the state down to the school level. The complexity of many factors at different layers makes it difficult to determine causality between the factors in the labor market and how individual teachers and teacher candidates make decisions regarding their careers.

REFERENCES

Achinstein, B., Ogawa, R.T., Sexton, D., and Freitas, C. (2010). Retaining teachers of color: A pressing problem and a potential strategy for "hard-to-staff" schools. *Review of Educational Research, 80*(1), 71–107.

Alderman, C. (2019). Why Aren't College Grads Becoming Teachers? *The Answer Seems to Be Economic—and the Labor Market May Be Starting to Improve.* Available: https://www.the74million.org/article/aldeman-why-arent-college-grads-becoming-teachers-the-answer-seems-to-be-economic-and-the-labor-market-may-be-starting-to-improve.

Allegretto, S., and Mishel, L. (2018). *The Teacher Pay Penalty Has Hit a New High: Trends in the Teacher Wage and Compensation Gaps Through 2017.* Economic Policy Institute. Available: https://www.epi.org/publication/teacher-pay-gap-2018.

Aragaon, S. (2016). *Teacher Shortages: What We Know.* Denver, CO: Education Commission of the States. Available: https://files.eric.ed.gov/fulltext/ED565893.pdf.

Backes, B., Goldhaber, D., Grout, C., Koedel, C., Ni, S., Podgursky, M., et al. (2016). Benefit or burden? On the intergenerational inequity of teacher pension plans. *Educational Researcher, 45*(6), 367–377.

Backes, B., Goldhaber, D., Cade, W., Sullivan, K., and Dodson, M. (2018). Can UTeach? Assessing the relative effectiveness of STEM teachers. *Economics of Education Review, 64*, 184–198.

Ballou, D., and Podgursky, M. (1995). Education policy and teacher efforts. *Industrial Relations, 34*, 21–39.

Bartanen, B., Grissom, J.A., and Rogers, L.K. (2019). The impacts of principal turnover. *Educational Evaluation and Policy Analysis, 41*(3), 350–374.

Betts, J.R., Zau, A., and Rice, L. (2003). *Determinants of Student Achievement: New Evidence from San Diego.* San Francisco: Public Policy Institute of California.

Blair, E.J. (Ed.). (2018). *By the Light of the Silvery Moon: Teacher Moonlighting and the Dark Side of Teachers' Work.* Gorham, ME: Myers Education Press.

Blom, E., Cadena, B.C., and Keys, B.J. (2015). *Investment over the Business Cycle: Insights from College Major Choice.* IZA Discussion Papers, No. 9167. Bonn: Institute for the Study of Labor.

Borman, G.D., and Dowling, N.M. (2008). Teacher attrition and retention: A meta-analytic and narrative review of the research. *Review of Educational Research, 78*(3), 367–409.

Boyd, D., Lankford, H., Loeb, S., and Wyckoff, J. (2005a). The draw of home: How teachers' preferences for proximity disadvantage urban schools. *Journal of Policy Analysis and Management: The Journal of the Association for Public Policy Analysis and Management, 24*(1), 113–132.

Boyd, D., Lankford, H., Loeb, S., and Wyckoff, J. (2005b). Explaining the short careers of high-achieving teachers in schools with low-performing students. *American Economic Review, 95*(2), 166–171.

Boyd, D., Goldhaber, D.D., Lankford H., and Wyckoff, J.H. (2007). The effect of certification and preparation on teacher quality. *The Future of Children, 17*(1), 45–68.

Boyd, D.J., Grossman, P.L., Lankford, H., Loeb, S., and Wyckoff, J. (2009). Teacher preparation and student achievement. *Educational Evaluation and Policy Analysis, 31*(4), 416–440.

Boyd, D.J., Lankford, H., Loeb, S., and Wyckoff, J. (2013). Analyzing the determinants of the matching of public school teachers to jobs: Disentangling the preferences of teachers and employers. *Journal of Labor Economics, 31*(1), 83–117.

Bristol, T.J. (2018). To be alone or in a group: An exploration into how the school-based experiences differ for Black male teachers across one urban school district. *Urban Education, 53*(3), 1–21.

Bristol, T.J., and Shirrell, M. (2019). Who is here to help me?: The work-related social networks of teachers of color. *American Educational Research Journal, 56*(3), 868–898.

Bruno, P., and Strunk, K.O. (2019). Making the cut: The effectiveness of teacher screening and hiring in the Los Angeles Unified School District. *Educational Evaluation and Policy Analysis*.

Buckley, J., Schneider, M., and Shang, Y. (2005). Fix it and they might stay: School facility quality and teacher retention in Washington, D.C. *Teachers College Record, 107*(5), 1107–1123.

Carver-Thomas, D., and Darling-Hammond, L. (2017). *Teacher Turnover: Why It Matters and What We Can Do About It.* Palo Alto, CA: Learning Policy Institute.

Chingos, M.M., and West, M.R. (2012). Do more effective teachers earn more outside the classroom? *Education Finance and Policy, 7*(1), 8–43.

Chingos, M.M., and West, M.R. (2015). Which teachers choose a defined contribution pension plan? Evidence from the Florida retirement system. *Education Finance and Policy, 10*(2), 193–222.

Clotfelter, C.T., Ladd, H.F., and Vigdor, J. (2005). Who teaches whom? Race and the distribution of novice teachers. *Economics of Education Review, 24*(4), 377–392.

Clotfelter, C.T., Ladd, H.F., and Vigdor, J.L. (2007). *How and Why Do Teacher Credentials Matter for Student Achievement.* NBER Working Paper 12828. Cambridge, MA: National Bureau of Economic Research. Available: https://www.nber.org/papers/w12828.pdf.

Corcoran, S.P., Evans, W.N., and Schwab, R.M. (2004). Changing labor-market opportunities for women and the quality of teachers, 1957–2000. *American Economic Review, 94*(2), 230–235.

Cowan, J., Goldhaber, D., Hayes, K., and Theobald, R. (2016). Missing elements in the discussion of teacher shortages. *Educational Researcher, 45*(8), 460–462.

Cowan, J., Goldhaber, D., and Theobald, R. (2017). *Teacher Equity Gaps in Massachusetts. Elementary and Secondary Education Policy Brief.* Available: http://www.doe.mass.edu/research/reports/2017/10teacher-equity.pdf.

Dee, T.S., and Goldhaber, D. (2017). Understanding and addressing teacher shortages in the United States. *The Hamilton Project at Brookings Institution, April.*

Dee, T.S., and Wyckoff, J. (2015). Incentives, selection, and teacher performance: Evidence from IMPACT. *Journal of Policy Analysis and Management, 34*(2), 267–297.

Editorial Projects in Education Research Center. (2004). Alternative teacher certification. *Education Week.* Available: http://www.edweek.org/ew/issues/alternative-teacher-certification/.

Engel, M., and Cannata, M. (2015). Localism and teacher labor markets: How geography and decision making may contribute to inequality. *Peabody Journal of Education, 90*(1), 84–92.

Engel, M., Jacob, B.A., and Curran, F.C. (2014). New evidence on teacher labor supply. *American Educational Research Journal, 51*(1), 36–72.

Feng, L., and Sass, T. (2011). *Teacher Quality and Teacher Mobility.* Urban Institute. Available: https://www.urban.org/research/publication/teacher-quality-and-teacher-mobility/view/full_report.

Figliio, D., Karbownik, K., and Salvanes, K.G. (2016). Chapter 2 – Education research and administrative data. *Handbook of the Economics of Education, 5*, 75–138.

Fitzpatrick, M.D. (2015). How much are public school teachers willing to pay for their retirement benefits?. *American Economic Journal: Economic Policy, 7*(4), 165–188.

Goldhaber, D. (2018). Evidence-based teacher preparation: Policy context and what we know. *Journal of Teacher Education,* 0022487118800712.

Goldhaber, D., and Grout, C. (2016). Which plan to choose? The determinants of pension system choice for public school teachers. *Journal of Pension Economics & Finance, 15*(1), 30–54.

Goldhaber, D., and Walch, J. (2014). Gains in teacher quality: Academic capabilities of the US teaching force are on the rise. *Education Next, 14*(1), 38–46.

Goldhaber, D., DeArmond, M., and DeBurgomaster, S. (2011). Teacher attitudes about compensation reform: Implications for reform implementation. *Industrial and Labor Relations Review,* 64(3), 441–463.

Goldhaber, D., Grout, C., and Holden, K.L. (2017a). Pension structure and employee turnover: Evidence from a large public pension system. *ILR Review, 70*(4), 976–1007.

Goldhaber, D., Grout, C., and Holden, K.L. (2017b). Why make it hard for teachers to cross state borders? *Phi Delta Kappan, 98*(5), 55–60.

Goldhaber, D., Grout, C., and Huntington-Klein, N. (2017). Screen twice, cut once: Assessing the predictive validity of applicant selection tools. *Education Finance and Policy List, 12*(2), 197–223.

Goldhaber, D., Lavery, L., and Theobald, R. (2015). Uneven playing field? Assessing the teacher quality gap between advantaged and disadvantaged students. *Educational Researcher, 44*(5), 293–307.

Goldhaber, D., Quince, V., and Theobald, R. (2018). Has it always been this way? Tracing the evolution of teacher quality gaps in US public schools. *American Educational Research Journal, 55*(1), 171–201.

Goldhaber, D., Grout, C., Holden, K.L., and Brown, N. (2015a). Crossing the border? Exploring the cross-state mobility of the teacher workforce. *Educational Researcher, 44*(8), 421–431.

Goldhaber, D., Krieg, J., Theobald, R., and Brown, N. (2015b). Refueling the STEM and special education teacher pipelines. *Phi Delta Kappan, 97*(4), 56–62.

Goldhaber, D., Strunk, K., Brown, N., Chambers, A., Naito, N., and Wolff, M. (2018). *Teacher Staffing Challenges in California: Exploring the Factors That Influence Teacher Staffing and Distribution.* Getting Down to Facts II Technical Report. Available: https://files.eric.ed.gov/fulltext/ED594738.pdf.

Goldring, R., Taie, S., and Riddles, M. (2014). *Teacher Attrition and Mobility: Results from the 2012–13 Teacher Follow-up Survey* (NCES 2014-077). U.S. Department of Education. Washington, DC: National Center for Education Statistics. Available: http://nces.ed.gov/pubsearch.

Gray, L., and Taie, S. (2015). *Public School Teacher Attrition and Mobility in the First Five Years: Results from the First Through Fifth Waves of the 2007–08 Beginning Teacher Longitudinal Study* (NCES 2015-337). U.S. Department of Education. Washington, DC: National Center for Education Statistics. Available: http://nces.ed.gov/pubsearch.

Grissom, J.A. (2008). But do they stay? Addressing issues of teacher retention through alternative certification. In P. Grossman and S. Loeb (Eds.), *Alternative Routes to Teaching: Mapping the New Landscape of Teacher Education* (pp. 499–534). Cambridge, MA: Harvard Education Press.

Grissom, J.A. (2011). Can good principals keep teachers in disadvantaged schools? Linking principal effectiveness to teacher satisfaction and turnover in hard-to-staff environments. *Teachers College Record, 113*(11), 2552–2585.

Grissom, J.A., and Bartanen, B. (2019). Strategic retention: Principal effectiveness and teacher turnover in multiple-measure teacher evaluation systems. *American Educational Research Journal, 56*(2), 514–555.

Grissom, J.A., Nicholson-Crotty, S., and Harrington, J.R. (2014). Estimating the effects of No Child Left Behind on teachers' work environments and job attitudes. *Educational Evaluation and Policy Analysis, 36*(4), 417–436.

Grissom, J.A., Viano, S.L., and Selin, J.L. (2016). Understanding employee turnover in the public sector: Insights from research on teacher mobility. *Public Administration Review, 76*(2), 241–251.

Guarino, C.M., Santibañez, L., and Daley, G.A. (2006). Teacher recruitment and retention: A review of the recent empirical literature. *Review of Educational Research, 76*(2), 173–280.

Hansen, M., and Quintero, D. (2019). *The Diversity Gap for Public School Teachers Is Actually Growing Across Generations.* Brookings Institution. Available: https://www.brookings.edu/blog/brown-center-chalkboard/2019/03/07the-diversity-gap-for-public-school-teachers-is-actually-growing-across-generations.

Hanushek, E.A., and Pace, R.E. (1995). Who chooses to teach (and why)? *Economics of Education Review, 14*(2), 101–117.

Hanushek, E.A., Kain, J.F., and Rivkin, S.G. (2004). Why public schools lose teachers. *Journal of Human Resources, 39*(2), 326–354.

Harris, D.N., and Adams, S. (2007). Understanding the level and causes of teacher turnover: A comparison with other professions. *Economics of Education Review, 26*(3), 325–337.

Hendricks, M.D. (2014). Does it pay to pay teachers more? Evidence from Texas. *Journal of Public Economics, 109*, 50–63.

Higgins, L. (2019). *Report: Michigan's Teacher Supply Is Dwindling and the State Is Doing Little About It.* Available: https://www.chalkbeat.org/posts/detroit/2019/02/12/report-michigans-teacher-supply-is-dwindling-and-the-state-is-doing-little-about-it.

Hill, A.J., and Jones, D.B. (2018). The impacts of performance pay on teacher effectiveness and retention: Does teacher gender matter? *Journal of Human Resources*, 0216-7719R3.

Hinrichs, P. (2014). *What Kind of Teachers Are Schools Looking For? Evidence from a Randomized Field Experiment.* Working Paper No. 14–36, Federal Reserve Bank of Cleveland. Available: https://www.clevelandfed.org/newsroom-and-events/publications/working-papers/2014-working-papers/wp-1436-what-kind-of-teachers-are-schools-looking-forevidence-from-a-randomized-field-experiment.aspx.

Holden, K. (2018). *Teacher Pensions and Labor Market Incentives.* CALDER Policy Brief No. 9-0918-1. Washington, DC: National Center for Analysis of Longitudinal Data in Education Research.

Hoxby, C.M., and Leigh, A. (2004). Pulled away or pushed out? Explaining the decline of teacher aptitude in the United States. *American Economic Review, 94*(2), 236–240.

Ingersoll, R.M. (2001). Teacher turnover and teacher shortages: An organizational analysis. *American Educational Research Journal, 38*(3), 499–534. Available: https://repository.upenn.edu/cgi/viewcontent.cgi?article=1093&context=gse_pubs.

Ingersoll, R.M. (2003). *Is There Really a Teacher Shortage?* Philadelphia: Consortium for Policy Research in Education, University of Pennsylvania.

Ingersoll, R.M., and May, H. (2012). The magnitude, destinations, and determinants of mathematics and science teacher turnover. *Educational Evaluation and Policy Analysis, 34*(4), 435–464.

Ingersoll, R.M. Merrill, L., and Stuckey, D. (2014). *Seven Trends: The Transformation of the Teaching Force April 2014.* CPRE Report (#RR-80). Philadelphia: Consortium for Policy Research in Education, University of Pennsylvania.

Ingersoll, R.M., Merrill, L., Owens, C., and Zukerberg, A. (2017). *A Quarter Century of Changes in the Elementary and Secondary Teaching Force: From 1987 to 2012*. Statistical Analysis Report (NCES 2017-092). U.S. Department of Education. Washington, DC: National Center for Education Statistics.

Ingersoll, R.M., Merrill, E., Stuckey, D., and Collins, G. (2018). Seven trends: The transformation of the teaching force, Updated October. *CPRE Research Reports*. Available: https://repository.upenn.edu/cgi/viewcontent.cgi?article=1109&context=cpre_researchreports.

Isenberg, E., Max, J., Gleason, P., Johnson, M., Deutsch, J., and Hansen, M. (2016). *Do Low-Income Students Have Equal Access to Effective Teachers? Evidence from 26 Districts* (NCEE 2017-4007). Washington, DC: Institute of Education Sciences.

Jacob, B.A., Rickoff, J.E., Taylor, E.S., Lindy, B., and Rosen, R. (2018). Teacher applicant hiring and teacher performance: Evidence from DC public schools. *Journal of Public Economics, 166*, 81–97.

Johnson, S.M., and Birkeland, S. (2003). Pursuing a "sense of success": New teachers explain their career decisions. *American Educational Research Journal, 40*(3), 581–617.

Johnson, S.M., Kraft, M.A., and Papay, J.P. (2012). How context matters: The effects of teachers' working conditions on their professional satisfaction and their students' achievement. *Teachers College Record, 114*.

Kabaker, J. (2012). *Alternative Teacher Training Programs Better at Attracting Male and Minority Trainees*. Available: https://www.newamerica.org/education-policy/federal-education-budget-project/ed-money-watch/alternative-teacher-training-programs-better-at-attracting-male-and-minority-trainees.

Kalogrides, D., and Loeb, S. (2013). Different teachers, different peers: The magnitude of student sorting within schools. *Educational Researcher, 42*(6), 304–316.

Khalil, D., and Griffen, M. (2012). An investigation of factors influencing pre-service mathematics teachers' preference to teach in urban settings. In L.R. Van Zoest, J.-J. Lo, and J.L. Kratky (Eds.), *Proceedings of the 34th Annual Meeting of the North American Chapter of the International Group for the Psychology of Mathematics Education*. Kalamazoo: Western Michigan University.

Khalil, D., and Chao, T. (forthcoming). I'm not going to teach there: A critical race quantitative analysis of prospective STEM teachers' preferences. In D. Ball and G. Ladson-Billings (Eds), *Multiple Perspectives on Disrupting Inequities in Mathematics Education*.

Killeen, K., Loeb, S., and Williams, I. (2015). *A Double Draw of Proximity: The Importance of Geography in Teacher Application and Hiring Decisions*. Stanford, CA: Center for Education Policy Analysis.

King, J.E., and Hampel, R. (2018). *Colleges of Education: A National Portrait*. Washington, DC: American Association of Colleges for Teacher Education.

Koedel, C., and Xiang, P.B. (2017). Pension enhancements and the retention of public employees. *ILR Review, 70*(2), 519–551.

Koedel, C., Li, J., Springer, M.G., and Tan, L. (2019). Teacher performance ratings and professional improvement. *Journal of Research on Educational Effectiveness, 12*(1), 90–115.

Koedel, C., Podgursky, M., and Shi, S. (2013). Teacher pension systems, the composition of the teaching workforce, and teacher quality. *Journal of Policy Analysis and Management, 32*(3), 574–596.

Kraft, M.A., and Gilmour, A.F. (2016). Can principals promote teacher development as evaluators? A case study of principals' views and experiences. *Educational Administration Quarterly, 52*(5), 711–753.

Kraft, M.A., Marinell, W.H., and Shen-Wei Yee, D. (2016). School organizational contexts, teacher turnover, and student achievement: Evidence from panel data. *American Educational Research Journal, 53*(5), 1411–1449.

Kraft, M.A., Brunner, E.J., Dougherty, S.M., and Schwegman, D. (2018). *Teacher Accountability Reforms and the Supply of New Teachers*. Brown University working paper. Available: https://scholar.harvard.edu/files/mkraft/files/kraft_et_al._2018_teacher_accountability_reforms.pdf.

Krieg, J.M. (2006). Teacher quality and attrition. *Economics of Education Review, 25*, 13–27.

Krieg, J.M., Theobald, R., and Goldhaber, D. (2016). A foot in the door: Exploring the role of student teaching assignments in teachers' initial job placements. *Educational Evaluation and Policy Analysis, 38*(2), 364–388.

Ladd, H.F. (2011). Teachers' perception of their working conditions: How predictive of planned and actual teacher movement? *Educational Evaluation and Policy Analysis, 33*(2), 235–261.

Lankford, H., Loeb, S., and Wyckoff, J. (2002). Teacher sorting and the plight of urban schools: A descriptive analysis. *Educational Evaluation and Policy Analysis, 24*(1), 37–62.

Lankford, H., Loeb, S., McEachin, A., Miller, L.C., and Wyckoff, J. (2014). Who enters teaching? Encouraging evidence that the status of teaching is improving. *Educational Researcher, 43*(9), 444–453.

Liu, M. (2013). Disrupting teacher education: High costs for brick-and-mortar degrees create opportunities for online programs. *Education Next, 13*(3), 26–32.

Liu, E., Rosenstein, J., Swann, A., and Khalil, D. (2008). When districts encounter teacher shortages? The challenges of recruiting and retaining math teachers in urban districts. *Leadership and Policy in Schools, 7*(3), 296–323.

Loeb, S., Darling-Hammond, L., and Luczak, J. (2005). How teaching conditions predict teacher turnover in California schools. *Peabody Journal of Education, 80*(3), 44–70.

Mansfield, R.K. (2015). Teacher quality and student inequality. *Journal of Labor Economics, 33*(3), 751–788.

Martin, L., and Mulvihill, T. (2016). Voices in education: Teacher shortage: Myth or reality? *Teacher Educator, 51*, 175–184.

Mihaly, K., McCaffrey, D.F., Staiger, D., and Lockwood, J.R. (2013). *A Composite Estimator of Effective Teaching*. Available: http://www.metproject.org/downloads/MET_Composite_Estimator_of_Effective_Teaching_Research_Paper.pdf.

Mosely, M. (2018). The Black Teacher Project: How racial affinity professional development sustains Black teachers. *Urban Review, 50*, 267–283.

Nagler, M., Piopiunik, M., and West, M.R. (forthcoming). Weak markets, strong teachers: Recession at career start and teacher effectiveness. *Journal of Labor Economics*.

Neumerski, C.M., Grissom, J.A., Goldring, E., Rubin, M., Cannata, M., Schuermann, P., and Drake, T.A. (2018). Restructuring instructional leadership: How multiple-measure teacher evaluation systems are redefining the role of the school principal. *The Elementary School Journal, 119*(2), 270–297.

Novy-Marx, R., and Rauh, J. (2011). Public pension promises: how big are they and what are they worth?. *The Journal of Finance, 66*(4), 1211–1249.

Papay, J.P., Taylor, E.S., Tyler, J.H., and Laski, M. (2016). *Learning Job Skills from Colleagues at Work: Evidence from a Field Experiment Using Teacher Performance Data* (No. w21986). Cambridge, MA: National Bureau of Economic Research.

Papay, J.P., Bacher-Hicks, A., Page, L.C., and Marinell, W.H. (2017). The challenge of teacher retention in urban schools: Evidence of variation from a cross-site analysis. *Educational Researcher, 46*(8), 434–448.

Partelow, L. (2019). *What to Make of Declining Enrollment in Teacher Preparation Programs*. Available: https://cdn.americanprogress.org/content/uploads/2019/12/04113550/TeacherPrep-report1.pdf.

Peske, H.G., Liu, E., Johnson, S.M., and Kauffman, D. (2001). The next generation of teachers: Changing conceptions of a career in teaching. *Phi Delta Kappan, 83*(4), 304–311.

Podgursky, M., and Springer, M.G. (2007). Teacher performance pay: A review. *Journal of Policy Analysis and Management, 26*(4), 909–950.

Podgursky, M., Ehlert, M., Lindsay, J., and Wan, Y. (2016). *An Examination of the Movement of Educators within and across Three Midwest Region States.* REL 2017-185. Regional Educational Laboratory Midwest. Washington, DC: Institute of Education Sciences.

Putnam, H., Hansen, M., Walsh, K., and Quintero, D. (2016). *High Hopes and Harsh Realities: The Real Challenges to Building a Diverse Workforce.* Brookings Institution. Available: https://www.nctq.org/dmsView/High_Hopes_Harsh_Realities.

Redding, C., and Smith, T.M. (2016). Easy in, easy out: Are alternatively certified teachers turning over at increased rates? *American Educational Research Journal, 53*(4), 1086–1125.

Reininger, M. (2012). Hometown disadvantage? It depends on where you're from: Teachers' location preferences and the implications for staffing schools. *Educational Evaluation and Policy Analysis, 34*(2), 127–145.

Sajjadiani, S., Sojourner, A.J., Kammeyer-Mueller, J.D., and Mykerezi, E. (2019). Using machine learning to translate applicant work history into predictors of performance and turnover. *Journal of Applied Psychology, 104*(110), 1207–1225.

Sartain, L., and Steinberg, M.P. (2016). Teachers' labor market responses to performance evaluation reform: Experimental evidence from Chicago public schools. *Journal of Human Resources, 51*(3), 615–655.

Sass, T.R., Hannaway, J., Xu, Z., Figlio, D.N., and Feng, L. (2010). *Value Added of Teachers in High-Poverty Schools and Lower-Poverty Schools.* CALDER Working Paper 52. Washington, DC: The Urban Institute.

Sawchuck, S. (2013). For-profits dominate market for online teacher prep. *Education Week, 33*(7), 1.

Southern Regional Education Board. (2018). *State Policies to Improve Teacher Preparation.* Report of the SREB Teacher Preparation Commission. Atlanta, GA: Author.

Springer, M.G., Pane, J.F., Le, V.N., McCaffrey, D.F., Burns, S.F., Hamilton, L.S., and Stecher, B. (2012). Team pay for performance: Experimental evidence from the Round Rock Pilot Project on Team Incentives. *Educational Evaluation and Policy Analysis, 34*(4), 367–390.

Springer, M.G., Swain, W.A., and Rodriguez, L.A. (2016). Effective teacher retention bonuses: Evidence from Tennessee. *Educational Evaluation and Policy Analysis, 38*(2), 199–221.

Startz, D. (2018). *Teachers Have Been Moonlighting in Texas—and Elsewhere—to Make Ends Meet.* Brookings Institution. Available: https://www.brookings.edu/blog/brown-center-chalkboard/2018/04/20/teachers-have-been-moonlighting-in-texas-and-elsewhere-to-make-ends-meet.

Steinberg, M.P., and Donaldson, M.L. (2016). The new educational accountability: Understanding the landscape of teacher evaluation in the post-NCLB era. *Education Finance and Policy, 11*(3), 340–359.

Sun, M., Saultz, A., and Ye, Y. (2017). Federal policy and the teacher labor market: Exploring the effects of NCLB school accountability on teacher turnover. *School Effectiveness and School Improvement, 28*(1), 102–122.

Sutcher, L., Darling-Hammond, L., and Carver-Thomas, D. (2016). *A Coming Crisis in Teaching? Teacher Supply, Demand, and Shortages in the U.S.* Palo Alto, CA: Learning Policy Institute.

Taylor, E.S., and Tyler, J.H. (2012). The effect of evaluation on teacher performance. *American Economic Review, 102*(7), 3628–3651.

Thompson, O. (2019). *School Desegregation and Black Teacher Employment.* NBER Working Paper No. 25990. Cambridge, MA: National Bureau of Economic Research. Available: https://www.nber.org/papers/w25990.pdf.

U.S. Department of Education. (2016). *Preparing and Credentialing the Nation's Teachers: The Secretary's Tenth Report on Teacher Quality.* Washington, DC: Author.

U.S. Department of Education, Office of Planning, Evaluation and Policy Development, Policy and Program Studies Service. (2016*). The State of Racial Diversity in the Educator Work-force.* Washington, DC: Author. Available: https://www2.ed.gov/rschstat/eval/highered/racial-diversity/state-racial-diversity-workforce.pdf.

U.S. Department of Education. (2019). *Title II Tips for Reporting.* Available: https://title2.ed.gov/public/TA/FAQ.pdf.

Villegas, A.M., Strom, K., and Lucas, T. (2012). Closing the racial/ethnic gap between students of color and their teachers: An elusive goal. *Equity & Excellence in Education, 45*(2), 283–302.

West, M.R., and Chingos, M.M. (2009). Teacher effectiveness, mobility, and attrition in Florida. In M.G. Springer (Ed.), *Performance Incentives: Their Growing Impact on American K–12 Education* (pp. 251–271). Washington, DC: Brookings Institution.

Will, M. (2016). Help wanted: Teacher-shortage hot spots. *Education Week, 36*(1), 10.

Wiswall, M. (2013). The dynamics of teacher quality. *Journal of Public Economics, 100,* 61–78.

Wolf, Z.B. (2019). *Why Teacher Strikes Are Touching Every Part of America.* Available: https://www.cnn.com/2019/02/23/politics/teacher-strikes-politics/index.html.

Yuan, K., Le, V.N., McCaffrey, D.F., Marsh, J.A., Hamilton, L.S., Stecher, B.M., and Springer, M.G. (2013). Incentive pay programs do not affect teacher motivation or reported practices: Results from three randomized studies. *Educational Evaluation and Policy Analysis, 35*(1), 3–22.

5

Preparing Teachers to Meet New Expectations: Preservice Teacher Education

As described in the previous chapters, student demographics and expectations for student learning have changed dramatically in the past two decades, and with them, the demands placed on teachers. Preservice teacher education—a vast and varied enterprise—plays a key role in preparing teacher candidates for these new conditions and increased responsibilities. Whether present approaches to teacher education fulfill that role well, and whether or not teacher education has changed in response to changes in expectations for students, have been the subjects of considerable debate. Given the size of the teacher workforce and the sheer scale of teacher education in the United States, it is perhaps not a surprise to find variation in the quality of programs or in their impact on individual graduates. Some past research has yielded critiques of teacher education as a weak intervention, largely ineffective in persuading teacher candidates of the need for deep specialized preparation or providing them with a sufficient understanding of the students they would likely be teaching (Book, Byers, and Freeman, 1983; Olsen, 2008). Policy makers,[1] academics, and advocacy groups alike have issued sweeping critiques (Levine, 2006; National Council on Teacher Quality [NCTQ], 2018).

Such all-encompassing critiques do not provide much empirically based guidance on the ways teacher preparation could be improved. There is evidence that some features of teacher preparation can make a difference with respect to teachers' sense of efficacy (Darling-Hammond, Chung, and

---

[1] For remarks by Education Secretary Arne Duncan at Teachers College, Columbia University, see https://www.ed.gov/news/speeches/teacher-preparation-reforming-uncertain-profession.

Frelow, 2002; Ronfeldt, Schwarz, and Jacob, 2014) and with teachers' retention in the profession (Ingersoll, Merrill, and May, 2014; Ronfeldt, Schwarz, and Jacob, 2014). For example, a requirement of a capstone project as part of teacher preparation is associated with teachers' students exhibiting greater test score gains (Boyd et al., 2009).

States and institutions have undertaken initiatives to strengthen the quality of preservice preparation and to develop systems of teacher accountability based on outcome measures (e.g., see Chief Council of State School Officers [CCSSO], 2017). Case study research supplies persuasive examples of programs and practices with the capacity to shape the knowledge, practices, and dispositions of novice teachers (Boerst et al., 2011; Darling-Hammond and Oakes, 2019; Lampert et al., 2013). Finally, the availability of large administrative datasets in some states has enabled quantitative research that seeks to uncover the relationship between a teacher's enrollment in a particular program and the learning subsequently demonstrated by that teacher's students. Although the last of these developments has been controversial on multiple grounds, it may spur additional research that could fruitfully inform improvements in preservice education.[2]

This chapter provides a "broad strokes" characterization of teacher education opportunities to meet new expectations and respond to changing student demographics, drawing on scholarship about what *does* happen in teacher preparation programs while also noting arguments about what *should* happen in teacher preparation programs (e.g., CCSSO, 2017; Darling-Hammond and Oakes, 2019; Espinoza et al., 2018), particularly with regard to producing novice teachers who are prepared to be successful with all students. It explores the range of visions promoted by teacher preparation programs and describes scholarship about preservice teacher preparation in general as well as highlights particular programs that are engaging in innovative approaches that show promise for recruiting—and supporting—teacher candidates from a diverse range of backgrounds.

The chapter also describes mechanisms for influencing preservice teacher education, provides illustrative cases of institutions and programs that represent deliberate and strategic responses to both the demographic changes and the evolving shifts in expectations for teaching and learning, and describes policies and practices designed to recruit, prepare, and retain teachers of color. It also highlights reform efforts in teacher education in recent years.

---

[2]Goldhaber, Liddle, and Theobald (2012, p. 34) conclude: "There is no doubt that evaluating teacher training programs based on the value-added estimates of the teachers they credential is controversial. It is true that the value-added program estimates do not provide any direct guidance on how to improve teacher preparation programs. However, it is conceivable that it is not possible to move policy toward explaining why we see these program estimates until those estimates are first quantified. Moreover, it is certainly the case that some of the policy questions that merit investigation . . . require additional data."

In this chapter and the following two chapters, discussion is framed around the capacity of teacher education, inservice professional development, and the school workplace to:

- Recruit, prepare, and retain a diverse teacher workforce.
- Prepare and support teachers to engage students in the kind of conceptually rich, intellectually ambitious, and meaningful experience encompassed by the term "deeper learning."
- Prepare and support teachers to work with a student population that is ethnically, racially, linguistically, culturally, and economically diverse.
- Prepare teachers to pursue equity and social justice in schools and communities.

The committee acknowledges that these goals of teacher education are closely intertwined. In particular, it is noted throughout Chapters 2 and 3 that achieving goals of "deeper learning" will require the capacity to work effectively within a diverse landscape of students, families, and communities.

A SPRAWLING LANDSCAPE

This section provides a brief overview of what might best be described (borrowing a phrase from Cochran-Smith et al., 2016) as a "sprawling landscape." Amid that sprawling landscape are the contributions and limitations of existing research. This chapter identifies cases in which preservice preparation programs seem particularly well positioned to attract and prepare teachers with the capacity and disposition to meet high expectations for an increasingly diverse student population. The chapter highlights programs that are part of colleges and universities as well as programs that have evolved in organizations outside institutions of higher education.

The Scale and Variability of Preservice Teacher Education

As noted above and described in Chapter 4, preservice teacher education is marked by a range of pathways into teaching, which vary considerably from state to state. The different interpretations of the term "alternative route" complicate how to analyze and report trends in preparation. The National Research Council (NRC; 2010) report *Preparing Teachers: Building Evidence for Sound Policy* concluded that distinctions between "traditional" and "alternative" routes are not clearly defined, and that more variation exists within the "traditional" and "alternative" categories than between them. States vary in the definition of "alternative" they use

---

BOX 5-1
Programs at Minority-Serving Institutions (MSIs)

A minority-serving institution (MSI) is defined by Title IV of the Higher Education Act (HEA) of 1965. There are seven kinds of MSIs: (1) historically black colleges and universities (HBCUs); (2) predominantly black institutions; (3) Hispanic-serving institutions (HSIs); (4) tribal colleges and universities (TCUs); (5) Native American non-tribal institutions; (6) Alaskan Native- or Native Hawaiian-serving institutions; and (7) Asian American- and Native American Pacific Islander-serving institutions. Together, these institutions educate 20 percent of college and university students (Gasman, Samayoa, and Ginsberg, 2016).

MSIs are responsible for preparing 14.2 percent of all public school educators; however the role they play in preparing teachers of color is disproportionately high: for example, 38.3 percent of all Black teachers and 48.0 percent of all Hispanic teachers earned their degrees from MSIs (Gasman, Samayoa, and Ginsberg, 2016). Here we focus on HBCUs, HSIs, and TCUs.

The HEA defines an HBCU as: "any historically black college or university that was established prior to 1964, whose principal mission was, and is, the education of black Americans, and that is accredited by a nationally recognized accrediting agency or association determined by the Secretary [of Education] to be a reliable authority as to the quality of training offered or is, according to such an agency or association, making reasonable progress toward accreditation" (e.g., Howard University and Spelman College). HBCUs were originally founded to provide education to Blacks who had gained their freedom during the pre- and post-Emancipation period. HBCUs have roots in teacher education as many were "normal schools"—teacher training institutions. Teaching was a highly valued career in the African American community; many students attended HBCUs specifically to become teachers (Robinson and Albert, 2008) and were employed in "Black schools." Although HBCUs are no longer the primary vehicle for educating Black teachers, they continue to train a significant percentage of the nation's

---

in federal Title II reports, and many of the "alternative" routes included in those reports are based in institutions of higher education. Yet it is worth noting that while the past 20–30 years have witnessed a proliferation of "alternative routes" (however defined—within or outside of institutions of higher education [IHEs]), the majority of prospective teachers continue to be prepared by traditional programs within IHEs. Eighty-eight percent of the organizations that offer teacher preparation programs are 2- and 4-year colleges and universities, including minority-serving institutions (see Box 5-1). The remaining 12 percent are school districts, nonprofit organizations, and other entities that run state-approved alternative teacher preparation programs. Alternative routes to teacher certification tend to enroll more racially diverse student populations than traditional programs (U.S. Department of Education, 2016). Finally, state-level data in California reveal the

Black teachers: HBCUs award nearly one-third of the bachelor's degrees in education conferred to African Americans in the 19 states, the District of Columbia, and the U.S. Virgin Islands where they are located (Anderson, 2017).

HSIs are institutions whose enrollment of undergraduate full-time-equivalent students comprises at least 25 percent Hispanic students (e.g., the University of Texas, El Paso and many of the California State University campuses). HSIs were formally recognized in 1986. "HSIs are specifically addressed in legislation through Title V's Developing Hispanic-Institutions Program which classifies eligible HSIs as those not-for-profit institutions whose full-time undergraduate enrollment is comprised of at least 25 percent Hispanic students and at least 50 percent low-income students" (Hispanic Association of Colleges and Universities, 2017, p. 2). In 2017–2018, there were 523 HSIs in 25 states, Puerto Rico, and the District of Columbia (Hispanic Association of Colleges and Universities, n.d.). In 2017, 172 4-year HSIs conferred education degrees.

In a report prepared for the American Association of Colleges for Teacher Education (AACTE), King and Hampel (2018) add tribal institutions of higher education to the list of MSIs that are making a contribution to the teacher workforce. They write, "Tribal colleges and universities, which are primarily 2-year institutions, are instrumental in preparing American Indians to become teachers. Twenty-six tribal colleges awarded 48 percent of all associate's degrees in education to American Indians and Alaska Natives nationwide" (King and Hampel, 2018, p. 52). Gasman, Samayoa, and Ginsberg (2016) spotlight Stone Child College's teacher education program, a tribally controlled community college of the Chippewa Cree Tribe in Montana. It offers a bachelor of science degree in elementary education. Its mission is represented by the image of a Cree medicine wheel (Stone Child College, 2017), which includes four "domains" of its education program, each represented by a season. Spring symbolizes the learner, and the physical and emotional environment that best supports student learning; summer is content knowledge needed to effectively teach; fall is emotional growth and professional development; winter represents reflection (Stone Child College, 2017).

prominent place now occupied by online teacher preparation programs; in data reported for 2016–2017, five of the top six producers in that state were online programs, and the top five online producers accounted for one-third of all completers.[3]

Like K–12 education in the United States, most preservice teacher education (with the exception of some online programs) is varied and localized: programs differ considerably among and within states. Programs are accredited by the states, which vary in terms of their requirements for preservice teacher candidates (Cochran-Smith et al., 2016; NRC, 2010). Even within states, where state standards and regulations govern program

---

[3] Detailed information can be found at https://www.ctc.ca.gov/docs/default-source/educator-prep/standards/adopted-tpes-2016.pdf?sfvrsn=0.

accreditation and teacher licensure, programs of teacher preparation vary in size, duration, curriculum, and the nature of field experience (NRC, 2010).

The discussion that follows describes general characteristics and trends in preservice teacher education over the past 20 years. It focuses in particular on characteristics that bear on the likelihood that teacher preparation programs will successfully recruit a more diverse teacher workforce and that they will develop the kind of curriculum, pedagogy, and learning experiences that are responsive to changing demographics and expectations.

What makes this task challenging is that the field lacks empirical evidence about what programs are effective, why, and for whom. Most state data systems fail to link preservice teacher candidates to inservice outcomes. Part of the problem has to do with the disagreement about what constitutes effectiveness (i.e., should indicators of effectiveness be student test scores, teacher retention rates, or closing achievement gaps among groups of students, or some other measure?). The NRC report *Preparing Teachers* (2010) called for research on the development of links between teacher preparation and outcomes for students, but that call has yet to be fulfilled. The problem also has to do with the difficulty in examining the causal effectiveness of teacher preparation programs, given all the confounding variables—including individual teacher traits—that might explain teacher success. The chapter instead examines qualitative research that dives deeply into program aims, characteristics of programs, innovations in practice, and accountability of programs.

The Visions of Teaching and Teachers Conveyed by Programs

The field lacks national data about the nature/substance of teacher preparation programs and the degree to which they have changed in any collective way over time, clearly signaling a critical area for research. There are, however, indicators of general shifts and developments in teacher preparation. For example, as highlighted in Chapter 2, the past two decades can be characterized as an "era of accountability" in education generally, and in teacher education specifically, in which federal, state, and professional association policy initiatives have been aimed at measuring outcomes such as student achievement (Cochran-Smith et al., 2018). This focus on outcomes is a shift from previous accountability emphases on measuring inputs (Cochran-Smith et al., 2018). Even if national data are lacking, there is evidence that increased attention to standards, accreditation, and the development and growing influence of new players committed to advancing equity and justice, such as the Education Deans for Justice and Equity (Cochran-Smith et al., 2018), have led to changes in teacher preparation, as reflected by case studies of programs.

A report by the National Academy of Education (Feuer et al., 2013) describes the variety of organizations that conduct evaluations of the quality of teacher preparation programs in the United States, including the federal government, state governments, national organizations (e.g., accreditors), private organizations (e.g., NCTQ), and individual programs themselves. It notes that selection or development of appropriate measures is a key component of designing a study of teacher preparation program quality. The measures might include assessments of program graduates' knowledge and skills, observations of their teaching practice, or assessments of what their pupils learn. Measures of program features could include analyses of course syllabi, qualifications of program faculty, and program uses of educational technology. The report describes general strengths and limitations of varying types of measures.

High-profile reports on teacher education (e.g., *Educating School Teachers* [Levine, 2006] and *Powerful Teacher Education: Lessons from Exemplary Programs* [Darling-Hammond, 2006]) have singled out specific programs as exemplars of excellence. Whereas these programs vary greatly in terms of program design, it is important to recognize that judgments about what constitutes "excellence" are often based on subjective assessments of what teacher preparation ought to look like rather than empirical, causal evidence on the effectiveness of teacher education.

Other reports describe programs that highlight particular approaches to program design, such as close connections to local communities (Guillen and Zeichner, 2018; Lee, 2018). Scholars looking at program similarities and differences across countries also have selected and described programs because of particular features they had, such as an intention to be coherent (Jenset, Klette, and Hammerness, 2018). The large international comparative study of preparation of mathematics teachers for elementary and lower secondary school (Tatto et al., 2012) described features of nationally representative samples of teacher preparation programs. All of these studies provide more information about what goes on in teacher preparation, but none can support causal claims about the effects of programs or program features on desired outcomes.

In the recent volume *Preparing Teachers for Deeper Learning* Darling-Hammond and Oakes (2019) identify seven "exemplars" that include public and private colleges and universities, a teacher residency program, and a "new graduate school of education" embedded in a charter management organization (see Box 5-2). These exemplars as described in the volume suggest that they are aligned with the five principles of deeper learning: (1) learning that is developmentally grounded and personalized; (2) learning that is contextualized; (3) learning that is applied and transferred; (4) learning that occurs in productive communities of practice; and (5) learning that is equitable and oriented to social justice (Darling-Hammond and

BOX 5-2
New Graduate Schools of Education (nGSEs)

The research study Teacher Preparation at nGSEs, funded by the Spencer Foundation and led by Marilyn Cochran-Smith, is examining a set of teacher preparation programs located at newly created graduate schools of education. By "New Graduate Schools of Education," Cochran-Smith and her team mean recent additions to the set of institutions doing preservice teacher preparation, distinguished by being located outside colleges and universities. The research team is focusing on institutions established since 2000, offering programs lasting at least nine months, and authorized by at least one state to grant master's degrees and recommend candidates for initial teacher certification. Several of these nGSEs, such as Relay and High Tech High, have received considerable attention, some positive and some critical, but little research has been done on these programs prior to this study. The study team identified nine such programs and decided to develop in-depth case studies of four programs: High Tech High, Sposato Graduate School of Education, TEACH-NOW, and the Richard Gilder Graduate School at the American Museum of Natural History. The aim of the research is to understand these programs, without intending to either defend or attack them. As a framework for characterizing the programs, the team will look at the following dimensions: mission, institutional context, funding models, and how they envision learning to teach. Preliminary analyses show that the case study schools vary substantially along each of the four dimensions. When the study is completed it will offer detailed analyses, within and across the cases, that could provide ideas for new approaches to the development of teacher preparation programs that are located in colleges and universities.

Oakes, 2019, pp. 13–14). The programs are diverse across many axes but all "have track records of developing teachers who are strongly committed to all students' learning—and to ensuring, especially, that students who struggle to learn can succeed" (Darling-Hammond and Oakes, 2019, p. 25). Common features of these programs are that they have a coherent set of courses and clinical experience (these programs have intensive relationships with schools and carefully matched student teaching placements that share the programs' commitments to deeper learning and equity); instructors model powerful practices rather than lecture and teach through textbooks; there is a strong connection between theory and practice; and they use performance assessments to evaluate teacher candidates' learning (pp. 323–324). Interpretation of key terms, such as "coherent," "intensive relationship," and "powerful practice," are still matters of judgment.

Pondering the question of what would constitute a "strong intervention" in preservice teacher education requires considering the conception of teachers and teaching conveyed by teacher preparation programs. *Preparing*

Teachers (NRC, 2010, p. 44) notes, "All teacher preparation programs presumably have the goal of preparing excellent teachers, but a surprising variation is evident in their stated missions." The sheer scale of preservice teacher education in the United States, combined with the fact that teacher preparation is governed at the state level, suggests wide variation in the degree to which a distinctive and coherent vision undergirds a given program. Although many web-based descriptions provide only vague and generic portraits of a program's conception of teachers and teaching, some institutions and programs articulate a goal to recruit and prepare teacher candidates who fit a strongly conceptualized and distinctive vision of teaching, and describe a program designed to embody that vision.

Program Coherence and Integration

Programs of teacher education confront the challenge of preparing prospective teachers for a complex and multi-faceted professional role, one that requires not only specialized knowledge related to the subjects, grades, and students they are likely to teach but also the capacity to assume responsibilities beyond the classroom and to engage in productive communication with professionals in other specializations (social work, school psychology, health professions). Yet long-standing criticisms of teacher education point to its fragmented or "siloed" character as a limitation on the quality of preparation experienced by teacher candidates (Ball, 2000; Grossman, Hammerness, and McDonald, 2009a; Harvey et al., 2010; Lanier and Little, 1986; Scruggs, Mastropieri, and McDuffie, 2007; Stone and Charles, 2018). This siloed nature takes the form of university coursework disconnected from clinical field experience; classroom teachers being trained separately from special education teachers, social workers, school psychologists, or other specialists focused on the development and well-being of students; elementary teachers prepared separately from early childhood educators, or from middle and high school teachers; and preservice preparation segmented from induction experiences and ongoing professional development. Achieving a conceptually coherent and experientially integrated program proves challenging for teacher education programs; Darling-Hammond terms this "probably the most difficult aspect of constructing a teacher education program" (2006, p. 305), but also underscores the importance of providing teacher candidates an "almost seamless experience of learning to teach" (p. 306).

The most prominent efforts to bridge the silos in the past two decades center on strengthening the relationship between university coursework and clinical practice, and on enhancing the quality of student teachers' field experiences. These efforts respond most directly to complaints that candidates receive little help in bridging theory and practice in their preparation, with training in content knowledge separate from training in classroom management and pedagogy (Ball, 2000). Some programs are addressing the chasm between university coursework and clinical practice by situating university courses within school sites (Zeichner, 2010), with results some scholars see as promising (Hodges and Baum, 2019). National associations have taken steps to promote higher quality approaches to clinical experience, closely integrated with other components of teacher preparation, as reflected most recently in the "proclamations" issued by AACTE's Clinical Practice Commission (2018).

CHARACTERISTICS OF TEACHER CANDIDATES

Every occupation must find ways of attracting newcomers to its ranks. The individuals who enroll in programs of teacher preparation bring with them a view of teaching as an occupation, and a set of experiences, perspectives, and motivations that shape their decision to enroll. Three developments in the past 20 years deserve particular attention, as they may shape both the capacity and motivation of new teachers to respond to changing student demographics and to expectations for teaching and learning in the 21st century. The committee offers a few illustrations of initiatives that have been started; however, the examples highlighted represent a small subset. Given time constraints, the committee was unable to offer a comprehensive review of all national efforts.

First, individuals who are now becoming teachers, with the possible exception of career changers (see Box 5-3), likely attended school during the era of test-based accountability. Their ideas of what it means to teach—the goals of learning, the nature of classroom instruction, the form and role of assessment, the relationships between teachers and students—may have been influenced strongly by the kinds of accountability-based instruction that evolved in the wake of No Child Left Behind (NCLB; see Chapters 2 and 3). Elementary instruction in particular shifted under NCLB to focus increasingly on math and reading at the expense of social studies, science, and the arts, and to emphasize narrowly defined, standardized forms of assessment (Dee and Jacob, 2010; Dee, Jacob, and Schwartz, 2013).

A second development conceives of teaching as short-term public service. The advent of Teach For America (TFA) introduced the premise that "that young, highly educated individuals will stimulate achievement and motivation in low-performing schools, even if they remain only a short period; a corollary but more implicit premise is that high turnover of such teachers will do no harm to students or schools, presuming that programs and schools are able to recruit a steady supply" (Little and Bartlett, 2010, p. 310). Although teachers recruited by TFA and by similar recruitment efforts (including the hiring of overseas-trained teachers) represent a small percentage of the teacher workforce (see Chapter 4), they are concentrated

BOX 5-3
Recent Innovative Recruitment Strategies

Some program leaders have capitalized on the market for teacher candidates by developing programs that target individuals seeking to switch careers. Some of these programs are post-baccalaureate programs within institutions of higher education. One example is Troops to Teachers, a program designed to assist transitioning members and veterans of the armed forces to careers as K–12 school teachers in public, charter, and Bureau of Indian Affairs schools. Since its establishment in 1993, more than 20,000 veterans have transitioned to education careers (Troops to Teachers, n.d.).

Other programs use innovative recruitment strategies such as providing debt-free education. The University of Mississippi has a program called the Mississippi Teacher Corps (MTC) that selects top college graduates to teach in high-poverty public schools in Mississippi. Teacher candidates, supported by a full scholarship, earn a debt-free master of arts degree in teaching (MAT), receive full pay and benefits from their school district, and attend graduate classes at the University of Mississippi.

Specific minority-serving institutions (MSIs) have successfully developed targeted recruitment strategies to recruit more teachers of color into their teacher education programs. These MSIs are reconsidering the use of GPA and standardized test scores as criteria for program admittance. While historically used as indicators of "quality," GPAs and exam scores may not fully represent a candidate's potential for teaching. In addition, students of color represent a higher proportion of first-generation college students and often have limited access to the same level of support as students from more advantaged backgrounds. Standardized tests also come with a significant price tag that must be paid even before students have been admitted into a program or allowed to enter the teaching labor force. Some programs have successfully increased their recruitment of teachers of color by providing multi-tiered testing support systems to help students prepare for these exams and providing stipends to cover the associated costs of taking them (Gasman, Samayoa, and Ginsberg, 2017).

Another successful strategy has been to recruit students early, even while they are still in high school. The Cheyney University of Pennsylvania and University of New Mexico recruit high school students from the same communities that those students will eventually return to as teachers—a Grow Your Own effort. Recruiting events such as teacher conferences for minoritized groups and campus visits are often elements of school-to-college pipelines with local communities to identify and recruit students interested in teaching before they exit grade 12. This early recruitment is often combined with tuition incentives and access to additional opportunities such as expanded residencies and culturally relevant coursework (Gasman, Samayoa, and Ginsberg, 2017).

in high-minoritized and high-poverty schools and districts (Bartlett, 2014; Clotfelder, Ladd, and Vigdor, 2005). More important than their numbers may be the staying power of the institutional logic of teaching as short-term service rather than a career for which one requires in-depth preparation and ongoing opportunity to learn (see Chapter 4).

A third development of the past two decades entails efforts to recruit a more diverse pool of teacher candidates, with respect to both teachers' demographic characteristics (more teachers of color and male teachers) and teachers' ability to help remedy chronic shortages in STEM fields, special education, and bilingual education (as discussed in Chapter 4). A report issued by the American Association of Colleges of Teacher Education (AACTE) (King and Hampel, 2018) identifies several initiatives intended to diversify the workforce, including Federal TEACH grants, state-level scholarships, foundation-supported initiatives, and AACTE initiatives. Most supply financial incentives or supports, but AACTE has also adopted the idea of a Networked Improvement Community to help institutions increase the number of Black and Hispanic/Latino men (see Carnegie Foundation for the Advancement of Teaching, 2019). TFA's current teacher corps is now half people of color (Teach For America, 2019), with active recruitment from MSIs, reflecting the organization's success in meeting one of the workforce's top agenda items.

PREPARING TEACHERS TO ENGAGE
STUDENTS IN DEEPER LEARNING

As described in Chapter 3, teaching for deeper learning arguably requires teachers to have deep command of content knowledge (i.e., disciplinary knowledge) and specialized content knowledge for teaching (i.e., knowing how to teach disciplinary knowledge and practices), as well as strong practical training in what it means to engage and empower learners from diverse communities through culturally relevant education. Intentional, purposeful instruction in disciplinary learning is critical to developing students' deep learning. Deeper learning also involves cultivating the disposition and ability to work effectively with a diverse population of students and families.

However, the constant refrain that teachers must be able to serve "all students" tends to emphasize academic competencies and render opaque some of the complex issues entailed in working for equity and social justice both in and beyond the classroom that in fact impact academic success (Cochran-Smith et al., 2016; Darling-Hammond, 2006). Some "deeper learning" documents focus learning outcomes principally on academic competencies, often characterizing this as a pursuit of "excellence." A notable example of this can be observed in the creation of particular standards such as computer science (e.g., Grover, Pea, and Cooper, 2015). In contrast, the five principles identified in the Darling-Hammond and Oakes (2019) book *Preparing Teachers for Deeper Learning* explicitly reference learning for equity and social justice. A substantial body of research suggests that each of these aims—achieving depth of understanding and skill, and catalyzing equity and social justice—present daunting challenges and tensions that may be compounded by the tendency to address "excellence" and "equity" as divergent rather than convergent aspects of an equitable learning ecology (Khalil and Kier, 2018).

Having acknowledged this dilemma, and having underscored the intersection of the preparation goals identified here, this section concentrates on approaches that teacher preparation programs have developed to supply novice teachers with deep specialized content knowledge for teaching (Ball, Thames, and Phelps, 2008) and with the ability to design and enact instruction that engages students in rich, complex, and authentic tasks. Three developments are highlighted: the movement to focus on professional practice, with particular focus on "core" or "high leverage" practices (and critiques of that movement); field experiences; and innovations in teacher education pedagogy.

Practice-Based Teacher Education

As described in Chapter 3, developing the knowledge, skills, and dispositions to support an increasingly diverse set of learners to engage in deeper learning requires significant shifts in what teaching looks and sounds like in most U.S. classrooms. It can be challenging to support preservice teachers in shifting their conceptions of instruction so as to be able to teach in ways substantially different from those experienced as K–12 students. Over the past two decades, a growing appreciation for the multi-faceted and specialized nature of teachers' knowledge has been joined to a richer conceptualization of the complexities of professional practice (see Box 5-4). Shulman (1987) introduced a taxonomy of teacher knowledge that in turn stimulated a substantial body of empirical research (especially on the nature of "pedagogical content knowledge") as well as further conceptual refinements (Ball, Thames, and Phelps, 2008; Gess-Newsome, 2015).

In a widely cited essay, Ball and Cohen (1999) present a compelling case for why this multi-faceted and specialized knowledge requires professional learning opportunities rooted in practice, especially if our educational system aspires to "deeper and more complex learning in students as well as teachers" (p. 5). Ball and Cohen envision professional education *centered in the critical activities of the profession—that is, in and about the practices of teaching,*" but caution that this does not entail a simplistic recommendation to locate more of teacher preparation in schools and classrooms, where the immediacy of classroom activity may limit teachers' ability to gain new insight into central problems of practice. Throughout, they urge (and illustrate) the thoughtful, collective analysis of well-chosen records of professional practice that include samples of student work, video-records

---

BOX 5-4
Woodrow Wilson Graduate School of Education

The Woodrow Wilson Graduate School of Education is an example of a teacher preparation program that was developed with the aim of having a national influence on teacher education through the power of the ideas and exemplars that it has constructed. The Woodrow Wilson Fellowship Foundation founded the program and is working with MIT to develop it further. The partnership presents itself as a laboratory for developing approaches to teacher preparation, which they hope that other programs will adapt and adopt. A central feature of the program is that teacher candidates progress through a series of design challenges to develop key competencies, rather than completing conventional courses. Program leaders have identified approximately 20 competencies and will recommend their students for licensure when they have demonstrated that they have mastered those competencies. One challenge, for example, is how to individualize learning, given the inevitable variation in student interests, skills, and knowledge. At the end of working on the challenge, the student submits a challenge solution, which is assessed by an outside evaluator who gauges the student's progress in mastering the competency.

By making the challenges and associated materials freely available online the program is providing exemplars that it hopes will influence other programs to move from a course-based model to a competency-based model.

Research also shows that facilitating discussion has potential in deepening teachers' understandings of students' ideas and personal experiences.

At the same time, research indicates that facilitating productive discussions, that is, discussions that advance student learning, is intricate, difficult work. Teachers are likely to engage students in whole-class discussions across a *range* of contexts (e.g., content domains, using different curricula). As such, the function of a discussion and therefore the form it may take varies—both within and across content areas (e.g., Boerst et al., 2011).

Thus, the idea of identifying a "core practice" is not to suggest that a particular form of practice—like facilitating a whole-class discussion—will look and sound the same in varied contexts, given different purposes for engaging in discussion, different disciplinary norms and practices, differences in students' experiences, and so forth. That said, proponents of core practices argue that there are some consistent features of planning for and facilitating a discussion (e.g., identifying goals for a discussion, anticipating student thinking, identifying key questions to pose in relation to goals and what's known about students' ideas, representing students' ideas publicly so that other students can make sense of them) that can fruitfully form the basis for curriculum in teacher education coursework. Novices are supported to study as well as try out the work of facilitating discussions that advance student learning.

---

of classroom lessons, curriculum materials, and teachers' plans and notes. Ball and Cohen nonetheless acknowledge that centering professional learning in an intensive consideration of practice would represent a fundamental, systemic change in the organization of teacher education and in the role of teacher educators.

Grossman and colleagues (2009b) developed a framework of the pedagogies of practice-based teacher education that elaborates on Ball and Cohen's (1999) call to center professional education on practice. The framework is grounded in a cross-field study that included teacher education together with preparation for the clergy and for clinical psychology. It distinguishes between *pedagogies of investigation,* which focus on analyzing and reflecting on records of practice (e.g., video recordings, student work), and *pedagogies of enactment,* or "opportunities to practice elements of interactive teaching in settings of reduced complexity" (Grossman and McDonald, 2008, p. 190). Analyzing records of practice to reflect upon and improve teaching, while necessary, is not sufficient for supporting novices to develop the *enact* the "contingent, interactive aspects of teaching" (Grossman, 2011, p. 2837)—especially when the goals of teaching are, for many novices, substantially different from what they experienced themselves as K–12 learners (see Box 5-5).

One issue in practice-based teacher education entails deciding what aspects of practice to focus on with novices, and when, and why. Grossman, Hammerness, and McDonald (2009a, p. 277) argued for the value in focusing teacher education on "core practices," which the authors describe as those that occur with high frequency in teaching; can be enacted in classrooms across different curricula or instructional approaches; allow teachers to learn more about students and about teaching; preserve the integrity and complexity of teaching; and are research-based and have the potential to improve student achievement. (See also Ball et al., 2009 for a discussion of "high-leverage practices.")

Facilitating whole-class discussions is an example of what might count as a "core" or "high-leverage" practice. Substantial research has indicated that engaging students in whole-class discussions, in which students are supported and pressed to reason about central ideas, and to connect their ideas to those of their peers, deepens students' understanding of content and competence with disciplinary forms of argument and reasoning (e.g., Fogo, 2014; Franke, Kazemi, and Battey, 2007; NASEM, 2018).

In 2012, a group of educators from multiple institutions and subject matter disciplines formed the Core Practices Consortium (CPC) to advance program innovations and a related research agenda. The premise underlying the work of the Consortium is that focusing on a selected set of core practices may better prepare novice teachers to "counter longstanding inequities in the schooling experiences of youth from historically marginalized communities in the U.S." (Core Practice Consortium, 2016). Although CPC participants share a set of commitments and understandings, the core practices they identify "vary in grain size, content-specificity, exhaustiveness, and other features" (Grossman, 2018, p. 4). For example, TeachingWorks, a center at the University of Michigan School of Education, identified

BOX 5-5
Pedagogies of Investigation and Enactment

Three concepts central to pedagogies of investigation and enactment are *representations of practice, decompositions of practice,* and *approximations of practice. Representations of practice* are records of teaching and learning, which might include video recordings of teaching, transcripts of instruction, student work, or lesson plans. Any representation makes some aspects of teaching visible, and thus available for investigation; however, representations also render other aspects invisible or opaque. *Decompositions of practice* entail "breaking down complex practice into its constituent parts for the purposes of teaching and learning" (Grossman, 2011, pp. 2838–2839). Identifying and then "decomposing" a component of teaching for deeper learning supports novices to attend to "essential" elements of teaching (p. 2939). Grossman and colleagues argue that it is important that teacher educators have a language for parsing elements of practice, for example, leading a text-based discussion in an English language arts class, so that they can, in turn, support novice teachers to attend to essential aspects of leading a discussion.

The third element of the framework, *approximations of practice,* are opportunities to enact aspects of teaching in settings that may "fall along a continuum, from less complete and authentic to more complete and authentic" (Grossman et al., 2009b, p. 2078). Such experiences may take the form of simulation, rehearsal, or supervised classroom teaching, where teacher educators purposefully press and support novices to "try out" important aspects of teaching. For example, in a coached rehearsal, a teacher candidate plays the role of rehearsing teacher while her peers typically play the role of students, and a teacher educator provides real-time feedback (Kazemi et al., 2015; Kelly-Petersen et al., 2018; Lampert et al., 2013). Rehearsals do not occur in the context of classrooms with students and instead tend to occur in a teacher education classroom. In that sense, they are intentionally inauthentic. Coached rehearsals allow teacher candidates the opportunity to try out new instructional moves without affecting students, and to collaborate with peers in problem solving around a problem of practice, with opportunities to apply feedback in multiple iterations.

A joint focus on pedagogies of investigation *and* enactment is intended to support novices to increasingly develop competency and comfort in enacting principled teaching in settings that are complex. McDonald, Kazemi, and Kavanagh (2013) put forth what they call the "learning cycle" as a model of one way to organize preservice teacher education to support novices to both investigate and enact contingent practice. The cycle includes developing a vision of the targeted aspect of instruction (e.g., leading a text-based discussion), as a whole and "decomposing" it in a self-reflective process that pairs action with analysis. The "decomposition" process might, for example, begin with teachers (1) experiencing the activity itself or analyzing video records of a discussion; (2) planning to enact instruction with students, which may include both developing a lesson plan and rehearsing the lesson; (3) trying out the lesson with students; and (4) analyzing the lesson (e.g., a video record, student work) in an effort to learn from and improve practice.

19 high-leverage practices that include leading a group discussion, building respectful relationships with students, and checking student understanding during and at the conclusion of lessons. A set of core science teaching practices in secondary classrooms was developed by a Delphi panel of expert science teachers and university faculty; these practices include engaging students in investigations, facilitating classroom discourse, and eliciting, assessing, and using student thinking about science (Kloser, 2014). Also using a Delphi panel, a set of core teaching practices for secondary history education were developed, including employing historical evidence, the use of history concepts, big ideas, and essential questions, and making connections to personal/cultural experiences (Fogo, 2014).

Some scholars have questioned the compatibility of organizing teacher education coursework around high-leverage practices with a commitment to advancing equity and social justice (Philip et al., 2018; Souto-Manning, 2019). Dutro and Cartun (2016) argue that calling some practices "core" necessarily suggests other practices are peripheral. They suggest that while choosing to focus on routine aspects of teaching can be of great value, it is important for teacher educators to remain vigilant in interrogating what is identified as central and what is less so. Moreover, they call for teacher educators to support novices to treat and approach teaching as complex, especially when narrowing focus to a particular form of practice. Similarly concerned with what is centered and what is pushed to the periphery, Philip et al. (2018) argue that a focus on core practices may result in the parsing of teaching into discrete, highly precise skills with not enough consideration into the character and complexity of local schooling contexts, and thus "decenter justice" (p. 6).

Recent research, including studies involving scholars affiliated with CPC, has begun to shed light on the impact of the core practices approach and issues related to equity. Several studies focus on determining whether and how core practices are evident in the planning and instruction of novice teachers. For example, Kang and Windschitl (2018) conducted a mixed-methods study of the lessons taught by two groups of first-year science teachers; one group had completed a "practice-embedded" program organized around core practices, and the second group completed a program that did not feature a core practices approach. The research team found that the graduates of the practice-embedded program were significantly different from the comparison group with respect to the opportunities for student learning embodied in the lesson plans (goals, tasks, tools) and in the level of active science sense-making evident in classroom discourse (see Chapter 6 for similar findings related to inservice professional development).

In an extension of that research, Kang and Zinger (2019) explicitly take up questions regarding the relationship between preparation in core practices and outcomes centered on equity and social justice. The authors draw on a longitudinal (3-year) case study of White women as they completed a program focused on core practices in science teaching and then in their first 2 years of teaching as they taught students from ethnically, linguistically, and economically diverse backgrounds. Even within a small case study sample of three teachers, they found variations in the teachers' use of ambitious science teaching practices (enabled or constrained in part by their workplace context), but also found that the awareness of core practices alone did not help novice teachers adopt teaching methods that reflect a critical consciousness about racism and systemic, structural inequity. The researchers attributed these results in part to a preparation program in which coursework focused on cultural diversity and equity remained separate from coursework on science teaching methods.

In a second example, Kavanagh and Danielson (2019) investigated novice elementary teachers' opportunities to attend to issues of social justice and facilitate text-based discussions in a literacy methods course, and the ways novices integrated the two domains when reflecting on their teaching practice. The literacy methods course was co-taught by a literacy methods instructor and a foundations instructor. Data included video recordings of the literacy methods course in which the novices prepared to teach text-based discussions (specifically in the context of interactive read-alouds), video recordings of the novices engaging elementary students in read-alouds, and novices' written reflections on their videos.

One finding concerned differences in teacher educator pedagogies as they relate to a focus on social justice issues or content. Kavanagh and Danielson found that when teaching about facilitating a text-based discussion, teacher educators supported the novices to both analyze and try out (e.g., rehearse) specific moves one might make during an interactive read-aloud, and to reason about their instructional decisions. However, while novices engaged in conversations about social justice in relation to *planning* for text-based discussions (e.g., which text to select in relation to their students' lived experiences), novices rarely engaged in discussions of social justice in relation to their actual *facilitation* of text-based discussions. Kavanagh and Danielson write: "When TEs . . . support[ed] teachers to attend to social justice in their teaching, justice was exclusively treated as an element of lesson planning rather than as a factor in in-the-moment instructional decision making, or instruction . . . Only on extremely rare occasions did novices discuss attending to social justice while making in-the-moment instructional decisions." (p. 19). Further, when reflecting on video recordings of their teaching, novices discussed issues of facilitating text-based discussions much more frequently than issues of attending to social justice (p. 19).

Kavanagh and Danielson suggest that novices' tendency to center issues of content and decenter issues of social justice when reflecting on their instructional decision-making is likely shaped by the pedagogies employed by the teacher educators. "While [Teacher Educators] frequently represented, decomposed, and approximated practice with novices, they rarely did so when supporting novices to attend to social justice" (p. 30). On the basis of these findings, and in relation to the ongoing debates about the relationships between "core practices" and advancing social justice and equity, Kavanagh and Danielson suggest the value in understanding more deeply how teacher educators might more purposefully integrate attention to specific forms of practice (e.g., facilitating a text-based discussion) and social justice concerns (e.g., representation of students, addressing classroom power relations during a discussion) in the context of practice-based teacher education.

The Field Experience

One hallmark of professional education in all fields is its reliance on practical experience to help novices develop key skills and cultivate professional judgment. Numerous correlational studies have shown some aspects of clinical experiences to be positively associated with measures of teacher effectiveness and retention (e.g., Boyd et al., 2009; Goldhaber, Krieg, and Theobold, 2017; Krieg, Theobold, and Goldhaber, 2016; Ronfeldt, 2012, 2015). Ronfeldt (2012, p. 4) points to variations in the degree to which programs take an active role in selecting and overseeing field placements, citing the NYC Pathways Study[4] conducted by Boyd and colleagues (2009) as an example.

> [P]rogram oversight of field experiences was positively and significantly associated with teacher effects. More specifically, new teachers who graduated from programs that were actively involved in selecting field placements had minimum experience thresholds for cooperating teachers and required supervisors to observe student teachers at least five times had higher student achievement gains in their first year as teacher of record.

Recent scholarship points to the relationship between field experience and teacher candidates' perceptions of the quality of their program and their preparedness to teach. Using longitudinal data from the Schools and Staffing Survey, Ronfeldt, Schwarz, and Jacob (2014) found that teachers who completed more methods-related coursework and practice teaching felt they were better prepared and were more likely to stay in teaching. These findings applied to teachers no matter what preparation route they

---

[4] The NYC Pathways Study reviewed the entry points for teachers in New York City through an analysis of more than 30 programs, including a survey of all first-year teachers. The study examined the differences in the components of the teacher preparation programs and examined the effects related to student achievement.

took. In an experimental study of a project called Improving Student Teaching Initiative (ISTI), Ronfeldt et al. (2018) found that teachers randomly assigned to placements evaluated as more promising rather than less promising (in terms of various measures of teacher and school characteristics) had higher perceptions of the quality of the instruction of their mentor teachers and the quantity and quality of the coaching they received. Additionally, candidates in the more promising placements were more likely to report better working conditions, stronger collaboration among teachers, more opportunities to learn to teach, and feeling better prepared to teach (Ronfeldt et al., 2018). In their study of six Washington State teacher education programs, Goldhaber, Krieg, and Theobald (2017) found that teachers are more effective when the student demographics of the schools where they did their student teaching and those of their current schools are similar. Scholarship also shows an association between the effectiveness of the mentor teacher and the future effectiveness of teacher candidates (Goldhaber, Krieg, and Theobald, 2018), using value-added as a measure of effectiveness.

Research on preservice preparation in multiple fields, including teacher education, points to the difficulties that novices may encounter in integrating their academic preparation with their clinical or field experience (Benner et al., 2010; Cooke, Irby, and O'Brien, 2010; Grossman et al., 2009b; Sheppard et al., 2009; Sullivan, 2005). Those difficulties may be compounded when novices lack access to clinical experiences in settings that reflect high standards of professional practice and that prepare novice professionals to take a reflective and questioning stance toward their own practice. As Ball and Cohen (1999) caution, some clinical experiences do little to disrupt or address the "apprenticeship of observation" (Lortie, 1975) that teachers bring with them to their field experiences and student teaching: that is, the thousands of hours in the classroom spent observing teaching as students. This apprenticeship of observation may reinforce the conservatism of teaching practice if teacher education, including clinical experience, does not offer opportunities for preservice teachers to seriously study their own experiences and practice, and engage in "substantial professional discourse" (Ball and Cohen, 1999, p. 5).

Concerns about the quality of clinical experience seem particularly warranted in situations where teacher candidates have little or no field experience, or where candidates are permitted or even required to find their own placement sites for early field experiences and/or student teaching (Levine, 2006). In a study of mathematics and science teachers using the 2003–2004 Schools and Staffing Survey, and the supplement, the 2004–2005 Teacher Follow-up Survey, Ingersoll, Merrill, and May (2012, 2014) found that 21 percent of new teachers did not have any practice or student teaching before their first job, and the rates were even higher for science teachers: 40 percent had no practice teaching. The latest data from the 2015–2016 National Teacher and Principal Survey indicate that this has not changed: 23 percent of first-year teachers in 2015 had no practice teaching (Ingersoll, personal communication, 2019). This matters because the amount of practice teaching teachers candidates have is associated with whether they remain in the field as teachers (Ingersoll, Merrill, and May, 2014). However, much is not known about how the student teaching experience contributes to teacher candidates' development (Anderson and Stillman, 2013). Much of the scholarship tends to focus on changing beliefs among teacher candidates rather than the development of teaching practice, and a more robust research base is needed to understand the role such development plays in teacher preparation (Anderson and Stillman, 2013).

Innovations in Teacher Preparation

Efforts to strengthen the quality of clinical experience have taken center stage in recent years, spurred in part by high-profile reports such as the Blue Ribbon Panel report, *Transforming Teacher Education through Clinical Practice: A National Strategy to Prepare Effective Teachers* (NCATE, 2010; see also the report of the AACTE Clinical Practice Commission, 2018). In addition, some studies have demonstrated the potential of field experiences to support teacher learning when well designed and coordinated with campus coursework (Darling-Hammond, 2006; Lampert et al., 2013; Tatto, 1996). Three recent innovations in the organization of clinical experience, discussed below, show promise for developing teacher candidates' practice, particularly in working in urban and high-need contexts.

Clinical Experiences

In an approach modeled after medical rounds attended by physicians in training, Robert Bain and Elizabeth Moje at the University of Michigan developed a project to integrate student teachers' discipline-specific preparation with their preparation to tackle problems of practice in the field (Bain, 2012; Bain and Moje, 2012). The Clinical Rounds Project was launched in 2005 with a pilot in the area of social studies; it has since expanded to include methods instructors, field instructors, interns, and practicing classroom teachers across five content areas: social studies, mathematics, science, English language arts, and world languages. The project seeks to integrate the disparate components of the teacher education program through a spiraling program of study. Teacher candidates rotate through classrooms of carefully selected mentor teachers (called "attending teachers") who model selected practices and intervene in the teaching of teacher candidates to offer real-time feedback. Based on video of preservice teachers working in the field and on other project documentation, Bain (2012) reports several changes evident in the "Rounds" cohorts compared to previous cohorts: a new conception of the teacher's role; a heightened appreciation for the kinds of curricular and instructional tools they would need to achieve their goals; a deeper understanding of the challenges their secondary students are likely to experience in the history classroom; and end-of-program perception that their coursework and field experiences had been fruitfully integrated.

Methods courses located at school sites (sometimes referred to as a hybrid space) can facilitate new connections between teacher candidates, practicing teachers, and university-based teacher educators in new ways that can address the historical divide that exists between campus and field-based teacher education and enhance teacher candidates' learning. This hybrid space has the potential of creating a partnership among key stakeholders (K–12 students, teacher candidates, university faculty, and mentor teachers) characterized by more egalitarian and collegial relationships than conventional school-university partnerships (Zeichner, 2010).

Different kinds of hybrid spaces exist. Some examples include having "studio days" focused on teaching English learners, with prospective teachers working jointly with experienced teachers to focus on language structures (Von Esch and Kavanagh, 2018); incorporating K–12 teachers and their knowledge bases into campus courses and field experiences (e.g., by having teachers with high levels of competence spend a residency working in all aspects of a preservice teacher education program); incorporating representation of teachers' practices in campus courses (through writing and research of K–12 teachers or multimedia representations of their teaching practice); and incorporating knowledge from communities into preservice teacher preparation (Zeichner, 2010).

Many other clinical innovations exist and are in various phases of development. Empirical research is needed to explore the effectiveness of these innovations on a range of outcome measures (e.g., teacher candidates' future effectiveness related to student achievement and in centering equity and justice in their teaching) as well as the feasibility and cost of implementing them. Some clinical approaches, such as microteaching, have been used for many years (Grossman, 2005) and continue to be common components of field instruction, with adaptions to make use of current contexts (Abendroth, Golzy, and O'Connor, 2011; Fernandez, 2010).

Technological Innovations

Teacher preparation programs are increasingly using technological innovations in a range of ways in attempts to better prepare teacher candidates (Hollett, Brock, and Hinton, 2017; Kennedy and Newman Thomas,

2012; Rock et al., 2009, 2014; Schaefer and Ottley, 2018; Scheeler et al., 2006; Sherin and Russ, 2014; Uerz, Volman, and Kral, 2018). eCoaching through bug-in-ear technology is a relatively new technology that allows for discreet coaching to be offered via an online coach or supervisor (Hollett, Brock, and Hinton, 2017; Rock et al., 2009, 2014; Schaefer and Ottley, 2018; Scheeler et al., 2006). Current research examines the way bug-in-ear technology can enhance teacher preparation programs (Hollett, Brock, and Hinton, 2017; Schaefer and Ottley, 2018; Scheeler et al., 2006), especially the long-term benefits for special education teachers-in-training (Rock et al., 2009, 2014).

Video recordings of practice are used for reflection, peer collaboration (e.g., through a "video club"), evaluation, and coaching. In response to the increased use of video recordings, there has been a corresponding development in video sharing platforms (e.g., Edthena, Torsh Talent, Class Forward, Iris Connect). For example, in one recent study of preparation for mathematics teaching, Sun and van Es (2015) designed a video-based secondary-level mathematics methods course, Learning to Learn from Teaching (LLFT), in which teacher candidates studied video cases of teaching to learn to notice features of ambitious pedagogy, with particular attention to analysis of student thinking. Researchers compared videos of teaching practice between teacher candidates enrolled in the LLFT course and teacher candidates in the same program from a prior year who did not take the LLFT course. They analyzed the videos along the dimensions of (1) making student thinking visible, (2) probing student thinking, and (3) learning in the context of teaching. Sun and van Es found that the teacher candidates in the LLFT course enacted responsive teaching practices attending to student thinking with more frequency.

Technology-supported simulations provide preservice teacher candidates opportunities to hone classroom management and instructional skills with multiple opportunities for practice without experimenting on actual students. This standardized tool is often found in other professions such as medicine, business, and the military. There are forms of simulations that are not aided by technology, such as work being done at Syracuse University in which actors play the part of students in the simulations (similar to the work being done within medical schools) and experimental efforts at the University of Michigan with an assessment that utilizes a "standardized student."

According to one teacher educator and researcher with extensive experience with this technology, an effective simulation needs to have three critical components: "(a) personalized learning, (b) suspension of disbelief, and (c) cyclical procedures to ensure impact" (Dieker et al., 2014, p. 22). For example, TLE TeachLivE, a mixed-reality teaching environment, provides a room for the teacher or teacher candidate to physically enter that simulates an actual classroom, with "virtual students" as avatars (played by a live "actor" offsite) (Dieker et al., 2014). Teachers interact with the virtual students (who represent a range of ages, cultures, backgrounds, and abilities), teach new content, and monitor students as they work independently. Following feedback or self-reflection, the teacher candidates may re-enter the virtual classroom to attempt different responses and strategies to support student learning (Dieker et al., 2014, p. 3).

PREPARING TEACHER CANDIDATES TO WORK WITH DIVERSE POPULATIONS

At their best, all of the approaches outlined above—developing a command of core practices in subject-specific teaching, participating in well-designed clinical experiences integrated with coursework, and capitalizing on new technologies—should aid in the preparation of teachers to work with a diverse student population. Some recent studies supply evidence that field experiences in local communities—beyond classrooms and schools, and where preservice teachers are carefully prepared and guided through mediation, debriefing of these experiences, and connecting these experiences to the rest of their program—may help teacher candidates develop a richer understanding of students whose backgrounds differ from their own (McDonald et al., 2011). Yet the charge that teacher preparation programs fail to effectively prepare teacher candidates for the students they teach remains a common theme in the scholarship on teacher preparation (Anderson and Stillman, 2010; Cochran-Smith et al., 2016).

As illustrated in Chapter 3, one response to the disconnect between teachers (who are predominantly White, middle class, and female) and their students has been to emphasize the tenets of culturally relevant pedagogy and culturally sustaining pedagogy that support multilingualism and multiculturalism. Although a full characterization of teacher education faculty was beyond the scope of this report, teacher education faculty including adjunct faculty (which as of 2007 were 78% White) may play a key role in "how urgently a program works to address race and ethnicity" (Sleeter, 2017, p. 158).

There is no shortage of approaches and programs designed to prepare teachers for increasing cultural diversity, conceptualized in terms of social class, ethnicity, culture, and language (Major and Reid, 2017). However, there is no single "formula" (Major and Reid, 2017, p. 8) for implementing these approaches because, as Gay (2013) argues, the sociocultural context in which instructional practices are taught should influence the approaches used: "Culturally responsive teaching, in idea and action, emphasizes localism and contextual specificity" (Gay, 2013, p. 63). As Major and Reid (2017) observe, "Cultural and linguistic difference is inevitably overlaid with larger historical and political issues of migration, indigeneity, invasion, economic power, citizenship and racism. All of these are realised differently in different contexts and require teachers to understand their own cultural positioning and power in relation to the varieties of cultural difference with which they are engaged" (p. 11).

To what extent do teacher preparation programs foreground approaches for teaching multilingual, multicultural students? Critics argue that most teacher programs fall short. In their review of the literature on culturally responsive schooling for indigenous youth, Castagno and Brayboy (2008) found that schools and classrooms were failing to meet the needs of Indigenous students; they also found that although much theory and scholarship has been devoted to culturally responsive schooling for Indigenous populations, the main tenets of such pedagogies are often essentialized or too generalized to be applicable and effective. Similarly, few teachers develop the required skills to effectively work with emergent bilinguals—skills such as gauging students' language development and content understanding and using informal and formal assessments to promote literacy development (López and Santibañez, 2018). Scholars who have examined these issues argue that the consequences of these failures are serious, with consequences for a range of indicators of student success, including achievement, classification as emergent bilinguals, and high school completion (López and Santibañez, 2018).

In one effort to advance the integration of culturally relevant pedagogy preparation into programs of teacher education, Allen and colleagues (2017) developed a conceptual framework that "requires teacher educators and candidates to pose questions that disrupt, deconstruct, reimagine, and develop concepts in an effort to promote academic rigor and higher-order thinking" (p. 18). The authors urge questions that challenge the "status quo" curriculum, the nature of classroom and field learning opportunities, the content of the program, instructional practices, and avenues for voice.

Given the demographic divide between teacher candidates and the students they teach, preparing teacher candidates to address issues of diversity and focus on equity in meaningful, authentic, and practical ways is critical. Teacher preparation programs vary dramatically in their approaches. Box 5-6 highlights two approaches that show promise for developing teacher candidates' will and capacity to value students' diverse backgrounds and engage in culturally sustaining pedagogy (Paris and Alim, 2017): (1) valuing students' funds of knowledge from outside of school and (2) building relationships with the students' communities.

This section highlights principles, commitments, and pedagogies that hold promise for preparing teachers to work for equity and social justice. Preparing teachers to work for equity and social justice is not the

---

BOX 5-6
Promising Approaches for Engaging Diverse Learners

Pedagogical approaches grounded in students' cultural backgrounds, experiences, out-of-school lives, and everyday knowledge make a difference in student learning. Recognizing and drawing on students' "funds of knowledge," defined as "historically accumulated and culturally developed bodies of knowledge and skills essential for household or individual functioning and well-being" (Moll et al., 1992, p. 133; also see Gonzalez and Moll, 2011), can help bridge students' cultural backgrounds with school curriculum. Moreover, approaches that invite families and community members to play a role in the preparation of teachers have promise for building teachers' candidates' self-efficacy, agency, and confidence, which are linked to higher rates of teacher retention (Lee, 2018).

Teacher candidates who lack knowledge about the communities of their students are limited in their effectiveness with students from different backgrounds from them (Honig, Kahne, and McLaughlin, 2002; Ladson-Billings, 2001). One approach to help teacher candidates, particularly those who are White and middle-class, have cross-cultural opportunities with their students and their students' families is through projects that build bridges between the university and communities in which teacher candidates are teaching. For example, Koerner and Abdul-Tawwab (2006) describe a project in which faculty at the University of Massachusetts-Boston collaborated with local community organizations to develop ways to deepen community participation. The faculty developed seven goals for their program that they think are portable to other institutions:

1. Make institutional and systemic changes in order to build the connection for community input into teacher education instruction and curriculum. 2. Provide a forum for discussion of the expectations and issues surrounding the preparation of teachers for urban children. 3. Make faculty aware of community resources for inclusion in their courses. 4. Use community organizations to help recruit future teachers.

---

same as preparing teachers to work with a diverse student population (Cochran-Smith, 2004). Rather, it involves preparation that fosters a deep understanding of the structures and processes that reproduce inequality, cultivates a disposition to act in ways that interrupt those structures and processes, and equips teachers for equity-oriented leadership.

Educators have been calling for teacher preparation that reflects commitments to equity for decades (Fraser, 2007). For example, a recent issue of *Teachers College Record* compiled articles devoted to the goal to "reclaim the power and possibility of university-based teacher education to engage in transformations that prioritize the preparation of asset-, equity-, and social justice-oriented teachers" (Souto-Manning, 2019, p. 2).

As discussed earlier, the philosophical approach of culturally sustaining pedagogy directly seeks to foster linguistic, literate, and cultural

5. Open up discussions so that faculty can have greater knowledge of community and greater understanding of the home and school life of urban students. 6. Validate and value community members and parents in the training of teachers. 7. Make community members and partnership schools more aware of and part of the underlying values of college of education conceptual framework. (Koerner and Abdul-Tawwab, 2006, p. 44)

The project led to new, innovative thinking about ways to build connections between these two spaces, but there were also barriers to the collaboration such as the differing levels of status of the university and the community and the university's resistance to change.

Another approach engages community members and parents in the preparation of teacher candidates. That is, some programs have community members serve as mentors for prospective teachers, providing direct access to the expertise of those in the community. For example, a program in the Pacific Northwest had a Community Teaching Strand as part of its program, where community members worked with prospective teachers, helping them understand the goals they had for the education of their children (Guillen and Zeichner, 2018). This community engagement is featured in programs elsewhere in the country (Richmond, 2017; Zygmunt et al., 2018). An additional example includes the Chicago Teacher Education Pipeline (CTEP), a partnership by Illinois State University and the Chicago Public School District, which is aimed at preparing teachers for high-need schools (Lee, 2018). The program uses a partnership among the university, schools, and community—which brings together academic, practitioner, and community-based knowledge—to build "community teachers." CTEP employs steps such as faculty training for redesigning courses, preparing teacher candidates to work in urban communities, and summer pre-teaching clinical programs that place teacher candidates with host families in urban communities. The program prioritizes community immersion and actively works against promoting a savior mentality (Lee, 2018).

pluralism with the aim of positive social transformation for education. Culturally sustaining pedagogy is an assets-based approach that addresses the colonial aspect of contemporary schooling and actively works to disrupt anti-Blackness, anti-Indigeneity, anti-Brownness, model minority myths, and other ways in which schools foster colonialism and seeks to provide an alternative to the dominant "White gaze" (Paris and Alim, 2017, pp. 2–3).

Contemporary teacher education scholarship continues to argue that programs are not adequately preparing teachers to enact teaching in ways that are informed by equity-oriented interpretive frames (Carter Andrews et al., 2019; Sleeter, 2017). Such programs may employ interpretive frameworks in coursework and field experience and engage in activity that deepens teacher candidates' understanding, skills, and commitments (e.g., asset mapping, placement in community-based organizations). Unfortunately, many scholars claim that most programs tend to fall short of equipping teacher candidates with a deep understanding of structural inequalities and tools needed to create more equitable opportunities (e.g., Carter Andrews et al., 2019; Cochran-Smith et al., 2014; Sleeter, 2017). Understanding how to prepare teacher candidates for this kind of work is an area for both research and innovation.

MECHANISMS FOR INFLUENCING PRESERVICE TEACHER EDUCATION

If preservice teacher education is to be a more uniformly coherent and demonstrably effective contributor to the quality of teachers and teaching in the 21st century, it will require change at multiples levels and in multiple respects. Thinking about levers for change proves challenging. Nonetheless, four (admittedly overlapping) categories of influence occupy a prominent place in the available research literature and in educational journalism.

First, teacher education has been increasingly shaped by regulatory and policy mechanisms including professional standards, program admission criteria, state licensure requirements, and program accreditation. Over the past two decades, policy makers supported new and flexible pathways into teaching while simultaneously moving to tighten accountability for program outcomes (Cochran-Smith et al., 2018a). States and other accrediting bodies have specified criteria for admission that emphasize both the academic qualifications of individuals and the formation of a diverse pool of teacher candidates. Standards of professional teaching practice encompass the expectations outlined in Chapter 3, although the field lacks the kind of empirical evidence to know with certainty how standards translate into preparation and practice outcomes. Nonetheless, changes in licensure requirements and program accreditation mark a shift from program inputs and components to teacher candidate outcomes, with some states requiring candidate performance assessment for licensure and/or program accreditation (AACTE, n.d.).

A second potential source of influence on teacher education are the multiple institutional or professional associations and networks that populate the teacher education terrain, as well as various policy-related organizations that include teacher education policies on a broader agenda of educational reform. Professional associations of teachers and teacher educators have served as mechanisms for developing and promoting research-based conceptions of learning that in turn have influenced programs of teacher preparation and professional development; a well-known example is the conception of mathematics learning advanced by the National Council of Teachers of Mathematics in the late 1980s (NRC, 2001). Professional associations with institutional (rather than individual) membership are more likely to promote broad programmatic priorities, as NCATE did by appealing to program to place field experience as the center of teacher preparation, and AACTE did in 2018 when it followed up with a set of proclamations regarding clinical practice (Little, 1993).[5]

A third source of influence takes the form of targeted change initiatives. Some initiatives have emerged from within the field of teacher education, led by teacher educators and teacher education researchers. Among the examples that span several decades are the Holmes Group and the more recent CPC. Other initiatives flow from initiatives or funding streams supported by the federal government (such as support for Teach For America and for alternatives to university-based teacher preparation). Still others stem from private corporations, venture capitalists, or foundations that have altered the landscape of teacher education through their investments in new institutional entities (such as new Graduate Schools of Education) and their ties to federal policy makers. Some private-sector initiatives recruit institutions that agree to pursue a particular reform agenda; Teachers for a New Era, launched by the Carnegie Corporation of New York, presents one well-funded example (see Box 5-7).

Finally, the committee acknowledges the potential of ideas, messaging, and exemplars to stimulate new organizational arrangements and practices. The rapid spread of terms such as "deeper learning" and "core practices" points to the potential for influence though the technology-aided and network-supported spread of new ideas and associated exemplars. Powerful ideas may be developed and spread by any number of entities, including public agencies, universities, reform organizations, private foundations, networks, and individuals—and by numerous means including social media, conferences, publications, as well as privately and publicly funded initiatives. Of course, the rapid spread of organizing ideas and images does not signal common definitions of what those terms mean (in fact, rapid spread may impede such common definition, complicating the conduct of related research), nor does it entail uniform endorsement of any given idea or approach (Aydarova and Berliner, 2018; Zeichner, 2014).

---

[5] More information regarding NCATE's appeal to place field experiences at the center of teacher preparation can be found at http://www.highered.nysed.gov/pdf/NCATECR.pdf. More on AACTE's proclamations can be found at https://secure.aacte.org/apps/rl/res_get.php?fid=3750&ref=rl.

BOX 5-7
Teacher Education Reform Initiatives

One approach to making improvements in teacher preparation is for programs themselves to work as a group to experiment with new approaches, with the long-term goal of having the approaches that are found to be successful adopted by programs outside of the group. In the past four decades, four notable groups of institutions fit this model. As with other education innovations, those initiating change often have high hopes for direct and dramatic general effects. Such dramatic direct effects are seldom detected, though the innovations may contribute to more diffuse changes.

In the mid-1980s, a nation-wide group of research universities banded together to form the Holmes Group. The organization, which grew to include 100 institutions, published a series of reports with recommendations for changes in initial teacher preparation (for the single volume, see Holmes Partnership, 2006). Beginning with the first report, *Teachers for Tomorrow's Schools* (1986), the organization combined recommendations for changes in initial preparation with recommendations for changes in schools as workplaces and for the creation of a staged career for teachers, with changing responsibilities for teachers who demonstrated a high level of knowledge and skill. (Significantly, this report was reprinted in the same year as *A Nation Prepared: Teacher for the 21st Century*, a report of the Carnegie Forum on Education and the Economy).

In that first report, the recommended changes in initial preparation were aimed at making the teacher preparation more intellectually solid, with stronger preparation in the academic disciplines and closer connections to the work of K–12 schools. The report's authors also called for development of new required examinations to be required for certification that would more closely align with both the content knowledge important for teaching and with the skills needed for high-quality instruction.

About a decade after the Holmes Group was created, it commissioned an independent study of its own history and effects. That report, *The Rise and Stall of Education Reform* (Fullan et al., 1998), was based on interviews and site visits to Holmes Group institutions and found that some, but not all, institutions had made program changes as called for in the reports. The study found that the most common changes made by schools resulted in the development of a "conceptual framework to guide the program, more rigorous standards of entry into teacher education programs, and improved assessments for preservice teacher candidates" (pp. 28–29). The authors also found that Professional Development Schools, a form of partnership that was the focus of the second Holmes Group report, had been created in all Holmes Group universities, as well as in other universities, with variation in implementation. The report also concluded that the group had a broad influence on connections between university preparation programs and K–12 schools and on the terms in which discussions of teacher education reform occur (e.g., on the most appropriate content in the disciplines). Yet the report does not see this influence as a "major impact on the field of teacher education" writ large, asserting that "substandard practices persist in the shadows of spotlighted reform efforts such as the Holmes Group" (p. 53) and others. In his history of teacher education, Fraser (2007) similarly reports on effects of the Holmes Group, together with other reform groups working at the same time, in some states, including Massachusetts and Illinois.

More recently, the Carnegie Corporation of New York secured funding for a collection of universities to make changes in their teacher preparation programs, with the hope that other preparation programs might adopt changes found to be successful. For this initiative, called Teachers for a New Era (TNE), Carnegie selected 11 institutions. While the Holmes Group was composed of leading research universities, the TNE institutions included a range of institutional types, from an elite private university (Stanford) with a small program, to a large regional university (California State University at Northridge), to a historically Black university (Florida A&M University).

In its prospectus for TNE, Carnegie stated that excellent teacher preparation programs should be guided by three principles: respect for evidence (including attention to learning gains for pupils taught by program graduates); full engagement of faculty in the arts and sciences; and close cooperation with faculty in K–12 schools. Carnegie arranged for $5 million in funding spread over 5 years for each of the institutions, which were required to generate an equal matching amount from other sources (e.g., grants from government agencies or philanthropy). Each TNE institution designed its own approach to addressing the three principles, with assistance and guidance from the Academy for Educational Development, which also served as the fiscal agent for the Carnegie grants.

The RAND Corporation and Manpower Demonstration Research Corporation jointly conducted an evaluation of the initiative over its first 3 years (Kirby et al., 2006). Their overall conclusion was that changes in the programs during the first 3 years (of a 5 or more year project) appeared to be small and incremental, a finding that was "not surprising" given that the institutions were selected in large part because they were already "among the best in their 'class,'" (p. xxi). Commenting on the likelihood of longer-term, more substantial changes, especially on other teacher preparation institutions, the authors were more optimistic about some goals (e.g., increasing awareness of the role or arts and sciences faculty in teacher preparation) than others (e.g., radical changes in teacher preparation or clear recommendations for other institutions).

A later study of TNE funded by the Gates Foundation (McDiarmid and Caprino, 2017) documented the progress made at each of the individual TNE sites but did not attempt to estimate the effect of the TNE initiative on the field as a whole. The authors point out that versions of the three TNE principles are present in many places, such as the requirement in the standards of the current accrediting agency, Council for the Accreditation of Educator Preparation, that institutions make use of evidence about the classroom performance of their graduates, a standard consistent with the TNE principle of respect for evidence. The authors note that they cannot claim that this standard is an outgrowth of TNE, but they do observe that "the debates and lessons from institutions as they worked to ground their preparation programs in evidence may well have accelerated the movement to set more rigorous program performance standards" (pp. 175–176). They also note that TNE led to the development of various data collection tools being used nationally. "Although consensus on a single set of instruments for all programs remains elusive, the field is moving, however grudgingly and haltingly, in this direction" (p. 176).

SUMMARY

The past 20 years has witnessed a proliferation in the pathways to teacher preparation and a range of innovations in teacher preparation programs including in the field and in technology. Preservice teacher education content, goals, and approaches have changed due in part to the accountability movement, increased attention to deeper learning, the changing nature of standards for what teachers should know and be able to do, and increased attention to equity. Qualitative studies of programs suggest that factors leading to stronger candidates include program coherence, instructors' modeling of powerful practices in methods courses, a strong connection between theory and practice, and intentional design of the field experience. However, the committee did not find evidence to support policies that would address questions about systems-level issues in preservice teacher preparation due to the high degree of variation in institutional type and mission, as well as decentralization of control that is built into the historical development of colleges and universities (Labaree, 2017).

In general, there is a lack of systematic research or evidence beyond anecdotes and case studies about teacher preparation programs' content and effectiveness, and whether these programs have changed over time. Despite a call nearly ten years ago (NRC, 2010) for an independent evaluation of teacher education approval and accreditation, no such evaluation has been initiated.

REFERENCES

Abendroth, M., Golzy, J.B., and O'Connor, E.A. (2011). Self-created YouTube recordings of microteachings: Their effects upon candidates' readiness for teaching and instructors' assessment. *Journal of Educational Technology Systems, 40*(2), 141–159.

Adler, S. (2008). The education of social studies teachers. In L.S. Levstik and C.A. Tyson (Eds.), *Handbook of Research in Social Studies Education* (pp. 329–351). New York: Routledge.

Allen, A., Hancock, S.D., W. Lewis, C., and Starker-Glass, T. (2017). Mapping culturally relevant pedagogy into teacher education programs: A critical framework. *Teachers College Record, 119*(1), 1–26.

American Association of Colleges for Teacher Educators (AACTE) (n.d.). *Participation Map.* Available: http://edtpa.aacte.org/state-policy.

American Association of Colleges for Teacher Educators Clinical Practice Commission. (2018). *A Pivot Toward Clinical Practice, Its Lexicon, and the Renewal of Educator Preparation.* Available: https://aacte.org/programs-and-services/clinical-practice-commission.

Anderson, L.M., and Stillman, J.A. (2013). Student teaching's contribution to preservice teacher development: A review of research focused on the preparation of teachers for urban and high-needs contexts. *Review of Educational Research, 83*(1), 3–69.

Anderson, M. (2017). *A Look at Historically Black Colleges and Universities as Howard Turns 150.* Washington, DC: Pew Research Center. Available: https://www.pewresearch.org/fact-tank/2017/02/28/a-look-at-historically-black-colleges-and-universities-as-howard-turns-150.

Aydarova, E., and Berliner D.C. (2018). Responding to policy challenges with research evidence: Introduction to special issue. *Education Policy Analysis Archives, 26*(32).

Bain, R.B. (2012). Using disciplinary literacy to develop coherence in history teacher education: The Clinical Rounds Project. *The History Teacher, 45*(4), 513–532.

Bain, R.B., and Moje, E.B. (2012). Mapping the teacher education terrain for novices. *Kappan, 93*(5), 62–66.

Ball, D. (2000). Bridging practices: Intertwining content and pedagogy in teaching and learning to teach. *Journal of Teacher Education, 51*(3), 241–247.

Ball, D.L., and Cohen, D.K. (1999). Developing practice, developing practitioners: Toward a practice-based theory of professional education. In L. Darling-Hammond and G. Sykes (Eds.), *Teaching as the Learning Profession: Handbook of Policy and Practice* (pp. 3–32). San Francisco: Jossey Bass.

Ball, D.L., and Forzani, F.M. (2009). The work of teaching and the challenge for teacher education. *Journal of Teacher Education, 60*(5), 497–511.

Ball, D.L., Thames, M.H., and Phelps, G. (2008). Content knowledge for teaching: What makes it special? *Journal of Teacher Education, 59,* 389–407.

Ball, D.L., Sleep, L., Boerst, T.A., and Bass, H. (2009). Combining the development of practice and the practice of development in teacher education. *Elementary School Journal, 109*(5), 458–474.

Banilower, E.R., Smith, P.S., Malzahn, K.A., Plumley, C.L., Gordon, E.M., and Hayes, M.L. (2018). *Report of the 2018 NSSME+.* Chapel Hill, NC: Horizon Research, Inc.

Bartlett, L. (2014). *Migrant Teachers: How American Schools Import Labor.* Cambridge: Harvard University Press.

Benner, P.E., Sutphen, M., Leonard, V., and Day, L. (2010). *Educating Nurses: A Call for Radical Transformation.* San Francisco: Jossey-Bass.

Bhabha, H. (1990). The third space: Interview with Homi Bhabha. In J. Rutherford (Ed.), *Identity, Community, Culture, Difference* (pp. 207–221). London: Lawrence & Wishart.

Boerst, T., Sleep, L., Ball, D., and Bass, H. (2011). Preparing teachers to lead mathematics discussions. *Teachers College Record, 113*(12), 2844–2877.

Book, C., Byers, J. and Freeman, D. (1983). Student expectations and teacher education traditions with which we can and cannot live. *Journal of Teacher Education, 34*(1), 9–13.

Boser, U. (2011). *Teacher Diversity Matters: A State-by-State Analysis of Teachers of Color.* Washington, DC: Center for American Progress. Available: https://cdn.americanprogress.org/wp-content/uploads/issues/2011/11/pdf/teacher_diversity.pdf.

Boser, U. (2014). *Teacher Diversity Revisited: A New State-by-State Analysis.* Center for American Progress. Available: https://www.americanprogress.org/issues/race/reports/2014/05/04/88962/teacher-diversity-revisited/.

Boyd, D.J., Grossman, P.L., Lankford, H., Loeb, S., and Wyckoff, J. (2009). Teacher preparation and student achievement. *Educational Evaluation and Policy Analysis, 31*(4), 416–440.

Boyd, D., Grossman, P., Lankford, H., Loeb, S., Wyckoff, J., McDonald, M., and Hammerness, K. (2012). *Stanford Center for Education Policy Analysis.* Available: https://cepa.stanford.edu/tpr/teacher-pathway-project-overview.

Carnegie Forum on Education and the Economy. (1986). *A Nation Prepared: Teachers for the 21st Century: The Report of the Task Force on Teaching as a Profession.* Hyattsville, MD: Author.

Carnegie Foundation for the Advancement of Teaching. (2019). *Our Ideas. Using Improvement Science to Accelerate Learning and Address Problems of Practice.* Available: https://www.carnegiefoundation.org/our-ideas.

Carter Andrews, D.J., Brown, T., Castillo, B.M., Jackson, D., and Vellanki, V. (2019). Beyond damage-centered teacher education: Humanizing pedagogy for teacher educators and preservice teachers. *Teachers College Record, 121*(6).

Carver-Thomas, D. (2018). *Diversifying the Teaching Profession: How to Recruit and Retain Teachers of Color.* Palo Alto, CA: Learning Policy Institute.

Carver-Thomas, D., and Darling-Hammond, L. (2017). *Teacher Turnover: Why It Matters and What We Can Do About It.* Palo Alto, CA: Learning Policy Institute.

Castagno, A.E., and Brayboy, B.M.J. (2008). Culturally responsive schooling for indigenous youth: A review of the literature. *Review of Educational Research, 78*(4), 941–993.

Clotfelder, C., Ladd, H., and Vigdor, J. (2005). Who teaches whom? Race and the distribution of novice teachers. *Economics of Education Review, 24*(4), 377–392.

Cochran-Smith, M. (2004). *Walking the Road: Race, Diversity, and Social Justice in Teacher Education.* New York: Teachers College Press.

Cochran-Smith, M. (2019). *Studying Teacher Preparation at New Graduate Schools of Education (nGSEs): Missions, Goals, and Logics.* Paper presentation at the annual meeting of the American Educational Research Association. Toronto, Canada.

Cochran-Smith, M., Carney, M.C., Keefe, E.S., Burton, S., Chang, W., Fernandez, M.B., Miller, A.F., Sanchez, J.G., and Baker, M. (2018). *Reclaiming Accountability in Teacher Education.* New York: Teachers College Press.

Cochran-Smith, M., Keefe, E.S., Chang, W.C., and Carney, M.C. (2018). *NEPC Review: 2018 State Teacher Policy Best Practices Guide.* Boulder, CO: National Education Policy Center. Available: http://nepc.colorado.edu/thinktank/review-teacher-quality.

Cochran-Smith, M., Piazza, P., and Power, C. (2013). The politics of accountability: Assessing teacher education in the United States. *The Educational Forum, 77*(1), 6–27.

Cochran-Smith, M., Ell, F., Grudnoff, L., Haigh, M., Hill, M., and Ludlow, L. (2016). Initial teacher education: What does it take to put equity at the center? *Teaching and Teacher Education, 57*, 67–78.

Cochran-Smith, M., Villegas, A.M., Abrams, L.W., Chavez-Moreno, L.C., Mills, T., and Stern, R. (2016). Research on teacher preparation: Charting the landscape of a sprawling field. In D.H. Gitomer and C.A. Bell (Eds.), *AERA Handbook of Research on Teaching, 5th Edition* (pp. 439–547). Washington, DC: AERA.

Conrad, C., and Gasman, M. (2015). *Educating a Diverse Nation: Lessons from Minority-Serving Institutions.* Cambridge, MA: Harvard University Press.

Cooke, M., Irby, D.M., and O'Brien, B.C. (2010). *Educating Physicians: A Call for Reform of Medical School and Residency.* San Francisco, CA: Jossey-Bass.

Core Practice Consortium. (2016). *The Problem We Are Trying to Solve.* Available: http://corepracticeconsortium.com/.

Council of Chief State School Officers. (2017). *Transforming Educator Preparation: Lessons Learned from Leading States.* Washington, DC: Author.

Darling-Hammond, L. (2006). *Powerful Teacher Education: Lessons from Exemplary Programs.* San Francisco, CA: Jossey-Bass.

Darling-Hammond, L. and Oakes, J. (2019). *Preparing Teachers for Deeper Learning.* Cambridge: Harvard Education Press.

Darling-Hammond, L., Chung, R., and Frelow, F. (2002). Variation in teacher preparation: How well do different pathways prepare teachers to teach? *Journal of Teacher Education, 53*(4), 286–302.

Dee, T.S., and Jacob, B.A. (2010). *The Impact of No Child Left Behind on Students, Teachers, and Schools.* Brookings Paper. Available: https://www.brookings.edu/wp-content/uploads/2010/09/2010b_bpea_dee.pdf.

Dee, T.S., Jacob, B., and Schwartz, N.L. (2013). The effects of NCLB on school resources and practices. *Educational Evaluation and Policy Analysis, 35*(2), 252–279.

Dieker, L.A., Rodriguez, J., Lingnugaris-Kraft, B., Hynes, M., and Hughes, C.E. (2014). The future of simulated environments in teacher education: Current potential and future possibilities. *Teacher Education and Special Education, 37*(1), 21–33.

Dilworth, M.E. (Ed.). (2018). *Millennial Teachers of Color*. Cambridge, MA: Harvard Education Press.

Dilworth, M.E., and Coleman, M.J. (2014). *Time for a Change: Diversity in Teaching Revisited*. Washington, DC: National Education Association. Available: https://www.nea.org/assets/docs/Time_for_a_Change_Diversity_in_Teaching_Revisited_(web).pdf.

Dutro, E., and Cartun, A. (2016). Cut to the core practices: Toward visceral disruptions of binaries in PRACTICE-based teacher education. *Teaching and Teacher Education, 58*, 119–128.

Espinoza, D., Saunders, R., Kini, T., and Darling-Hammond, L. (2018). *Taking the Long View: State Efforts to Solve Teacher Shortages by Strengthening the Profession*. Palo Alto, CA: Learning Policy Institute.

Evans, C.M. (2017). Predictive validity and impact of CAEP standard 3.2: Results from one master's-level teacher preparation program. *Journal of Teacher Education, 68*(4), 363.

Fernandez, M.L. (2010). Investigating how and what prospective teachers learn through microteaching lesson study. *Teaching & Teacher Education, 26*(2), 351–362.

Feuer, M.J., Floden, R.E., Chudowsky, N., and Ahn, J. (2013). *Evaluation of Teacher Preparation Programs: Purposes, Methods, and Policy Options*. Washington, DC: National Academy of Education.

Fogo, B. (2014). Core practices for teaching history: The results of a Delphi Panel Survey. *Theory and Research in Social Education, 42*(2), 151–196.

Franke, M.L., Kazemi, E., and Battey, D. (2007). Mathematics teaching and classroom practice. In F.K. Lester (Ed.), *Second Handbook of Research on Mathematics Teaching and Learning* (pp. 225–256). Greenwich, CT: Information Age Publishers.

Fraser, J.W. (2007). *Preparing America's Teachers: A History*. New York: Teachers College Press.

Fraser, J.W., and Lefty, L. (2018). *Teaching Teachers: Changing Paths and Enduring Debates*. Baltimore, MD: Johns Hopkins University Press.

Fraser, J.W., and Watson, A.M. (2014). *Why Clinical Experience and Mentoring Are Replacing Student Teaching on the Best Campuses*. Princeton, NJ: The Woodrow Wilson National Fellowship Foundation. Available: http://woodrow.org/wp-content/uploads/2014/11/WoodrowWilson_FraserWatson_StudentTeaching_Nov20141.pdf.

Freeman, H.R. (2018). Millennial teachers of color and their question for community. In M.E. Dilworth, (Ed.), *Millennial Teachers of Color* (pp. 63–72). Cambridge, MA: Harvard Education Press.

Fullan, M., Galluzzo, G., Morris, P., and Watson, N. (1998). *The Rise and Stall of Teacher Education Reform*. Washington, DC: American Association of Colleges for Teacher Education.

Gasman, M., Baez, B., Sotello, C., and Turner, V. (2008). *Understanding Minority-Serving Institutions*. Albany, NY: SUNY Press.

Gasman, M., Samayoa, A.C., and Ginsberg, A., (2016). *A Rich Source for Teachers of Color and Learning: Minority Serving Institutions*. Available: https://cmsi.gse.upenn.edu/sites/default/files/MSI_KelloggReportR5.pdf.

Gasman, M., Samayoa, A.C., and Ginsberg, A. (2017). Minority-serving institutions: Incubators of teachers of color. *The Teacher Educator,52*(2), 84–98.

Gay, G. (2002). Preparing for culturally responsive teaching. *Journal of Teacher Education, 53*, 106–116.

Gay, G. (2013). Teaching to and through cultural diversity. *Curriculum Inquiry, 43*(1), 48–70.

Gess-Newsome, J. (2015). A model of teacher professional knowledge and skill including PCK: Results of the thinking from the PCK Summit. In P.F.A. Berry and J. Loughran (Ed.), *Re-examining Pedagogical Content Knowledge in Science Education* (pp. 28–42). NewYork: Routledge.

Gitomer, D.H., Brown, T.L., and Bonett, J. (2011). Useful signal or unnecessary obstacle? The role of basic skills test in teacher preparation. *Journal of Teacher Education, 62*(5), 431–445.

Glazerman, S., Isenberg, E., Dolfin, S., Bleeker, M., Johnson, A., Grider, M., and Jacobus, M. (2010). *Impacts of Comprehensive Teacher Induction: Final Results from a Randomized Controlled Study* (NCEE 2010-4027). Washington, DC: U.S. Department of Education.

Goldhaber, D., and Hansen, M. (2010). Race, gender, and teacher testing: How informative a tool is teacher licensure testing? *American Educational Research Journal, 47*(1), 218–251.

Goldhaber, D., Gross, B., and Player, D. (2010). Teacher career paths, teacher quality, and persistence in the classroom: Are public schools keeping their best? *Journal of Policy Analysis and Management, 30,* 57–87.

Goldhaber, D., Liddle, S. and Theobald, R. (2012). *The Gateway to the Profession: Assessing Teacher Preparation Programs Based on Student Achievement* CEDR Working Paper 2012-4. Seattle, WA: University of Washington Press.

Goldhaber, D., Krieg, J.M., and Theobald, R. (2017). Does the match matter? Exploring whether student teaching experiences affect teacher effectiveness. *American Educational Research Journal, 54*(2), 325–359.

Goldhaber, D., Krieg, J., and Theobald, R. (2018). *Effective Like Me? Does Having a More Productive Mentor Improve the Productivity of Mentees?* CEDR Work Paper No. 11232018-1-1. Seattle, WA: University of Washington Press. Available: http://www.cedr.us/papers/working/CEDR%20Working%20Paper%20No.%2011232018-1-1.pdf.

Gonzalez, N., and Moll, L.C. (2001). Cruzando el Puente: Building bridges to funds of knowledge. *Educational Policy, 16*(4), 623–641.

Gonzales, N., Moll, L., and Amanti, C. (Eds.). (2005). *Funds of Knowledge: Theorizing Practices in Households, Communities, and Classrooms.* Mahwah, NJ: Erlbaum.

Grant, C., and Gibson, M. (2011). Diversity and teacher education: Historical perspective on research and policy. In A. Ball and C. Tyson (Eds.). *Studying Diversity in Teacher Education* (pp. 19–62). Lanham, MD: Rowman and Littlefield.

Grossman, P. (2005). Research on pedagogical approaches in teacher education. In M. Cochran-Smith and K.M. Zeichner (Eds.), *Studying Teacher Education* (pp. 425–476). Washington, DC: American Educational Research Association.

Grossman, P. (2011). Framework for teaching practice: A brief history of an idea. *Teachers College Record, 113*(12), 2836–2843.

Grossman, P. (Ed.). (2018). *Teaching Core Practices in Teacher Education.* Cambridge, MA: Harvard Education Press.

Grossman, P., Hammerness, K., and McDonald, M. (2009a). Redefining teaching, re-imagining teacher education. *Teachers and Teaching: Theory and Practice, 15*(2), 273–289.

Grossman, P., Compton, C., Igra, D., Ronfeldt, M., Shahan, E., and Williamson, P. (2009b). Teaching practice: A cross-professional perspective. *Teachers College Record, 111*(9), 2055–2100.

Grossman, P., and McDonald, M. (2008). Back to the future: Directions for research in teaching and teacher education. *American Educational Research Journal, 45*(1), 184–205.

Grover, S., Pea, R., and Cooper, S. (2015). Designing for deeper learning in a blended computer science course for middle school students. *Computer Science Education, 25*(2), 199–237.

Guillen, L., and Zeichner, K. (2018). A university-community partnership in teacher education from the perspectives of community-based teacher educators. *Journal of Teacher Education, 69*(2), 140–153.

Haddix, M.M. (2017). Diversifying teaching and teacher education: Beyond rhetoric and toward real change. *Journal of Literacy Research, 49*(1), 141–149.

Hansen, M., and Quintero, D. (2019). *The Diversity Gap for Public School Teachers is Actually Growing Across Generations.* Brookings Institution. Available: https://www.brookings.edu/blog/brown-center-chalkboard/2019/03/07/the-diversity-gap-for-public-school-teachers-is-actually-growing-across-generations/.

Harris, D., and Sass, T. (2011). Teacher training, teacher quality and student achievement. *Journal of Public Economics, 95*(7), 798–812.

Harvey, M.W., Yssel, N., Bauserman, A.D., and Merbler, J.B. (2010). Preservice teacher preparation for inclusion: An exploration of higher education teacher-training institutions. *Remedial and Special Education, 31*, 24–33.

Henry, G.T., Thompson, C.L., Bastian, K.C., Kershaw, D.C., Purtell, K.M., and Zulli, R.A. (2011). *Does Teacher Preparation Affect Student Achievement?* Chapel Hill, NC: Carolina Institute for Public Policy.

Hiebert, J., and Morris, A.K. (2012). Teaching, rather than teachers, as a path toward improving classroom instruction. *Journal of Teacher Education, 63*(2), 92–102.

Higher Education Act of 1965 (HEA) (Pub.L. 89–329). Available: https://www.govinfo.gov/content/pkg/STATUTE-79/pdf/STATUTE-79-Pg1219.pdf.

Hispanic Association of Colleges and Universities. (n.d.). Available: https://www.hacu.net/hacu/HSIs.asp.

Hispanic Association of Colleges and Universities. (2017). *Tomorrow's Teachers Today: Hispanic-Serving Institutions and Education Degrees.* Available: https://cqrcengage.com/hacu/file/jG5pfovg7Pe/HACU%20Report%20on%20HSI%20and%20Education%20Degrees.pdf.

Hodges, T.E., and Baum, A.C. (2019). *Handbook of Research on Field-Based Teacher Education.* Hershey, PA: ICI Global.

Hollett, N.L., Brock, S.J., and Hinton, V. (2017). Bug-in-ear technology to enhance preservice teacher training: Peer versus instructor feedback. *International Journal of Learning, Teaching, and Educational Research, 16*(2), 1–10.

Holmes Group. (1986). *Tomorrow's Teachers.* East Lansing: Michigan State University, College of Education.

Holmes Partnership. (2006). *The Holmes Partnership Trilogy: Tomorrow's Teachers, Tomorrow's Schools, Tomorrow's Schools of Education* (2nd ed.). New York: Peter Lang.

Honig, M.I., Kahne, J., and McLaughlin, M.W. (2002). School community connections: Strengthening opportunity to learn and opportunity to teach. In W.R. Houston (Ed.), *Handbook of Research on Teaching* (pp. 998–1028). Washington, DC: American Educational Research Association.

Howard, T.C. (2001). Powerful pedagogy for African American students: Conceptions of culturally relevant pedagogy. *Journal of Urban Education, 36*(2), 179–202.

Ingersoll, R., and May, H. (2011). *Recruitment, Retention, and the Minority Teacher Shortage.* Philadelphia: University of Pennsylvania.

Ingersoll, R., and Strong, M. (2011). The impact of induction and mentoring programs for beginning teachers: A critical review of the research. *Review of Educational Research, 81*(2), 201–233.

Ingersoll, R., Merrill, L., and May, H. (2014). *What Are the Effects of Teacher Education and Preparation on Beginning Teacher Attrition? Research Report* (#RR-82). Philadelphia: Consortium for Policy Research in Education, University of Pennsylvania.

Ingersoll, R.M., Merrill, E., Stuckey, D., and Collins, G. (2018). *Seven Trends: The Transformation of the Teaching Force–Updated October 2018.* CPRE Research Reports. Available: https://repository.upenn.edu/cpre_researchreports/108.

Ingersoll, R., May, H., and Collins, G. (2019). Recruitment, employment, retention and the minority teacher shortage. *Education Policy Analysis Archives, 27*(37).

Ingvarson, L., Elliott, A., Kleinhenz, E., and McKenzie, P. (2006). *Teacher Education Accreditation: A Review of National and International Trends and Practices.* Available: http://research.acer.edu.au/teacher_education/1.

Jenset, I. S., Klette, K., and Hammerness, K. (2018). Grounding teacher education in practice around the world: An examination of teacher education coursework in teacher education programs in Finland, Norway, and the United States. *Journal of Teacher Education, 69*(2), 184–197.

Kang, H. (2017). Preservice teachers' learning to plan intellectually challenging tasks. *Journal of Teacher Education*, 68(1), 55–68.

Kang, H., and Windschitl, M. (2018). How does practice-based teacher preparation influence novices' first-year instruction? *Teachers College Record*, 120. Available: https://www.tcrecord.org/content.asp?contentid=22279.

Kang, H., and Zinger, D. (2019). What do core practices offer in preparing novice science teachers for equitable instruction? *Science Teacher Education*, 1–31.

Kavanagh, S., and Danielson, K. (2019). Practicing justice, justifying practice: Toward critical practice teacher education. *American Educational Research Journal*, 1–37.

Kazemi, E., Ghousseini, H., and Cunard, A., and Turrou, A. (2015). Getting inside rehearsals: Insights from teacher educators to support work on complex practice. *Journal of Teacher Education*, 1–14.

Kelly-Petersen, M., Davis, E.A., Ghousseini, H., Kloser, M., and Monte-Sano, C. (2018). Rehearsals as examples of approximation. In P. Grossman (Ed.), *Teaching Core Practices in Teacher Education* (pp. 85–105). Cambridge, MA: Harvard Education Press.

Kennedy, M., and Newman Thomas, C. (2012). Effects of content acquisition podcasts to develop preservice teachers' knowledge of positive behavioral interventions and supports. *Exceptionality*, 20(1), 1–19.

Khalil, D., and Kier, M. (2018). Critical race design: Designing a community of practice for urban middle school students through a critical race perspective. In E. Mendoza, B. Kirshner, and K. Gutiérrez (Eds.) *Designing for Equity: Bridging Learning and Critical Theories in Learning Ecologies for Youth*. Charlotte, NC: Information Age Press.

King, J.E., and Hampel, R. (2018). *Colleges of Education: A National Portrait*. Washington, DC: American Association of Colleges for Teacher Education.

Kirby, S.N., McCombs, J.S., Barney, H., and Naftel, S. (2006). *Reforming Teacher Education: Something Old, Something New*. Available: http://www.rand.org/pubs/monographs/MG506.

Kloser, M. (2014). Identifying a core set of science teaching practices: A Delphi Expert Panel approach. *Journal of Research in Science Teaching*, 51(9), 1185–1217.

Koerner, M.E., and Abdul-Tawwab, N. (2006). Using community as a resource for teacher education: A case study. *Equity & Excellence in Education*, 39(1), 37–46.

Krieg, J. M., Theobald, R., and Goldhaber, D. (2016). A foot in the door: Exploring the role of student teaching assignments in teachers' initial job placements. *Educational Evaluation and Policy Analysis*, 38(2), 364–388.

Labaree, D.F. (2004). *The Trouble with Ed Schools*. New Haven: Yale University Press.

Labaree, D.F. (2017). *A Perfect Mess: The Unlikely Ascendancy of American Higher Education*. Chicago: University of Chicago Press.

Ladson-Billings, G. (2001). *Crossing Over to Canaan: The Journey of New Teachers in Diverse Classrooms*. San Francisco: Jossey- Bass.

Ladson-Billings, G.J. (1995). Toward a theory of culturally relevant pedagogy. *American Education Research Journal*, 35, 465–491.

Lamb, C. (2016). Struggle and success: The state of teacher education at tribal colleges and universities. *Journal of American Indian Higher Education*, 27(3). Available: https://tribalcollegejournal.org/struggle-and-success-the-state-of-teacher-education-at-tribal-colleges-and-universities.

Lampert, M. (2001). *Teaching Problems and the Problems of Teaching*. New Haven: Yale University Press.

Lampert, M., Franke, M.L., Kazemi, E., Ghousseini, H., Turrou, A.C., Beasley, H., Cunard, A., and Crowe, K. (2013). Keeping it complex using rehearsals to support novice teacher learning of ambitious teaching. *Journal of Teacher Education*, 64(3), 226–243.

Lanier, J.E., and Little, J.W. (1986). Research on teacher education. In M. Wittrock (Ed.), *Handbook of Research on Teaching* (3rd ed., pp. 527–569). New York: Macmillan Publishing Company.

Lee, C.D. (2007). *Culture, Literacy, and Learning.* New York: Teachers College Press.

Lee, R.E. (2018). Breaking down barriers and building bridges: Transformative practices in community- and school-based urban teacher preparation. *Journal of Teacher Education, 69*(2), 118–126.

Levine, A. (2006). *Educating School Teachers.* Available: http://edschools.org/pdf/Educating_Teachers_Report.pdf.

Little, J.W. (1993). Teachers' professional development in a climate of educational reform. *Educational Evaluation and Policy Analysis, 15*(2), 129–151.

Little, J.W., and Bartlett, L. (2010). The teacher workforce and problems of educational equity. *Review of Research in Education, 34*, 285–328.

López, F., and Santibañez, L. (2018). Teacher preparation for emergent bilingual students: Implications of evidence for policy. *Education Policy Analysis Archives, 26*(36).

Lortie, D.C. (1975). *Schoolteacher: A Sociological Study.* Chicago: University of Chicago Press.

Lynch, K., Hill, H.C., Gonzalez, K., and Pollard, C. (2019). Strengthening the research base that informs STEM Instructional improvement efforts: A meta-analysis. *Educational Evaluation and Policy Analysis, 41.* doi: 10.3102/0162373719849044.

Major, J., and Reid, J. (2017). Culturally relevant teacher education pedagogical approaches. In D.J. Clandinin and Jukka Husu (Eds.), *SAGE Handbook of Research on Teacher Education* (Ch. 35, Sec. III). London, England: SAGE.

Mason, J. (2011). Noticing: Roots and branches. In M. Sherin, V. Jacobs, and R. Philipp (Eds.), *Mathematics teacher noticing: Seeing through teachers' eyes* (pp. 35–50). New York: Routledge.

McDiarmid, G.W., and Caprino, K. (2017). *Lessons from the Teachers for a New Era Project: Evidence and Accountability in Teacher Education.* New York: Routledge.

McDonald, M., Kazemi, E., and Kavanagh, S.S. (2013). Core practices and pedagogies of teacher education: A call for a common language and collective activity. *Journal of Teacher Education, 64*(5), 378–386.

McDonald, M., Tyson, K., Brayko, K., Bowman, M., Delport, J., and Shimomura, F. (2011). Innovation and impact in teacher education: Community-based organizations as field placements for preservice teachers. *Teachers College Record, 113*(8), 1668–1700.

Mentzer, G.A., Czerniak, C.M., and Duckett, T.R. (2019). Comparison of two alternative approaches to quality STEM teacher preparation: Fast-track licensure and embedded residency programs. *School Science and Mathematics, 119*, 35–48.

Moje, E.B., Ciechanowski, K.M., Kramer, K., Ellis, L., Carrillo, R., and Collazo, T. (2004). Working toward third space in content area literacy: An examination of everyday funds of knowledge and Discourse. *Reading Research Quarterly, 39*(1), 38–70.

Moll, L., Amanti, C., Neff, D., and Gonzalez, N. (1992). Funds of knowledge for teaching: Using a qualitative approach to connect homes and classrooms. *Theory Into Practice, 31*(2), 132–141.

National Academies of Sciences, Engineering, and Medicine. (2018). *How People Learn II: Learners, Contexts, and Cultures.* Washington, DC: The National Academies Press.

National Academies of Sciences, Engineering, and Medicine. (2019). *Minority-Serving Institutions: America's Underutilized Resource for Strengthening the STEM Workforce.* Washington, DC: The National Academies Press.

National Council for Accreditation of Teacher Education. (2001). *Professional Standards for the Accreditation of Schools, Colleges, and Departments of Education.* Washington, DC: National Council for Accreditation of Teacher Education.

National Education Association. (2004). *Assessment of Diversity in America's Teaching Force: A Call to Action*. Washington, DC: Author.

National Research Council. (NRC). (2000). *Educating Teachers of Science, Mathematics, and Technology: New Practices for the New Millennium*. Washington, DC: The National Academies Press.

———. (2001). *Adding It Up: Helping Children Learn Mathematics*. Washington, DC: The National Academies Press.

———. (2010). *Preparing Teachers: Building Evidence for Sound Policy*. Washington, DC: The National Academies Press.

Neville, S., and Cohen, (2005). *Preparing and Training Professionals Comparing Education to Six Other Fields*. Washington, DC: The Finance Project.

Olsen, B. (2008). *Teaching What They Learn, Learning What They Live: How Teachers Personal Histories Shape Their Professional Development*. Boulder, CO: Paradigm Publishers.

Paris, D., and Alim, H.S. (2017). *Culturally Sustaining Pedagogies: Teaching and Learning for Justice in a Changing World*. New York: Teachers College Press.

Perna, L., Lundy-Wagner, V., Drezner, N.D., Gasman, M., Yoon, S., Bose, E., and Gary, S. (2009). The contribution of HBCUs to the preparation of African American women for stem careers: A case study. *Research in Higher Education, 50*(1), 1–23.

Philip, T., Souto-Manning, M., Anderson, L., Horn, I.S., Andrews, D.J.C., Stillman, J., and Varghese, M. (2018). Making justice peripheral by constructing practice as "core": How the increasing prominence of core practices challenges teacher education. *Journal of Teacher Education*, 1–14.

Richmond, G. (2017). The power of community partnership in the preparation of teachers. *Journal of Teacher Education, 68*(1), 6–8.

Robinson, B.B., and Albert, A.R. (2008). HBCU's institutional advantage. In M. Gasman, B. Baez, and C.S.V. Tuner (Eds.), *Understanding Minority-Serving Institutions* (pp. 183–199). Albany: State University of New York.

Rock, M.L., Gregg, M., Thead, B.K., Acker, S.E., Gable, R.A., and Zigmond, N.P. (2009). Can you hear me now? Evaluation of an online wireless technology to provide real-time feedback to special education teachers-in-training. *Teacher Education and Special Education, 32*(1), 64–82.

Rock, M.L., Schumacker, R.E., Gregg, M., Howard, P.W., Gable, R.A., and Zigmond, N. (2014). How are they now? Longer term effects of e-coaching through online bug-in-ear technology. *Teacher Education and Special Education, 37*(2), 161–181.

Ronfeldt, M. (2012). Where should student teachers learn to teach? effects of field placement school characteristics on teacher retention and effectiveness. *Educational Evaluation and Policy Analysis, 34*(1), 3–26.

Ronfeldt, M. (2015). Field placement schools and instructional effectiveness. *Journal of Teacher Education, 66*(4), 304–320.

Ronfeldt, M., Schwarz, N., and Jacob, B. (2014). Does preservice preparation matter? Examining an old question in new ways. *Teachers College Record, 116*(10).

Ronfeldt, M., Brockman, S.L., and Campbell, S.L. (2018). Does cooperating teachers' instructional effectiveness improve preservice teachers' future performance? *Educational Researcher, 47*(7), 405–418.

Ronfeldt, M., Goldhaber, D., Cowan, J., Barelli, E., Johnson, J. and Tien, C.D. (2018). *Identifying Promising Clinical Placements Using Administrative Data: Preliminary Results from ISTI Placement Initiative Pilot*. CALDER Working Paper 189. Available: https://caldercenter.org/sites/default/files/WP%20189.pdf.

Sawchuk, S. (2016). Teacher-prep accreditation group seeks traction. *Education Week, 36*(1).

Schaefer, J.M., and Ottley, J.R. (2018). Evaluating immediate feedback via bug-in-ear as an evidence-based practice for professional development. *Journal of Special Education Technology, 33*(4), 247–258.

Scheeler, M.C., McAfee, J.K., Ruhl, K.L., and Lee, D.L. (2006). Effects of corrective feedback delivered via wireless technology on preservice teacher performance and student behavior. *Teacher Education and Special Education, 29*(1), 12–25.

Scruggs, T.E., Mastropieri, M.A., and McDuffie, K.A. (2007). Co-teaching in inclusive classrooms: A meta-synthesis of qualitative research. *Exceptional Children, 73,* 392–416.

Sheppard, S., Macatangay, K., Colby, A., and Sullivan, W.M. (2009). *Educating Engineers: Designing for the Future of the Field.* San Francisco, CA: Jossey-Bass.

Sherin, M.G., and Russ R. (2014). Teacher noticing via video: The role of interpretive frames. In B. Calandra and P. Rich (Eds.), *Digital Video for Teacher Education: Research and Practice.* New York: Routledge.

Shulman, L.S. (1987). Knowledge and teaching: Foundations of the new reform. *Harvard Education Review, 57*(1), 1–22.

Sleeter, C. E. (2017). Critical race theory and the whiteness of teacher education. *Urban Education, 52*(2), 155–169.

Souto-Manning, M. (2019). Transforming university-based teacher education preparing asset equity and justice oriented teachers within the contemporary political context. *Teachers College Record, 121*(6), 1–26.

Stone Child College. (2017). Available: https://www.stonechild.edu.

Stone, S.I., and Charles, J. (2018). Conceptualizing the problems and possibilities of interprofessional collaboration in schools. *Children & Schools,* 1–8.

Sullivan, W. (2005). *Work and Integrity: The Crisis and Promise of Professionalism in America.* San Francisco: Jossey-Bass.

Sun, J., and van Es, E.A. (2015). An exploratory study of the influence that analyzing teaching has on preservice teachers' classroom practice. *Journal of Teacher Education, 66*(3), 201–214.

Tatto, M.T. (1996). Examining values and beliefs about teaching diverse students: Understanding the challenges for teacher education. *Educational Evaluation and Policy Analysis, 18*(2), 155–180.

Tatto, M.T., Schwille, J., Senk, S.L., Ingvarson, L., Rowley, G., Peck, R., Bankov, K., Rodriguez, M., and Reckase, M. (2012). *Policy, Practice, and Readiness to Teach Primary and Secondary Mathematics in 17 Countries: Findings from the IEA Teacher Education and Development Study in Mathematics.* Amsterdam: International Association for the Evaluation of Educational Achievement.

Teach For America. (2019). *Who We Are.* Available: https://www.teachforamerica.org/what-we-do/who-we-are.

Troops to Teachers. (n.d.). Available: https://proudtoserveagain.com.

Uerz, D., Volman, M., and Kral, M. (2018). Teacher educators' competences in fostering student teachers' proficiency in teaching and learning with technology: An overview of relevant research literature. *Teaching and Teacher Education, 70,* 12–23.

U.S. Department of Education. (2016). *The State of Racial Diversity in the Educator Workforce, Washington, D.C. 2016.* Available: http://www2.ed.gov/rschstat/eval/highered/racial-diversity/state-racial-diversityworkforce.pdf.

van Es, E.A. (2012). Using video to collaborate around problems of practice. *Teacher Education Quarterly, 39*(2), 103–116.

Von Esch, K.S., and Kavanagh, S.S. (2018). Preparing mainstream classroom teachers of English learner students: Grounding practice-based designs for teacher learning in theories of adaptive expertise development. *Journal of Teacher Education, 69*(3), 239–251.

Will, M. (2018). Colleges grapple with teacher-prep standards. *Education Week, 38*(2).

Yuen, T.T., Bonner, E.P., and Arreguín-Anderson, M.G. (Eds.) (2018). *(Under)represented Latin@s in STEM: Increasing Participation Throughout Education and the Workplace.* New York: Peter Lang.

Zeichner, K. (2010). Rethinking the connections between campus courses and field experiences in college and university-based teacher education. *Journal of Teacher Education, 61*(1–2), 89–99.

Zeichner, K. (2014). The struggle for the soul of teaching and teacher education in the U.S. *Journal of Education Teaching, 40*(5), 551–568.

Zeichner, K., and Conklin, H.G. (2016). Beyond knowledge ventriloquism and echo chambers: Raising the quality of the debate in teacher education. *Teachers College Record, 118*(12), 1–38.

Zygmunt, E., Cipollone, K., Tancock, S., Clausen, J., Clark, P., and Mucherah, W. (2018). Loving out loud: Community mentors, teacher candidates, and transformational learning through a pedagogy of care and connection. *Journal of Teacher Education, 69*(2), 127–139.

6

Opportunities for Learning Through Inservice Professional Development

Well-designed preservice teacher preparation may supply new teachers with a significant foundation for the work of teaching in the 21st century, but cannot, in a short period of time, aspire to preparing teachers for all they must know and do. Meanwhile, an array of classroom studies provides evidence that many practicing teachers are not prepared to teach in ways that align with new expectations or that are responsive to a more diverse student population. Most teachers will require substantial changes to what they do on a daily basis if they are to respond productively to changing demographics and to new expectations for student learning (e.g., see Cobb et al., 2018; Osborne et al., 2019). Studies of professional development (PD) in key content domains (mathematics, science, literacy, social studies) demonstrate the challenges that teachers experience in shifting their stance from one of supplying explanations to one that engages students in collaborative inquiry (Kazemi and Franke, 2004; Osborne et al., 2019; Roth et al., 2011). Making substantial changes to teachers' perspectives and practices will require significant and sustained opportunities for professional learning (Borko, 2004; National Academies of Sciences, Engineering, and Medicine, 2015).

This chapter concentrates on the contribution to teacher learning that may be made by formally structured PD programs, including both those located at school sites and a wide range of programs and experiences outside the school context. The committee notes that schools with a record of improvement tend to be those where teachers have access to high-quality PD and also experience a workplace culture marked by strong professional community (Bryk et al., 2010; McLaughlin and Talbert, 2001). Thus, this chapter and the following chapter on workplace-embedded opportunities are intended to be complementary.

Following a brief introduction, this chapter begins by characterizing patterns of teacher participation in designated PD activity as reported in national surveys. It then takes up the question of how emerging forms and foci of PD represent responses to shifting student demographics and evolving expectations for what students should know and be able to do. The next section considers evidence for the effectiveness of PD with respect to desired teacher and student outcomes. The final section of the chapter turns attention to the role of the larger system and the policies and practices that bear on the availability and quality of PD for teachers.

As a preface to the discussion in this chapter and in the following chapter on teacher learning in the workplace, the committee notes that the category of "practicing teachers" and the corresponding category of "in-service education" may be too broad to help educators and policy makers think productively about implications derived from changing student demographics and expectations for student learning. Teachers vary with respect to the PD needs they experience and the interests they may express. In particular, teachers' career stages may affect how they encounter current conditions and expectations, as well as what they find to be relevant and meaningful learning opportunities.

Newly prepared (or novice) teachers may enter teaching having been well grounded in new expectations for pursuing greater conceptual depth, enabling student inquiry and sense-making, integrating new forms of technology, and working effectively with a diverse group of students (as articulated in Chapter 3). For these teachers, inservice learning demands likely center on how to enact the ideas and practices they have encountered in their preparation while mastering classroom management and navigating the school workplace culture. This may also include balancing these demands against an increasing push to utilize differing forms of technology during teaching while also responding to the continued paperwork burden that is prevalent. Relevant supports include well-designed systems of induction and mentoring, as well as the preparation of principals and other school leaders to aid beginning teachers.

In contrast, more experienced teachers who are faced with new expectations for student learning and new images of teaching practice confront a problem of change. Relevant supports for these teachers may take the form of structured PD, coaching, access to relevant instructional resources, the opportunity to work with colleagues to shift ideas and practice, and the support of principals or other leaders in managing change.

Finally, teachers increasingly take on an array of leadership roles, some of which (e.g., instructional coach, writing curriculum pacing guides) may be a direct response to the changing expectations for student learning out-lined in Chapter 3. Such roles may reflect the broader response to the move toward more in-depth learning and innovative instruction or they may reflect the vestiges of narrowly defined test-based accountability systems. A growing body of research examines how these roles have been defined and enacted, but few studies explore how teachers are recruited into these roles and how they are prepared and supported to succeed in them.

THE GROWTH OF PROFESSIONAL DEVELOPMENT OPPORTUNITIES

Educators, education scholars, school and system leaders, and policy makers treat teacher PD as a vehicle for advancing a more ambitious vision of teaching and learning for all students. Although estimates of the financial investment in PD vary widely depending on the model used to construct them, they add up to thousands of dollars per teacher per year (The New Teacher Project, 2015; Odden et al., 2002; Rice, 2001). In principle, such programs constitute a significant complement to learning opportunities embedded in teachers' daily work in classrooms and schools.

A dramatic proliferation of PD providers dates back to the advent of the federal Elementary and Secondary Education Act in the mid-1960s; opportunities for PD escalated in the wake of the 1983 *Nation at Risk* report (Little, 1989). Districts emerged during that period as significant decision makers regarding the form and content of PD and as PD providers in their own right. By the mid-1980s, the National Education Association reported a 15-year decline in teachers' participation in university course work and a corresponding increase in attendance at district-sponsored workshops and conferences (National Education Association, 1987). Reform movements multiplied in the 1980s and 1990s, culminating in the standards and accountability movement that has induced some states to require continuing education units from teachers; during this period of increased reform, a marketplace of PD providers emerged, many of them (including universities) packaging their services for district or school consumption. In the 21st century, the landscape has grown still more diversified as PD providers capitalize on technological advances to offer online PD options to individual teachers as well as to their employing organizations. Indeed, the landscape of inservice PD is just as sprawling as that of preservice preparation; observers have repeatedly noted its fragmented or nonsystemic character (e.g., Borko, 2004; Dede et al., 2009; Wilson and Berne, 1999), although recent research supplies examples of coherent approaches at the school and district level (Bryk et al., 2010; Cobb et al., 2018; Coburn and Russell, 2008).

PATTERNS OF TEACHER PARTICIPATION

As detailed below, nationally representative surveys supply a partial picture of teachers' participation in formal PD. The Fast Response Survey System survey of 2000 and the Schools and Staffing Survey (SASS) questionnaires for 2003–2004, 2007–2008, and 2011–2012 include items that focus on the amount and type of PD in which teachers participated in a 1-year period and on teachers' perceptions of the usefulness of selected PD. Unfortunately, the National Teacher and Principal Survey (successor to SASS), conducted in 2015–2016, preserved questions about teachers' preservice preparation but eliminated items related to teachers' subsequent participation in PD. The 2018 National Survey of Science and Mathematics Education (NSSME+), conducted by Horizon Research, Inc., reports data on PD for teachers of science, technology, engineering, and mathematics (STEM) subjects, but there appears to be no comparable national survey of teachers in other subject areas.

Teachers' Participation in PD

Rotermund, DeRoche, and Ottem (2017) draw on the 2011–2012 SASS data to provide the most recent descriptive national profile of teachers' participation in PD. Overall, 99 percent of teachers reported participating in some form of PD in 2011–2012. Subject-specific PD constituted the predominant focus (85% of teachers), followed by the instructional use of computers (67%). On the whole, elementary and secondary teachers reported that subject-specific PD and PD on computers was useful (see Table 6-1).

The 2011–2012 SASS data also provide indications of teachers' participation in PD targeted at two specific student populations: English learners and students with disabilities. Relatively few teachers reported participating in PD focused on teaching students with disabilities (37%) or English learners (27%). On the whole, the majority of teachers reported that PD on teaching students with disabilities was useful (44%) or very useful (22%), while 30 percent indicated it was somewhat useful. Teachers' perceptions

TABLE 6-1 Teachers' Reported Perceptions of Professional Development (PD) in Percentage, by Usefulness

	Not Useful	Somewhat Useful	Useful	Very Useful
Subject-Specific PD	2	28	43	28
PD Focused on the Use of Computers	4	31	41	24

SOURCE: 2011–2012 SASS data.

of the usefulness of PD on teaching English learners indicated they found it slightly less useful than other PD; 18 percent very useful, 41 percent useful, and 34 percent only somewhat useful. Subject-matter PD tended to be longer in duration (nearly 80% more than 8 hours), while about two-thirds of PD related to teaching students with disabilities or English learners was less than 8 hours. A comparison of these patterns with those reported earlier by Parsad et al. (2001) based on a 2000 survey suggests that the investment in PD for a diverse student population has remained relatively low even though teachers in the earlier survey reported feeling inadequately prepared to teach students from diverse cultural backgrounds. This is important as some states (e.g., Florida) license renewal requirements include a specific number of hours for retooling in special education or English learning for license renewal.

Mathematics, Science, and Computer Science Teachers' Participation in PD

According to the 2018 NSSME+ Report (Banilower et al., 2018), mathematics, science, and computer science teachers report that participating in discipline-specific PD programs or workshops is the most common form of PD in which they participate. On the whole, about 80 percent or more of science, mathematics, and computer science teachers have participated in content-specific PD in the past 3 years (Banilower et al., 2018, p. 47). However, elementary science teachers are an exception; less than about 60 percent reported participating in discipline-specific PD in the past 3 years (p. 47). Perhaps not surprisingly, high school teachers report having participated in more hours of discipline-specific PD than elementary teachers in both science and mathematics. The authors summarized trends in number of discipline-specific hours as follows:

> [A]bout a quarter of middle school and about a third of high school science teachers have participated in 36 hours or more of science professional development in the last three years; very few elementary teachers have had this amount of professional development in science. A similar pattern exists in mathematics, with about 2 in 5 secondary teachers having participated in at least 36 hours of mathematics-focused professional development in the last three years compared to fewer than 1 in 6 elementary teachers. (p. 48)

Importantly, both science and mathematics teachers across elementary, middle, and secondary indicated that a focus on how to incorporate students' cultural backgrounds into instruction was relatively rare, with only about a quarter of science teachers and 20 percent of math teachers indicating having received PD with this focus (p. 56).

In addition, the 2018 NSSME+ Report indicated "differences in the extent to which science and mathematics classes with different demographic characteristics have access to teachers who have had a substantial amount of professional development" (p. 49). Namely, in science, classes that serve a high proportion of historically underrepresented students in STEM and classes composed mostly of students who previously achieved at lower levels "are significantly less likely than classes serving high prior achievers [and students who have been historically well-represented in STEM] to be taught by teachers who have participated in more than 35 hours of professional development in the last three years" (p. 49). Further, students attending small schools, on average, have less "access to teachers who have participated in a substantial amount of professional development" (p. 49). However, "mathematics classes with the highest proportion of students from race/ethnicity groups historically underrepresented in STEM are more likely than their counterparts to be taught by teachers who have participated in more than 35 hours of professional development in the last three years" (p. 49).

Overall, most teachers report having had access to PD in recent years, and most report that the PD they have experienced has been at least somewhat useful. However, survey data also signal areas in which PD opportunities may be under developed or unevenly distributed (e.g., with respect to teaching science, teaching students with special needs, or supporting English learners).

EMERGING FORMS OF PROFESSIONAL DEVELOPMENT

The past two decades have witnessed not only a steadily growing marketplace of providers, but also new developments in the type of PD experience available to teachers and in their orientation to changing expectations for teachers and teaching. These developments include the emergence of online programs and platforms and learning from practice by way of video and other artifacts of teaching and learning.

Online Programs and Platforms

In the past two decades, one prominent development in inservice PD, as in preservice teacher education, has been the growing turn to online programs and platforms to support teacher learning and innovation. A review of the extant literature about online PD turns up multiple studies focused on programs and platforms targeted to particular populations of teachers: special education teachers (including teacher of both students identified as having "disabilities" and "gifted"), rural teachers, and teachers of particular subjects. Although a thorough review of these studies extends beyond the scope of this report, the sheer number of them attests to the growth of online programs and platforms.

Online platforms, such as those offering teaching videos and other resources, are multiplying faster than the research; although not yet validated by research, this includes teachers sharing resources using a variety of platforms (e.g., Pinterest, Teachers Pay Teachers). A literature review published by Dede and colleagues (2009) predates a number of the currently available studies, but the authors noted at the time that the available research suffered from an overemphasis on short-term program evaluation and a reliance on self-reported experiences and outcomes. The authors recommended a more rigorous approach to research design, more of a focus on actual learner interactions, a mix of qualitative and quantitative methods suitable to the research questions, multiple outcome measures, and a longitudinal timeframe to capture trajectories of learning and subsequent practice.

In one empirical study that might be judged at least partially responsive to these recommendations, Fishman and colleagues (2013) employed a randomized experiment to compare teacher and student outcomes associated with teachers' participation in a face-to-face PD or an online version of the same PD.[1] They acknowledge the critiques put forward by Dede and colleagues (2009) but observe that since 2009, "Studies of teachers learning from online PD that employ experimental design with randomization and control groups have started to address the linkages between teachers' learning, practice, and student learning outcomes" (p. 3). They nonetheless caution:

> Online PD is not monolithic. It makes little sense to ask questions about whether "it" is more or less effective than any other PD modality. . . . Thus, when considering questions of comparative effectiveness, it is critical to clearly identify design features of PD opportunities in question. (p. 4)

Fishman and colleagues (2013) found no difference in outcomes between the group engaged in face-to-face PD and the group participating in an online program. "In online and face-to-face PD conditions, teachers reported increased confidence with new curriculum materials, enacted those materials consistently with curriculum designers' intent, and their students learned from curriculum successfully and in equal amounts" (p. 2).[2]

Some models of PD have capitalized on advances in technology-aided simulation in other fields ranging from military and flight training to medicine. In an experimental design study in 10 sites in six states, Dieker and

---

[1] The program was designed to prepare high school teachers to implement a year-long environmental science curriculum.

[2] Teachers in the online condition first received a face-to-face orientation to the online platform.

colleagues (2014) investigated the contributions of avatar-based simulation and supplemental online PD to improvements in the performance of middle school mathematics teachers. Researchers randomly assigned teachers to one of four groups: (1) a treatment group that received lesson plans aligned with the Common Core for the teaching of linear equations, together with a 40-minute online PD focused on five strategies for formative assessment; (2) a treatment group that received the lesson plans and participated in the TeachLivE simulator, including an "after-action-review" segment; (3) a treatment group that received the lesson plans, the online PD experience, and the TeachLivE simulator experience without the after-action-review; and (4) control. All teachers were observed teaching the designated lesson and their students tested (using items derived from National Assessment of Educational Progress data) prior to the random assignment and again following completion of the treatment series. Analysis of teaching observations focused on teachers' use of questioning to elicit student thinking, their use of wait time, and their feedback to students. Researchers found that treatment teachers in both groups that included a TeachLivE experience increased their use of higher order questions to elicit student thinking and their specific feedback to students across the four virtual events and in their real classrooms. The highest gains in classroom performance accrued to the TeachLivE-only condition that included an after-action-review segment.

The emergence of online programs and other technological tools give rise to the question of how these new resources and opportunities fit with the organizational environment that teachers inhabit in their schools and districts. In a book addressed to school and district leaders, Rodman (2019) observes that teachers have responded to the persistence of "sit-and-get" PD by turning to online opportunities to secure new instructional resources and to learn from and with other teachers:

> Teachers . . . have begun to speak out against this unilateral system and form their own professional learning networks (PLNs) via Twitter and Voxer chats, edcamps, massive open online courses (MOOCs), blogs, and podcasts. Such networks not only connect teachers with like-role peers beyond their school but also provide on-demand professional learning in a variety of different formats. As PLNs continue to grow, so does an unprecedented wealth of text, video, and planning resources. However, while these experiences may help individual educators who have the drive and commitment to seek them out, they do little to foster a community of professional inquiry within a school or district. (pp. 1–2)

As Rodman notes, teachers have turned to a wide array of online venues for ideas, resources, and assistance. To the committee's knowledge, these venues—some of which assert that they are research-based—have not yet been the focus of empirical investigations. However, research on the use of online platforms in the context of structured PD programs suggests that this technological resource may help to expand teachers' access to opportunities specifically designed to meet changing expectations.

Learning in and from Practice Through Artifacts of Teaching and Learning

For the past two decades, advances in PD practice and research have been prominently marked by the potential for teachers' learning in and from practice. As noted in the previous chapter on preservice teacher education, Ball and Cohen (1999) supplied a compelling rationale for learning in and from practice as a means of joining a teacher's subject matter knowledge to a specialized knowledge for teaching. Roth and colleagues (2011) add,

> A key feature of analysis-of-practice approaches is teacher inquiry into their own practice as a vehicle for learning and PD. However, it is difficult in a real-time context for teachers to conduct inquiries into their teaching practices in a way that addresses all their complexity. One solution to this realistic problem is to use artifacts of practice, such as student work and assessment products, teacher lesson plans and notes, and lesson videos. (p. 118)

In the evolving landscape of PD, two approaches to learning in and through practice have gained particular prominence over the past two decades: Lesson Study and video clubs and other forms of video-based PD.

Lesson Study

The instructional improvement strategy termed "Lesson Study" gained popularity in the United States following the publication of the findings from the Third International Mathematics and Science Study. In their book *The Teaching Gap*, Stigler and Hiebert (1999) characterized this Japanese form of PD—a collaborative inquiry approach strongly embedded in the culture of teaching and schools—as a model worthy of emulation. More specifically, as practiced in Japan:

> Lesson study consists of cycles of instructional improvement in which teachers work together to: formulate goals for student learning and long-term development; collaboratively plan a "research lesson" designed to bring to life these goals; conduct the lesson in a classroom, with one team member teaching and others gathering evidence on student learning and development; reflect on and discuss the evidence gathered during the lesson, using it to improve the lesson, the unit, and instruction more generally; and, if desired, teach, observe, and improve the lesson again in one or more additional classrooms. (Lewis, 2009, p. 95)

Early studies of Lesson Study illuminated both the potential benefits of and the challenges associated with introducing a model that in certain key respects runs against the grain of U.S. teachers' accustomed interactions with one another (Fernandez, 2002, 2005). Although Lesson Study shares some features with previously implemented practices of learning from student work in the United States, it differs centrally in the place occupied by the collective observation of live classroom practice. In an essay that took stock of this evolving innovation, Lewis, Perry, and Murata (2006) noted that "the simple practice of observation in colleagues' classrooms for the purpose of professional learning is rare in the United States" (p. 3).

Over time, research has come to focus on the adaptation of Lesson Study to a range of contexts. However, Lewis and Perry (2017) note that "lesson study has been researched mainly through small-scale, qualitative studies by investigators directly involved in lesson study implementation" (p. 265). In a significant exception, one recent randomized, controlled trial (RCT) study examines the role of Lesson Study as an intervention in the scale-up of efforts to improve the teaching and learning of fractions in grades 2–5 (Lewis and Perry, 2017).[3] More than 200 educators (87% of them classroom teachers) from 27 school districts were randomly assigned to one of three conditions: (1) an experimental condition in which teams conducted lesson study focused on fractions, aided by a research-based mathematics (fractions) resource kit; (2) a "business as usual" condition in which teachers in teams chose their own approach to learning and their own focus, but were asked not to pursue lesson study on fractions; and (3) a lesson study condition in which teacher teams could choose their topic and were supplied with lesson study tools but not with the mathematics resource kit. The kit was designed to help teachers delve into the instructional affordances of different mathematical tasks, grapple with what students are likely to find difficult, and plan an approach to the cycle of planning, implementation, observation, and reflection.

Lewis and Perry (2017) assessed gains in educators' own knowledge of fractions for teaching with a 33-item instrument derived from previously tested item banks and focused mainly on conceptual knowledge as required to navigate particular teaching contexts (e.g., "how to adjudicate a disagreement between two students about whether 1/2 of Andrew's books was more than 1/5 of Steve's books" (p. 274)). Student learning was measured by a grade-appropriate test including items drawn from national and state assessments, published curricula, and research publications. In addition,

---

[3] The design of this RCT study permits researchers to examine the processes (video recorded) and outcomes of a lesson study on a large scale, managed and led by local educators rather than experts; it also permits a test of the lesson study cycle integrated with curricular resources of the sort commonly available in Japan.

participating educators completed an end-of-project self-report survey on which they rated the quality of their experience.

Results show a statistically significant effect on educators' fractions knowledge for the treatment condition (lesson study plus resource kit; effect size = 0.19). Students of teachers in the treatment condition also significantly outperformed students in the other conditions (effect size = 0.49). Analysis of a subset of PD meeting videos indicates which elements of the mathematics resource kit compelled most attention (e.g., videos of fractions lessons taught in Japanese classrooms), and otherwise suggests how the availability of the resource kit may have contributed to the measured outcomes. Students of teachers who adopted the Japanese lesson demonstrated higher learning gains than those whose teachers pursued an alternative approach. Written reflections provided examples of particular insights that emerged from the discussions in the experimental condition (Lewis and Perry, 2017):

> In the past, I have worked hard to make fractions very hands-on and visual, but not once did I consider using a linear model.
>
> A great deal of our discussions prior to beginning this lesson study was spent on how we . . . teach fractions . . . here at our school. Each of us used the typical pizza cut up or candy cut up to show . . . fractional parts. However . . . this . . . didn't lead to full understanding. . . . Teaching fractions in a linear manner was a real aha moment for all of us on the team. (p. 287)

Although the most prominent outcomes of this RCT study were associated with the experimental condition, educators' own reported perceptions of professional learning quality show nearly equivalent high ratings from educators in the two lesson study conditions, and substantially lower ratings from those in the "business as usual" condition. Overall, Lewis and Perry (2017, p. 289) report that "lesson study supported by a mathematical resource kit showed a significant impact on both educators' fractions knowledge and students' fractions knowledge after controlling for baseline fractions knowledge, hours of instruction, and other relevant variables."

Video-Based Collaborative Professional Development

Since 2000, and especially in the past decade, video-based PD has occupied an increasingly prominent place in the published research on PD, especially in mathematics and science (Borko, Koellner, and Jacobs, 2011; Luna and Sherin, 2017; Roth et al., 2011; Santagata, 2009; Seago, 2004; Sherin and Han, 2004; van Es et al., 2014; van Es, Tekkumru-Kisa, and

Seago, in press). Roth and colleagues (2011) underscore the particular virtues of video as an artifact for teachers' collective attention:

> Using video and other artifacts also provides a common point of reference for teachers' collaborative discussions and anchors teachers' discourse, keeping it focused on content, teaching, and learning. . . . For example, shared analysis of the same lesson video challenges each member to provide evidence from the video to support claims and judgments which can then be evaluated by others in the group. (p. 118)

One of the earliest and most widely cited contributions detailed teachers' gradual transition from a focus on teachers' actions to a focus on students' mathematical reasoning over the course of year-long participation in a "video club" facilitated by expert mathematics educators (Sherin and Han, 2004). In that video club project, facilitators invited teachers to establish a focus for their attention and discussion and noted the shift in focus over time. In other PD projects, facilitators have oriented teachers to specific aspects of teaching and learning, such as the nature of students' science argumentation (Zembal-Saul, 2005).

Although several studies trace changes in teachers' ability to notice and analyze selected aspects of classroom interaction, few have attempted to relate teachers' participation in video-based PD to changes in classroom practice and student learning. In one exception, Borko and colleagues (2015) report the changes in mathematics instruction and student achievement associated with teachers' participation in the Problem-Solving Cycle (PSC) PD, in which video analysis plays a central role. The PSC model engages teachers in a series of interconnected workshops built around a common "rich mathematical task," as defined by several criteria (e.g., tasks that encompass important mathematical concepts and skills, have multiple entry points and solution paths, are accessible to learners with varying levels of mathematical knowledge). Teachers begin each cycle by working together to solve the selected mathematical task and to develop lesson plans for teaching the task in their own classrooms. Video recordings of the teachers' implementation of the lessons form the basis of the second and third workshops in the cycle, in which teachers devote close attention to the nature of students' mathematical reasoning and consider the role of the teacher in supporting student learning. Over the course of the three workshops, teachers learn how to elicit and respond to student thinking and consider a range of instructional strategies for cultivating rich mathematical discourse in the classroom.

Borko and colleagues (2015) draw on data collected over 5 years to assess changes in teacher knowledge and instructional practice and to examine impact on student achievement. Pre- and post-administration of the

Mathematical Knowledge for Teaching (MKT) assessment for middle school teachers showed significant positive gains on average for 62 participating teachers, although the absence of a control group necessarily limits claims regarding effectiveness of the PD in this respect.

To investigate changes in classroom practice, the researchers employed the Mathematical Quality of Instruction (MQI) instrument to analyze 51 videotaped lessons taught by 13 teachers; the analysis compared implementation of the collaboratively developed PSC lessons with "typical" lessons taught by the same teacher. Overall, teachers' instruction over time was demonstrably stronger when they were teaching the collaboratively developed PSC lessons built around a "mathematically rich task" than when they were teaching their typical lessons. Teachers made the greatest improvement on the MQI dimension labeled "working with mathematics and students," with gains evident in both the PSC and typical lessons. Borko and colleagues (2015) report that "over time, the teachers were better able to understand and build on their students' mathematical ideas and help them work through their errors in a conceptual manner" (p. 54). Teachers showed a gain in the richness of the mathematics tasks in PSC lessons, but not in typical lessons, suggesting that availability of well-designed tasks and the collaborative setting of the PSC may be important factors in teachers' ability to enact more ambitious instruction. Student participation ratings were high in both types of lessons and across time, but ratings dropped somewhat as the richness of tasks and conceptual focus increased. In judging the promise of the PSC model, the researchers note, "One especially encouraging finding is the fact that the teachers in our study improved their ability to listen to students' ideas and make sound instructional decisions based on those ideas" (pp. 64–65).

Finally, Borko and colleagues (2015) examined student achievement on the Colorado Student Achievement mathematics assessment, comparing the students of PSC teachers, the students of middle school teachers in the same district who were not participating in the PSC, and middle school students across the state. In 4 of the 5 PSC years, students of the participating PSC teachers outperformed other students in the district. (Both groups in this district outperformed the state average in all years.) The achievement results are suggestive but not conclusive, given the absence of random assignment and changes in the composition of the PSC cohort from year to year.

In the domain of science, Roth and colleagues (2011) employed videocases in a year-long PD program for elementary teachers (Science Teachers Learning from Lesson Analysis, or STeLLA) to investigate changes in teachers' science content knowledge, ability to analyze science teaching, classroom instruction, and student learning. The study's quasi-experimental design entailed a comparison of two groups of teachers, both of which had completed the same 3-week summer institute focused on science content, and one of which elected to participate in additional summer and school-year analysis-of-practice activity. Although the teachers were not randomly assigned, they did not differ with respect to their education, science background, or teaching experience. Teachers in the experimental group showed significantly greater gains in content and pedagogical content knowledge and in their ability to analyze video-based lessons (although they showed some decline in that ability during the school year). Both groups completed a science content test and a video-based lesson analysis task, but only the experimental group was observed in the classroom. In pre-post observations, experimental teachers showed increased use of the recommended science teaching strategies associated with both a "science content storyline" lens and a "student thinking" lens emphasized in the PD, and their students outperformed the students in the comparison content-only group.

Especially given its increasing prominence, further research is needed to understand crucial aspects of designing and implementing video-based collaborative PD that supports teachers to meet changing expectations and to serve an increasingly diverse student population. Van Es and colleagues (in press) offer a comprehensive framework to guide the design, implementation, and study of video-based collaborative PD. Their framework includes what they refer to as six dimensions, or "critical features of video-based activity systems for teachers" (p. 5): audience, goals/purpose, video selection, task design, planning/facilitation, and assessing learning. As they cogently argue, most studies of video-based PD foreground a specific dimension (e.g., the role of the facilitator), resulting in a limited understanding of the broader activity system in which the use of video is embedded, and thus a limited understanding of how and why a particular video-based PD program results, or does not, in the intended learning outcomes. An additional advantage of the application of a comprehensive framework for the study of video-based PD is that it can support the field to engage in comparative analysis across studies, and thus accumulate knowledge across studies.

PROFESSIONAL DEVELOPMENT THAT SUPPORTS TEACHERS TO MEET CHANGES IN EXPECTATIONS AND IN STUDENT POPULATIONS

As indicated above, nationally representative samples indicate that on the whole, practicing teachers participate in formally structured programs of PD. However, little is known about the *quality* of PD that the average teacher receives, especially in relation to heightened expectations for teaching and student learning, and changes in the student populations that the average teacher serves. While the evidence remains mixed regarding the extent to which PD results in desired changes to teachers' knowledge and practice, and in student learning, there has been some progress in the field in the past two decades in discerning features and theories of action of PD that appear to impact teachers' practice and student learning.

Research published in the 1990s and early 2000s resulted in a purported "emerging consensus" on selected design features of effective PD. Desimone (2009) summarized the basis for this consensus and argued that research would be strengthened by attending more systematically to five distinguishing features of effective PD: the depth of focus on subject matter content and how students learn it; sufficient provision for teachers to engage in "active learning;" a coherent connection to teachers' own work and to prevailing local and state policy; "collective participation" by teachers of the same school, department, or grade level; and adequate duration for teachers to develop new understandings and instantiate them in their teaching. She posited a conceptual model in which these five design features constitute foundational conditions that in turn enhance teacher knowledge, skill, and dispositions; stimulate and enable related changes in instructional practice; and ultimately generate positive student learning outcomes.

At the time it was first touted a decade ago, this "emerging consensus" rested on somewhat tenuous ground, especially when tested against expectations for gains in student learning. Desimone (2009, p. 183) acknowledged that only a "handful of studies" had included measurement of student outcomes. In addition, some experimental-design research framed by the recommended "PD design features" yielded mixed results, leading reviewers to cast doubt on the power of PD programs to advance teacher knowledge and practice or to enhance student learning. Mixed or null results from some studies—studies that employed randomized experimental designs and that measured both teacher and student outcomes—posed a particular threat to the reported consensus. Two widely cited experimental design studies, one focused on second-grade reading (Garet et al., 2008) and the second on middle school mathematics (Garet et al., 2010), found only minimal positive results for teachers and no significant positive results for students despite implementing PD interventions closely aligned with the features in the "consensus" model.

Such studies suggest the complexity of pursuing significant change in teachers' knowledge, beliefs, dispositions, and practices through programs of organized PD; however, they may also point to the limitations of the conceptual model and some aspects of the research design. With respect to the latter, for example, Garet and colleagues (2010) note that, "The observation protocol measured the degree to which each provider's plan was implemented but it did not measure the quality of the delivery or the accuracy of the mathematics presented" (p. 24). That is, design features alone may not serve well as proxies for the quality of teachers' PD experience, and the resulting research may not have uncovered aspects of implementation that could account for weak results.

More recent empirical studies, literature reviews, and meta-analyses have found consistent evidence of positive outcomes while also suggesting the limitations of a conceptual model oriented principally to generic features of PD design (e.g., opportunities for "active learning"). Kennedy (2016), in a review of 28 experimental design studies of PD in core academic subjects conducted between 1975 and 2014, rejected the focus on design features and defined programs instead in terms of "underlying theories of action" that addressed a "central problem of practice" in teaching. Similarly, in a study of elementary grades science PD, Grigg and colleagues (2013) focused not on PD design fidelity but on the degree to which learners (teachers in the PD; students in the classroom) demonstrably engaged in five features of scientific inquiry: defining scientifically oriented questions, giving priority to evidence in responding to questions, formulating explanations from evidence, connecting explanations to scientific knowledge, and communicating and justifying explanations. By specifying these features of scientific inquiry as their focal point, Grigg and colleagues theorized the mechanism by which they predicted students' learning gains would be realized. Their analysis suggests that conceptual, empirical, and practical gains from PD research likely require that the meaning of key design features (e.g., "active learning" or "collective participation") be more fully theorized and specified, and that they be probed in-depth at the level of both PD and classroom practice.

The discussion that follows centers on two bodies of research that bear particularly on the capacity of the teacher workforce to respond to heightened expectations for student learning and changing student demographics: content-focused PD and PD targeted at teachers' capacity for working with a diverse student population.

Impact of Content-Focused Professional Development

Over the past two decades, and despite mixed results in some studies, the field has accumulated a body of increasingly rigorous research on organized programs of PD, especially in math, science, and literacy. Studies employing experimental and quasi-experimental research designs and studies incorporating measures of student learning outcomes have multiplied. Rotermund, DeRoche, and Ottem (2017), in their preface to a National Center for Education Statistics summary of the 2011–2012 SASS survey results on teachers' participation in PD, write:

> Although past literature on professional development has found little causal evidence of its impact on student achievement, recent research on the effects of individual programs of professional development has found some positive effects on student outcomes (DeMonte, 2013; Heller et al., 2012; Polly et al., 2015; Yoon et al., 2007). In addition, two meta-analyses of research on professional development found statistically significant effects (Blank and de las Alas, 2009; Gersten et al., 2014, p. 1).

More recently, a meta-analysis of 95 experimental or quasi-experimental studies of the impacts of preK–12 STEM-related curriculum and/or PD programs on student learning indicate that, on the whole, PD with the following characteristics yields benefits for teachers and students (Lynch et al., 2019): "the use of professional development along with new curriculum materials; a focus on improving teachers' content and pedagogical content knowledge, or understanding of how students learn; and specific formats, including meetings to troubleshoot and discuss classroom implementation of the program, the provision of summer workshops to begin the professional development learning process, and same-school collaboration" (p. 294). The authors highlight advances in research design over the past two decades, writing that "following calls in the early 2000s for stronger research into the impact of educational interventions . . . federal research portfolios began to prioritize research methods that allow causal inference and to use student outcomes as the major indicator of program success" (p. 260).

In some respects, the meta-analysis findings paralleled those identified in previous reviews as elements of the "emerging consensus" regarding PD design (Desimone, 2009; Wei et al., 2009). For example, programs achieved stronger outcomes when teachers participated in PD programs with colleagues from their school. This finding is consistent with the broader research base, and likely reflects the benefit of a shared commitment to trying out what was learned in a PD program, and of having colleagues with whom to determine how to employ or adapt what was learned in a specific teaching context. In addition, Lynch and colleagues (2019) found that outcomes were stronger when the PD programs included what they refer to as "implementation meetings," or opportunities to "convene briefly with other activity participants to troubleshoot and discuss obstacles and aids to putting the program into practice" (p. 276).

More generally, Lynch and colleagues note that the "programs studied recently contain more varied delivery methods and features (e.g., coaching, online learning components) than those of a decade ago" (p. 264). On average, they found that programs that included an online component had positive effects on student outcomes but that such programs "yielded significantly smaller effects" on student outcomes, as compared to programs that did not include an online component (p. 276).

In another echo of prior research, Lynch and colleagues (2019) found that average effect sizes were larger when the PD "focused on improving teachers' content and pedagogical content knowledge and/or how students learned the content" (p. 275). Their findings underscore the importance that PD be content-specific; PD focused on "content-generic instructional strategies was not a significant predictor of effect size magnitude" (p. 275). On the whole, the authors also found that effect sizes were largest where programs combined PD with new curriculum materials (as compared to PD only, absent curriculum materials). This finding is consistent with qualitative studies of PD as well, which have suggested that it is important that PD be "close to practice" and that it support teachers to make sense of the actual materials they teach with (e.g., Ball and Cohen, 1999; Kazemi and Franke, 2004).

However, Lynch and colleagues (2019) found that not all PD involving new curriculum materials yielded desired effects. For example, they cite a comprehensive review by Slavin and colleagues (2014), who report "programs that used science kits did not show positive outcomes on science achievement measures (weighted ES=0.02 in 7 studies), but inquiry-based programs that emphasized professional development but not kits did show positive outcomes (weighted ES=0.36 in 10 studies)" (p. 870). Science kits supply teachers with materials for hands-on science activities and guidelines for their use, but the accompanying PD (if any) may or may not include a focus on underlying science concepts and processes or guidance with respect to inquiry-oriented instructional practices. Slavin and colleagues (2014) report,

> A surprising finding from the largest and best-designed of the studies synthesized in the present review is the limited achievement impact of elementary science programs that provide teachers with kits to help them make regular use of hands-on, inquiry-oriented activities. These include evaluations of the well-regarded FOSS, STC, Insights, Project Clarion, and Teaching SMART programs, none of which showed positive achievement impacts. (p. 894)

The lack of effects associated with kit-based science PD suggests that future research would benefit from closer attention to the relationship between PD emphases and the local curriculum-in-use, as well as the measures used to assess learning outcomes.

Finally, Lynch and colleagues (2019) found "no evidence of a positive association between the duration of professional development," which included both number of hours and timespan, and "program impacts" (p. 285). Although this finding is contrary to what some prior reviews have suggested (Desimone, 2009; Scher and O'Reilly, 2009; Yoon et al., 2007), it is consistent with Kennedy's (2016) review of PD for teachers of core academic subjects (language arts, mathematics, the sciences, and the social sciences). As Lynch and colleagues (2019) write, "Our findings echo those of Kennedy (1999, 2016), who did not find a clear benefit of contact hours or program duration, and concluded that the core condition for program effectiveness was valuable content; more hours of a given intervention will not help if the intervention content is not useful" (p. 285).

Although Lynch and colleagues (2019) meta-analysis focused exclusively on studies in the STEM fields, RCT studies in the domain of literacy have also shown significant positive results for teacher and student learning. For example, an IES-funded RCT study of the National Writing Project's College-Ready Writers Program (Gallagher, Arshan, and Woodworth, 2017) examined the implementation and outcomes of a 2-year initiative to enhance students' argument writing in 44 districts served by 12 National Writing Project (NWP) sites in 10 states (see also Olson et al., 2012). The researchers found a positive, statistically significant impact on students' argument writing in the 22 treatment districts (effect size 0.20).

In another example, Vernon-Feagans and colleagues (2015) conducted an IES-funded RCT study of the Targeted Reading Intervention (TRI) in high-poverty rural schools. The intervention tested face-to-face vs. webcam-based instructional coaching of kindergarten and first grade teachers as they worked one-on-one with struggling readers. Researchers found that the struggling readers receiving TRI treatment outperformed those struggling readers in the control group on all measured outcomes (letter-word identification, word attack, comprehension), with effect sizes ranging from 0.15 to 0.26. Although both treatment conditions produced positive results, gains were stronger in the webcam version of coaching, in which webcam footage formed the basis of feedback that teachers received for 20–30 minutes every other week. Researchers in a follow-up study of the treatment teachers found that those who had participated in 2 years of implementation produced stronger gains than those with only 1 year of participation.

Most of the research in the domain of social studies consists of small-scale studies (Crocco and Livingston, 2017), and the available research supplies little evidence of the relationship between PD participation and teacher learning and student outcomes. De La Paz and colleagues (2011) acknowledge that the social studies field has been slow to develop research that could credibly examine the relationships among teachers' participation in PD, their subsequent classroom practice, and student learning (p. 497). In one effort to advance the research in this area, De La Paz and colleagues conducted a study of 5th-, 8th-, and 11th-grade teachers who had all participated in a summer workshop designed to enhance students' experience of historical inquiry and argumentation; following the summer workshop, teachers were randomly assigned to a follow-up school-year "networking group" (with grade-level cohorts) or to a group that would teach based on the workshop experience alone. The networking group was invited to participate in seven additional PD events during the school year and also received other supports: paid time for lesson planning, opportunities to observe other teachers, and the assistance of district librarians in locating print and online resources. In their analysis, the researchers further distinguished between teachers who logged 30 or more hours in networking and other follow-up activities and those who logged fewer than 30 hours. The researchers found that teachers characterized as "high networking" more often employed classroom practices consistent with the PD, and that their students out-performed students of low-networking or no-networking teachers on Document-Based Questioning essays. The differences in student performance were especially pronounced at the 11th-grade level.

On a still larger scale, Barr and colleagues (2016) conducted an RCT of more than 100 teachers and their 9th- and 10th-grade students in 60 high schools in eight metropolitan areas of the United States to examine the impact of the program Facing History and Ourselves. Facing History provides PD to support teachers' use of historical case studies and related instructional activities focused on engaging students in "informed civic reflection" and, more specifically, "in an examination of racism, prejudice, and antisemitism in order to promote the development of a more humane and informed citizenry" (Barr et al., 2016, p. 4, citing Facing History and Ourselves, 2012). They found that teachers receiving PD in Facing History and Ourselves reported significantly greater self-efficacy than control teachers with respect to four discipline-specific aims: promoting historical understanding, promoting tolerance and psychosocial development, promoting deliberation, and promoting student civic literacy. Further, students of the intervention teachers demonstrated stronger skills in historical thinking and greater self-reported civic efficacy and tolerance for different perspectives than students of the control teachers.

Still other research has found that PD has the potential to positively influence history teachers' practices. Saye and colleagues have demonstrated the potential of scaffolded lesson study in increasing teachers' content knowledge and instructional strategies in Problem-based Historical Inquiry (Saye et al., 2017), and Howell and Saye (2016) found that participation in lesson study cycles can help 4th-grade teachers develop a shared professional teaching knowledge culture.

Impact of Professional Development Targeted at Increasing Teachers' Capacity to Work with a Diverse Student Population

The section above details what is known in the field about characteristics of subject-specific PD that is associated with positive impacts on students' learning. In light of the committee's task, it is also critical to ask what the field knows about the impact of PD that aims squarely to support teachers to better serve an increasingly diverse student population. Parkhouse, Lu, and Massaro's (2019) recent literature review on "multicultural education professional development" is especially helpful in understanding the landscape of research in this area, including its impact on teachers and students. Parkhouse et al. defined "multicultural education" as "an overarching term for the various historical and contemporary reform efforts to create more inclusive and equitable schooling for all children" (p. 420), which includes culturally relevant pedagogy (Ladson-Billings, 1995), culturally responsive teaching (Gay, 2002), and culturally sustaining pedagogy (Paris and Alim, 2017). There is debate in the education research community regarding the language to use to describe initiatives that are focused on furthering educational equity and justice. Scholars have identified limitations in the use of the term "multicultural education," suggesting that over the course of several decades, in practice, "multicultural education" has come to "mean adapting how one teaches, but not necessarily what one teaches or for what purposes" (Sleeter, 2018, p. 11). In what follows, we draw on the important findings offered by Parkhouse et al.'s comprehensive review; however, we refer to PD supporting teachers to work with diverse groups of students (rather than multicultural education PD) when identifying implications for the field.

In their review, Parkhouse, Lu, and Massaro hoped "to better understand the forms and features of [PD] programs that contribute to teachers' self-efficacy and success in working with culturally diverse students" (p. 416). They identified 40 (of 1,602) studies, inclusive of 33 unique PD programs from the United States, as well as other countries, that met the following criteria:

> (a) the study examined a PD program on one or more topics related to cultural diversity, such as intercultural competence, culturally relevant and responsive pedagogies, or [multicultural education]; (b) the study used original qualitative and/or quantitative data; (c) the PD in the study was designed for in-service teachers or other school professionals in PK12 settings; and finally, (d) the study reported the outcomes of the PD, such as its impact on participants and/or student academic performance. (p. 421)

However, upon review of these studies, Parkhouse, Lu, and Massaro found that the designs of the PD and of the research were both so variable that it was impossible to discern particular forms and features of PD programs that contribute to effectiveness. Even so, their review offers important insights.

Parkhouse, Lu, and Massaro found that culturally responsive teaching or culturally relevant pedagogy was identified as the leading framework for most of the PD. However, they also identified what they termed as "significant inconsistencies" across programs in terms of how these frameworks were operationalized. Namely, in many cases, Parkhouse, Lu, and Massaro found that what was described lacked a "critical stance;" for example, there was often no mention of engaging teachers in making sense of broader structural inequities or processes of racialization in relation to culturally and linguistically non-dominant students' schooling opportunities. Moreover, there was not necessarily evidence that such PD focused on identifying and building on students' cultural resources in substantive ways. In fact, Parkhouse, Lu, and Massaro found several instances in which what was billed as culturally responsive or relevant teaching appeared to reflect generally effective teaching strategies, like "scaffolding, using a variety of formative assessments, pointing out misconceptions, and building lessons on prior learning" (p. 426).

Another set of findings regarded whether PD programs concentrated on specific groups of students; they found that about half did, "whereas the other half discussed cultural responsiveness in more general terms" (p. 425). Particular groups of students included, for example, speakers of non-dominant languages, American Indian students, and students with disabilities. In reviewing findings across the studies, Parkhouse, Lu, and Massaro found that teachers generally reported greater benefit from those programs that specified particular groups of students. However, Parkhouse, Lu, and Massaro also found that it appeared that at times specific groups of students and their cultural histories were being stereotyped through the PD. They identify this tension as critical to wrestle with in the design and enactment of PD that aims to advance educational equity and justice.

Parkhouse, Lu, and Massaro also found that by and large, PD that focused on working with a diverse student population was separate from subject-matter PD. This finding fits with what teachers tended to report in nationally representative surveys, as described above. In the few cases in which the PD was tied to specific subject matter (e.g., science, math, social studies), the PD appeared to lack attention to developing a critical perspective on equity and schooling.

In terms of impacts on teachers, Parkhouse, Lu, and Massaro found that, on the whole, studies reported benefits to teachers' perspectives and/or knowledge about how to support a diverse student body, mostly on the basis of self-report data derived from teacher surveys, questionnaires, or interviews. For example, teachers reported being more aware of their students' cultural backgrounds, as well as of their own biases and their potential impact on instruction. However, Parkhouse, Lu, and Massaro also found that while some studies reported changes in teachers' awareness of their students' backgrounds, there was minimal attention to whether, and if so, how, teachers changed their practice. In fact, based on the challenges identified across the studies in changing practice, Parkhouse, Lu, and Massaro wrote: "These studies caution against assuming that raising awareness of diversity and inequities will naturally lead to transformed teaching practices or that teachers will develop culturally responsive lessons without specific guidance on how to connect cultural assets to their curriculum (e.g., Brown and Crippen, 2016; Lee et al., 2007)" (p. 451; on this point, see also Sleeter, 1997).

Lee and colleagues' (2007) study of a 2-year elementary science PD program is one of the few studies that integrated a focus on content and supporting culturally and linguistically diverse students to track changes in both teachers' beliefs *and* practices. The intervention consisted of four 1-day workshops provided throughout the school year, and the provision of curriculum materials for two units that explicitly focused on attention to students' home language and culture. The overwhelming majority of the 43 participating teachers were female; however, they were racially and ethnically diverse. Eighteen of the teachers reported speaking English as their home language, while 13 reported Spanish, 6 reported English and Spanish, 1 reported Haitian Creole, and 5 teachers did not respond.

Lee and colleagues' analysis of changes in beliefs and practices over the 2 years is sobering. At the start of the intervention, many teachers expressed the view that students' home language is an important resource for instruction, and there was modest improvement in the presence of this belief at the end of year two. However, on the whole, based on quantitative coding of two video-recorded classroom observations each year of teachers' teaching the specially designed units, researchers found that most teachers did "not use students' home language in instruction, and [did] not allow or invite students to use their home language" (p. 1,283); there was no significant change in this over the course of the 2 years. In addition, there was no significant change in teachers' beliefs or practices related to attending to students' home cultures in instruction. Lee and colleagues write, "[A]lthough [teachers] emphasized the importance of incorporating students' culture into science instruction . . ., [t]hey generally did not incorporate diverse cultural experiences or materials into their teaching" (p. 1,284). Lee and colleagues offer thoughtful reflection on the implications of their findings, including suggesting the value in connecting the 1-day workshops with ongoing support in teachers' classrooms to modify their instruction. They suggest, more broadly, the importance of attending to how PD interfaces with other aspects of teaching and the workplace (e.g., accountability systems, expectations about treating students' linguistic and cultural backgrounds as resources for instruction).

In their review, Parkhouse, Lu, and Massaro (2019) explicitly call for more coordinated research on PD programs that target teachers' capacity to work with diverse groups of students. They write: "The studies reviewed here lack sufficient consistency across theoretical approaches, PD designs, and data collection methods to draw definitive conclusions about the characteristics of effective [multicultural education] PD" (p. 451). While recognizing the value in studying a diverse set of PD programs, Parkhouse, Lu, and Massaro also caution that absent some consistency, whether it be to a specific underlying theory of action of the PD, theory of teacher learning, PD design, or research methodology, it is difficult to discern critical features of designing and implementing effective PD in this crucial area.

In addition, on the basis of their review, the authors identify several important research questions to explore. One entails investigating how PD can "both challenge teachers to reflect on inequities within education while also recognizing that some teachers may meet such discussions with defensiveness, reluctance to change, or skepticism" (p. 451). A second question concerns investigating ways to attend to the tension discussed above "between providing specific knowledge about students' cultures—for instance, through partnering with community members—and guarding against pro-moting stereotypes or broad generalizations" (p. 451). Parkhouse, Lu, and Massaro also argue for the value in investigating how to design and implement PD targeting teachers' work with culturally diverse students that explicitly takes into account variation in teachers' knowledge, skills, beliefs, and experience.

SUMMARY

Teachers in the 21st century encounter an increasingly diverse popula-tion of students and escalating expectations for what those students should know and be able to do as they progress through school. The world that those teachers, students, and their families inhabit—with its rapid techno-logical advances, environmental dilemmas, social and political disruptions, and global interconnectedness—presents both compelling new opportu-nities and daunting challenges. This chapter responds to those require-ments by highlighting the ideas, materials, and guidance offered through structured PD.

Nationally representative surveys indicate that most teachers have ac-cess to PD related to their teaching assignment; however, teachers report having minimal opportunities to learn how to support a broader student population, including students with disabilities and students identified as English learners. PD that targets teachers' capacity to support a diverse student population tends to remain separate from content-focused PD, even though research indicates it is important that they be integrated.

Formally structured PD, like that of preservice teacher education, pres-ents a "sprawling landscape" of programs and an equally sprawling array of research. New forms of PD have emerged in recent years, prominently in-cluding online programs and platforms, as well as approaches such as Lesson Study that invite teachers to learn in and from their own practice. Research has yielded mixed evidence regarding the outcomes of PD with respect to gains in teacher knowledge, classroom practice, and student outcomes. However, a growing number of studies demonstrate that well-designed, content-focused PD can achieve positive outcomes, especially when the PD helps teachers integrate new ideas or strategies with curriculum and when teachers engage with others in the same grade level, department, or school. Less is known about the outcomes of PD targeted at teachers' capacity for working with a diverse student population. Moreover, evidence of effec-tive PD tends to come from research on small-scale interventions designed and led by experts (or in some instances, PD designed by experts and led by local facilitators trained by experts). Little is known about the quality of the PD that *most* teachers receive or the degree to which programs of PD prove responsive to the needs and interests arising from teachers' main teaching assignments and from the changing expectations they encounter. In the chapter that follows, the committee considers the learning opportunities rooted in teachers' daily experience in the classroom and school.

REFERENCES

Ball, D.L., and Cohen, D.K. (1999). Developing practice, developing practitioners: Toward a practice-based theory of professional education. In L. Darling-Hammond and G. Sykes (Eds.), *Teaching as the Learning Profession: Handbook of Policy and Practice* (pp. 3–32). San Francisco: Jossey Bass.

Banilower, E.R., Smith, P.S., Malzahn, K.A., Plumley, C.L., Gordon, E.M., and Hayes, M.L. (2018). *Report of the 2018 NSSME+.* Chapel Hill, NC: Horizon Research, Inc.

Barr, D., Boulay, B., Selman, R.L., McCormick, R., Lowenstein, E., Gamse, B., et al. (2015). A randomized controlled trial of professional development for interdisciplinary civic education: Impacts on humanities teachers and their students. *Teachers College Record, 117*(4), 1–52.

Blank, R.K., and de las Alas, N. (2009). *The Effects of Teacher Professional Development on Gains in Student Achievement: How Meta Analysis Provides Scientific Evidence Useful to Education Leaders.* Washington, DC: Council of Chief State School Officers.

Borko, H. (2004). Professional development and teacher learning: Mapping the terrain. *Educational Researcher, 33*(8), 3–15.

Borko, H., Koellner, K., and Jacobs, J. (2011). Using video representations of teaching in practice-based professional development programs. *Mathematics Education, 43*, 175–187.

Borko, H., Jacobs, J., Koellner, K. and Swackhamer, L.E. (2015). *Mathematics Professional Development: Improving Teaching Using the Problem-Solving Cycle and Leadership Preparation Models.* New York: Teachers College Press.

Brown, J.C., and Crippen, K.J. (2016). Designing for culturally responsive science education through professional development. *International Journal of Science Education, 38*, 470–492.

Bryk, A.S., Sebring, P.B., Allensworth, E., Luppescu, S., and Easton, J.Q. (2010). *Organizing Schools for Improvement.* Chicago: University of Chicago Press.

Cobb, P., Jackson, K., Henrick, E., Smith, T., and MIST team. (2018). *Systems for Instructional Improvement: Creating Coherence from the Classroom to the District Office.* Cambridge, MA: Harvard Education Press.

Coburn, C.E., and Russell, J.L. (2008). District policy and teachers' social networks. *Educational Evaluation and Policy Analysis, 30*(3), 203–235.

Crocco, M.S., and Livingston, E. (2017). Becoming an "expert" social studies teacher: What we know about teacher education and professional development. In M.M. Manfra and C.M. Bolick (Eds.), *The Wiley Handbook of Social Studies Research* (pp. 360–384). Malden, MA: Wiley-Blackwell.

Dede, C., Ketelhut, D.J., Whitehouse, P.L., Breit, L.A., and McCloskey, E.M. (2009). A research agenda for online teacher professional development. *Journal of Teacher Education, 60*(1), 8–19.

De La Paz, S., Malkus, N., Monte-Sano, C., and Montanaro, E. (2011). Evaluating American history teachers' professional development: Effects on student learning. *Theory & Research in Social Education, 39*, 494–540.

DeMonte, J. (2013). *High-Quality Professional Development for Teachers: Supporting Teacher Training to Improve Student Learning.* Washington, DC: Center for American Progress.

Desimone, L.M. (2009). Improving impact studies of teachers' professional development: Toward better conceptualizations and measures. *Educational Researcher, 38*, 181–199.

Dieker, L.A., Rodriguez, J.A., Lignugaris/Kraft, B., Hynes, M.C., and Hughes, C.E. (2014). The potential of simulated environments in teacher education: Current and future possibilities. *Teacher Education and Special Education, 37*(1), 21–33.

Fernandez, C. (2002). Learning from Japanese approaches to professional development: The case of lesson study. *Journal of Teacher Education, 53*(5), 393–405.

Fernandez, C. (2005). Lesson Study: A means for elementary teachers to develop the knowledge of mathematics needed for reform-minded teaching? *Mathematical Thinking and Learning 7*(4), 265–289.

Fishman, B., Konstantopoulos, S., Kubitskey, B.W., Vath, R., Park, G., Johnson, H., and Edelson, D.C. (2013). Comparing the impact of online and face-to-face professional development in the context of curriculum implementation. *Journal of Teacher Education, 64*(5), 426–438.

Gallagher, H.A., Arshan, N., and Woodworth, K. (2017). Impact of the National Writing Project's College-Ready Writers Program in High-Need Rural Districts. *Journal of Research on Educational Effectiveness, 10*(3), 570–595.

Garet, M.S., Cronen, S., Eaton, M., Kurki, A., Ludwig, M., Jones, W., Uekawa, K., Falk, A., Bloom, H., Doolittle, F., Zhu, P., and Sztejnberg, L. (2008). *The Impact of Two Professional Development Interventions on Early Reading Instruction and Achievement.* (NCEE 2008–4030). Washington, DC: National Center for Education Evaluation and Regional Assistance, Institute of Education Sciences, U.S. Department of Education.

Garet, M., Wayne, A., Stancavage, F., Taylor, J., Walters, K., Song, M., Brown, S., Hurlburt, S., Zhu, P., Sepanik, S., and Doolittle, F. (2010). *Middle School Mathematics Professional Development Impact Study: Findings after the First Year of Implementation.* (NCEE 2010–4009). Washington, DC: National Center for Education Evaluation and Regional Assistance, Institute of Education Sciences, U.S. Department of Education.

Gay, G. (2002). Preparing for culturally responsive teaching. *Journal of Teacher Education, 53,* 106–116.

Gersten, R., Taylor, M.J., Keys, T.D., Rolfhus, E., and Newman-Gonchar, R. (2014). *Summary of Research on the Effectiveness of Math Professional Development Approaches.* Washington, DC: National Center for Education Evaluation and Regional Assistance, Institute of Education Sciences, U.S. Department of Education.

Grigg, J., Kelly, K.A., Gamoran, A., and Borman, G.D. (2013). Effects of two scientific inquiry professional development interventions on teaching practice. *Educational Evaluation and Policy Analysis, 35*(1), 38–56.

Heller, J.I., Daehler, K.R., Wong, N., Shinohara, M., and Miratrix, L. (2012). Differential effects of three professional development models on teacher knowledge and student achievement in elementary science. *Journal of Research in Science Teaching, 49*(3), 333–362.

Howell, J., and Saye, J. (2016). Using lesson study to develop a shared professional teaching knowledge culture among 4th grade social studies teachers. *The Journal of Social Studies Research, 40*(1), 25–37.

Kazemi, E., and Franke, M.L. (2004). Teacher learning in mathematics: Using student work to promote collective inquiry. *Journal of Mathematics Teacher Education, 7*(3), 203–235.

Kennedy, M.M. (1999). *Form and Substance in In-service Teacher Education.* (Research Monograph No. 13). Arlington, VA: National Science Foundation.

Kennedy, M.M. (2016). How does professional development improve teaching? *Review of Educational Research, 86*(4), 945–980.

Ladson-Billings, G.J. (1995). Toward a theory of culturally relevant pedagogy. *American Education Research Journal, 35,* 465–491.

Lee, O., Luykx, A., Buxton, C., and Shaver, A. (2007). The challenge of altering elementary school teachers' beliefs and practices regarding linguistic and cultural diversity in science instruction. *Journal of Research in Science Teaching, 44,* 1269–1291.

Lewis, C. (2009). What is the nature of knowledge development in lesson study? *Educational Action Research, 17*(1), 95–110.

Lewis, C., and Perry, R. (2017). Lesson study to scale up research-based knowledge: A randomized, controlled study of fractions learning. *Journal for Research in Mathematics Education, 48*(3), 261–299.

Lewis, C., Perry, R., and Murata, A. (2006). How should research contribute to instructional improvement? The case of lesson study. *Educational Researcher, 35*(3), 3–14.

Little, J.W. (1989). District policy choices and local professional development opportunities. *Educational Evaluation and Policy Analysis, 11*(2), 165–179.

Gallagher, H.A., Arshan, N., and Woodworth, K. (2017). Impact of the National Writing Project's College-Ready Writers Program in high-need rural districts. *Journal of Research on Educational Effectiveness, 10*(3), 570–595.

Luna, M.J., and Sherin, M.G. (2017). Using a video club design to promote teacher attention to students' ideas in science. *Teaching and Teacher Education, 66,* 282–294.

Lynch, K., Hill, H.C., Gonzalez, K., and Pollard, C. (2019). Strengthening the research base that informs STEM instructional improvement efforts: A meta-analysis. *Educational Evaluation and Policy Analysis, 41*(3), 260–293.

McLaughlin, M.W., and Talbert, J.E. (2001). *Professional Communities and the Work of High School Teaching.* Chicago: Chicago University Press.

National Academies of Sciences, Engineering, and Medicine. (2015). *Science Teachers' Learning: Enhancing Opportunities, Creating Supportive Contexts.* Washington, DC: The National Academies Press.

National Center for Education Statistics. (2018). *Characteristics of Public Elementary and Secondary School Teachers in the United States: Results from the 2015–2016 National Teacher and Principal Survey First Look.* Washington, DC: Author.

National Education Association. (1987). *The Status of the American Teacher 1985–1986.* Washington, DC: Author.

Odden, A., Archibald, S., Fermanich, M., and Gallagher, H.A. (2002). A cost framework for professional development. *Journal of Education Finance, 28*(Summer), 51–74.

Olson, C.B., Kim, J.S., Scarcella, R., Kramer, J., Pearson, M., van Dyk, D.A., Collins, P., and Land, R.E. (2012). Enhancing the interpretive reading and analytic writing of mainstreamed English learners in secondary school: Results from a randomized field trial using a cognitive strategies approach. *American Educational Research Journal, 49*(2), 323–355.

Osborne, J.F., Borko, H., Fishman, E., Zaccarelli, F.G., Berson, E., Busch, K.C., et al. (2019). Impacts of a practice-based professional development program on elementary teachers' facilitation of and student engagement with scientific argumentation. *American Educational Research Journal, 56*(4), 1067–1112.

Paris, D., and Alim, H.S. (2017). *Culturally Sustaining Pedagogies: Teaching and Learning for Justice in a Changing World.* New York: Teachers College Press.

Parkhouse, H., Lu, C.Y., and Massaro, V. (2019). Multicultural education professional development: A review of the literature. *Review of Educational Research, 89*(3), 416–458.

Parsad, B., Lewis, L., Farris, E., and Greene, B. (2001). *Teacher Preparation and Professional Development: 2000.* Washington, DC: National Center for Education Statistics.

Polly, D., McGee, J., Wang, C., Martin, C., Lambert, R., and Pugalee, D. (2015). Linking professional development, teacher outcomes, and student achievement: The case of a learner-centered mathematics program for elementary school teachers. *International Journal of Educational Research, 72,* 26–37.

Rice, J.K. (2001). *Cost Framework for Teacher Preparation and Professional Development.* New York: Finance Project.

Rodman, A. (2019). *Personalized Professional Learning: A Job-Embedded Pathway for Elevating Teacher Voice.* Alexandria, VA: ASCD.

Rotermund, S., DeRoche, J., and Ottem, R. (2017) *Teacher Professional Development by Selected Teacher and School Characteristics: 2011–2102*. Washington, DC: National Center for Education Statistics.

Roth, K.J., Garnier, H.E., Chen, C., Lemmens, M., Schwille, K., and Wickler N.I.Z. (2011) Videobased lesson analysis: Effective science PD for teacher and student learning. *Journal of Research in Science Teaching, 48*(2), 117–148.

Santagata, R. (2009). Designing video-based professional development for mathematics teachers in low-performing schools. *Journal of Teacher Education, 60*(1), 38–51.

Saye, J.W., Kohlmeier, J., Howell, J.B., McCormick, T.M., Jones, R.C., and Brush, T.A. (2017). Scaffolded lesson study: Promoting professional teaching knowledge for problem-based historical Inquiry. *Social Studies Research and Practice, 12*(1), 95–112.

Scher, L., and O'Reilly, F. (2009). Professional development for K–12 math and science teachers: What do we really know? *Journal of Research on Educational Effectiveness, 2*(3), 209–249.

Seago, N. (2004). Using video as an object of inquiry for mathematics teaching and learning. In J. Brophy (Ed.), *Using Video in Teacher Education* (pp. 259–286). Amsterdam: Elsevier.

Sherin, M.G., and Han, S.Y. (2004). Teacher learning in the context of a video club. *Teaching and Teacher Education, 20*(2), 163–183.

Slavin, R.E., Lake, C., Hanley, P., and Thurston, A. (2014). Experimental evaluations of elementary science programs: A best-evidence synthesis. *Journal of Research in Science Teaching, 51*(7), 870–901.

Sleeter, C.E. (1997). Mathematics, multicultural education, and professional development. *Journal for Research in Mathematics Education, 28*(6), 680–696.

Sleeter, C.E. (2018). Multicultural education past, present, and future: Struggles for dialog and power-sharing. *International Journal of Multicultural Education, 20*(1), 5–20.

Stigler, J.W., and Hiebert, J. (1999). *The Teaching Gap: Best Ideas from the World's Teachers for Improving Education in the Classroom*. New York: Summit Books.

The New Teacher Project. (2015). *The Mirage: Confronting the Hard Truth about Our Quest for Teacher Development*. New York: Author.

van Es, E.A., Tunney, J., Goldsmith, L.T., and Seago, N. (2014). A framework for the facilitation of teachers' analysis of video. *Journal of Teacher Education, 65*(4), 340–356.

van Es, E.A., Tekkumru-Kisa, M., and Seago, N. (in press). Leveraging the power of video for teacher learning: A design framework for teacher educators. In S. Llinares and O. Chapman (Eds.), *International Handbook of Mathematics Teacher Education* (Vol. 2). Boston, MA: Brill.

Vernon-Feagans, L., Bratsch-Hines, M., Varghese, C., Bean, A., and Hedrick, A. (2015). The targeted reading intervention: Face-to-face vs. webcam literacy coaching of classroom teachers. *Learning Disabilities Research & Practice, 30*(3).

Wei, R.C., Darling-Hammond, L., Andree, A., Richardson, N., and Orphanos, S. (2009). *Professional Learning in the Learning Profession: A Status Report on Teacher Development in the United States and Abroad*. Dallas, TX: National Staff Development Council.

Wilson, S.M., and Berne, J. (1999). Teacher learning and the acquisition of professional knowledge: An examination of research on contemporary professional development. *Review of Research in Education, 24*, 173–209.

Yoon, K.S., Duncan, T., Lee, S.W.Y., Scarloss, B., and Shapley, K. (2007). *Reviewing the Evidence on How Teacher Professional Development Affects Student Achievement* (Issues and Answers Report, REL 2007-No. 033). Washington, DC: National Center for Education Evaluation and Regional Assistance, Regional Educational Laboratory Southwest, Institute of Education Sciences, U.S. Department of Education.

Zembal-Saul, C. (2009). Learning to teach elementary science as argument. *Science Education, 93*(4), 687–719.

7

Opportunities for Teacher Learning in the Workplace

The committee was charged with considering the role of preservice and inservice education in responding to changing student demographics and evolving expectations for teaching and learning. However, the committee concluded that programs of teacher preparation and continuing professional development (PD), while important, are insufficient in and of themselves to equip teachers to meet these expectations. Teachers hone their instructional practices and develop their ways of relating to students and families in the context of daily work in schools. Research supplies consistent and compelling evidence that what teachers do in their classrooms, as well as whether teachers stay in their schools and the profession, writ large, is shaped by the nature of the social relations, material resources, and organizational conditions of the schools and districts in which teachers work (Bryk et al., 2010; Cobb et al., 2018; Coburn, 2003; Johnson, 2019; Johnson, Kraft, and Papay, 2012; McLaughlin and Talbert, 2001; Nasir et al., 2014; National Academies of Sciences, Engineering, and Medicine, 2015).

For example, based on analysis of a statewide survey of a representative sample of Massachusetts teachers focused on working conditions, paired with an analysis of student demographic and achievement data, Johnson, Kraft, and Papay (2012) found that "the seeming relationship between student demographics and teacher turnover is driven not by teachers' responses to their students, but by the conditions in which they must teach and their students are obliged to learn" (p. 1). Johnson, Kraft, and Papay investigated the impact of a number of working conditions, including material resources (e.g., facilities, instructional resources), planning time, and social relationships on teacher satisfaction and intent to remain teaching at their current school, as well as on growth in student achievement. While all of the working conditions on which teachers were surveyed mattered, it was the *social relationships* that mattered most in explaining teachers' satisfaction and intent to remain teaching at their school. Specifically, three elements stood out, in explaining teachers' satisfaction:

> (1) *collegial relationships*, or the extent to which teachers report having productive working relationships with their colleagues; (2) the *principal's leadership*, or the extent to which teachers report that their school leaders are supportive and create school environments conducive to learning; and (3) *school culture*, or the extent to which school environments are characterized by mutual trust, respect, openness, and commitment to student achievement. (p. 24, italics added)

In fact, as Johnson, Kraft, and Papay (2012) report, the magnitudes of the effects of these social relationships "were almost twice as large as those of school resources and facilities" (p. 24). Further, they found that after teachers' perception of community support (defined as the extent to which families and the broader community support teachers and students in the school), these same three elements—collegial relationships, principal's leadership, and school culture—were also most strongly related to growth in student achievement at the school level, including when comparing schools serving similar student populations.

As a second example, in a study employing a large administrative data set spanning 10 years from Charlotte-Mecklenburg Schools, Kraft and Papay (2014) pose questions about the relationship between teacher improvement and aspects of a school's professional environment (order and discipline, principal leadership, peer collaboration, PD, school culture, and teacher evaluation). They conclude that

> policies aimed at improving teacher effectiveness that focus on the individual, ignoring the role of the organization, fail to recognize or leverage the potential importance of the school context in promoting teacher development. We show that the degree to which teachers become more effective over time varies substantially by school. In some schools, teachers improve at much greater rates than in others. We find that this improvement is strongly related to the opportunities and supports provided by the professional context in which they work. (p. 494)

In light of these findings, this chapter turns attention to the role of the workplace in supporting individual teachers and in building teachers' collective capacity to create robust learning opportunities for all the children they serve. It poses the question: In a context of changing demographics and heightened expectations, to what extent are schools and school systems organized for teachers to learn from and with each other about how to improve instruction and support student learning? For purposes of clarity and focus, this chapter and the preceding chapter distinguish between external PD and internal job-embedded/workplace professional learning opportunities; however, the available research indicates that these various opportunities intersect in the daily lives of teachers with varying degrees of coherence. Research spanning decades points to the gains that follow when schools are organized both to support workplace-based learning *and* to capitalize on well-designed formal PD (Bryk et al., 2010; Cobb et al., 2018; Horn, 2005; Little, 1984, 2006; Nasir et al., 2014).

JOB-EMBEDDED PROFESSIONAL LEARNING OPPORTUNITIES IN THE WORKPLACE

This chapter begins by highlighting three strategic investments that school and system leaders have made in recent decades to strengthen the knowledge, skill, and professional identity of teachers: systems of induction and mentoring for beginning teachers, opportunities for teachers to learn from and with colleagues, and the development of instructional coaching roles, relationships, and practices. The chapter concludes by taking up the broader question of how schools as organizations build the capacity to respond to changing conditions and expectations. School-level leadership figures prominently in that discussion.

Induction and Mentoring for Beginning Teachers

Over the past several decades, in response to teacher attrition among beginning teachers, there has been a marked increase in the presence of induction programs, whether at the state, district, or school level; national survey data indicate that 90 percent of teachers in 2008 reported having participated in an induction program in their first year of teaching, up from 50 percent in 1990 (Ingersoll and Strong, 2011; Ronfeldt and McQueen, 2017). As Ingersoll and Strong (2011) explain, the goals of induction programs are to "improve the performance and retention of beginning teachers . . . with the ultimate aim of improving the growth and learning of students" (p. 203). What counts as "induction" varies; it can include orientation sessions, time to collaborate with other faculty, workshops, meetings with supervisors, extra assistance in the classroom, reduced workloads, and mentoring (Ingersoll and Strong, 2011). In theory, induction is different from other forms of inservice PD, in that it is targeted only at beginning teachers and is likely to encompass support for new teachers that extends beyond classroom performance (e.g., achieving work-life balance or navigating the school culture). However, in practice and in research, the lines between induction and other forms of in-service PD are blurry (e.g., provision of common planning time).

The expansion of induction and mentoring programs has prompted a corresponding growth in descriptive studies that characterize the nature of such programs and in evaluative studies that attempt to trace the effects of mentoring and induction on teachers' confidence, performance, and retention (Evertson and Smithey, 2000; Fletcher, Strong, and Villars, 2008; Ingersoll and Strong, 2011; Kang and Berliner, 2012; Ronfeldt and McQueen, 2017; Schwille, 2008; Smith, Desimone, and Porter, 2012; Stanulis and Floden, 2009). The most ambitious large-scale, experimental design study to date compared a randomly assigned treatment group of beginning elementary school teachers who received "comprehensive" induction supports provided by Educational Testing Services or the New Teacher Center to a control group who received "business as usual" district induction support (Glazerman et al., 2010). Teachers across both groups reported on surveys that they received similar kinds of supports (e.g., PD, mentor); however, teachers in the treatment group reported receiving significantly greater amounts of support. That study found no significant differences between the groups with respect to retention or teachers' instructional practice in the first year. Other studies, including some with comparison group designs, have found positive effects of induction and mentoring on teachers' instructional practice (Evertson and Smithey, 2000; Stanulis and Floden, 2009) and on student achievement (Fletcher, Strong, and Villars, 2008).

The most recent comprehensive study of the prevalence of induction programs, including mentoring and its impact on retention of beginning teachers, utilizes data from nationally representative samples of beginning teachers, specifically three administrations of the Schools and Staffing Survey (SASS) and Teacher Follow-Up Survey (2003–2004, 2007–2008, 2011–2012) and the Beginning Teacher Longitudinal Study for full- and part-time public school teachers (Ronfeldt and McQueen, 2017). Ronfeldt and McQueen found that the vast majority of teachers in the full sample reported participating in an induction program in their first year.[1] The most prevalent form of professional learning support was mentoring (79%), followed by participation in seminars (73%) and common planning time with same-subject teachers (about 62%). In addition, 88 percent of teachers reported supportive communication with leadership.

In the 2011–2012 SASS, comparable percentages of elementary and secondary teachers reported receiving similar first-year supports, with one

---

[1] An induction program was defined on the 2011–2012 SASS as "a program for beginning teachers that may include teacher orientation, mentoring, coaching, demonstrations, and/or assessments aimed at enhancing teachers' effectiveness" (p. 19).

TABLE 7-1 Percentage of Teachers Reporting Receipt of Induction Supports, by School Setting

	Rural	City	Suburb	Town
Common Planning Time	49	60	62	59
Mentor	75	72	79	82
Seminar	56	63	66	61

SOURCE: 2011–2012 Schools and Staffing Survey.

exception: 65 percent of elementary teachers reported receiving common planning time as compared to 50 percent of secondary teachers. Teachers' reports about first-year supports varied slightly in relation to their school setting (see Table 7-1): fewer teachers in rural settings reported receiving common planning time with their same-subject teachers, as compared to teachers in a city, setting, or town setting. Teachers' report of supportive communication from leadership was similar (72–77% of teachers) regardless of school setting.

In terms of teacher migration and attrition, Ronfeldt and McQueen (2017) found that all induction supports reduced the odds that a beginning teacher would move schools the following year. However, certain supports appeared to be more important than others. Namely, receiving supportive communication from school leadership, having a mentor, attending a beginning seminar, and having common time for collaborating/planning significantly reduced the odds that a beginning teacher would *move* schools the following year. Supportive communication from school leadership was significantly associated with reducing the odds of migrating schools between 43 and 52 percent, depending on the model they ran, *across 5 years*. In terms of attrition, attending a beginner's seminar, receiving supportive communication from leadership and having a mentor significantly reduced the odds of teachers *leaving* the profession after 1 year, as well as up to 5 years later. Moreover, with both teacher migration and with attrition, Ronfeldt and McQueen (2017) found *the more supports, the better*. Across cohorts of teachers as well as various data sources and models, they found that "teachers who received more extensive induction supports[2] were significantly less likely to migrate or leave the profession" (p. 395).

Importantly, the provision of extensive supports did not appear to vary by teacher or school characteristic, with a few exceptions. "Black teachers were significantly more likely than White teachers to receive extensive

---

[2]Ronfeldt and McQueen (2017) distinguished between teachers who received zero to three supports, and those who received four to six supports. Fifty-six percent of the sample received four to six supports, or what Ronfeldt and McQueen characterized as "extensive supports."

induction supports; in fact, the odds of receiving extensive induction supports were between 80% and 100% greater" (p. 402). Ronfeldt and McQueen hypothesize that this may be due to the fact that beginning Black teachers leave teaching at a much faster rate than their peers (see Ingersoll, May, and Collins, 2019). Ronfelt and McQueen also found that the school characteristics significantly related to receiving extensive induction supports were "teachers in schools with (a) higher percentages of LEP students and (b) smaller enrollments (less than 350)" (p. 402).

Ronfeldt and McQueen's (2017) study clearly suggests that providing multiple induction supports to first-year teachers, including mentoring, is an important policy lever for retaining teachers and reducing turnover between schools (see Chapter 4) in their early years. However, there has been little research on how the *content* or *quality* of induction supports impacts teacher migration and attrition and about the impact of supports on other outcomes, such as the quality of teaching or student learning. Moreover, whereas Ronfeldt and McQueen's findings suggest that Black teachers receive significantly more extensive supports than their colleagues, little is known about the impact of the quality or quantity of supports on Black teachers or other teachers of color.

Opportunities for Learning with and from Colleagues

The physical and social organization of schools in the United States remains largely akin to what sociologist Dan Lortie (1975, p. 14) characterized as an "egg crate," with teachers and their students encapsulated in individual classroom spaces. Such an arrangement tends to isolate teachers and to place a premium on learning alone in the confines of the classroom. However, evidence from large-scale survey data (Banilower et al., 2018; Rotermund, DeRoche, and Ottem, 2017) and studies of instructional improvement at scale (Bryk et al., 2010; Cobb et al., 2018; Coburn and Russell, 2008) suggest that school and system leaders increasingly recognize the potential benefit to be realized from opportunities for teachers to collaborate within the workplace and to learn from watching one another teach through voluntary peer observation. In addition, efforts to enrich the academic and social experience for students with disabilities have included co-teaching arrangements in which special education teachers share classroom responsibility with their "general education" colleagues (Friend et al., 2010). Initiatives to establish Professional Learning Communities, or PLCs, have become commonplace in recent years, although the term is now so widespread and refers to so many different configurations and purposes as to render comparisons among studies challenging (Vangrieken et al., 2017; Vescio, Ross, and Adams, 2008). Several decades worth of studies point to the variability in teachers' professional interactions within and across schools.

Research conducted in the 1980s and 1990s highlighted the potential value in teachers' having regular opportunities to make sense of teaching together, identifying and working to resolve common dilemmas in teaching and patterns of student learning (Little, 1982; McLaughlin and Talbert, 2001; Rosenholtz, 1989; Siskin, 1994). Few of the early workplace studies investigated the relationship between robust professional community and student outcomes. However, a multiyear study of Chicago elementary schools identified "professional capacity"[3] as one of five essential elements that accounted for improvements in student achievement and attendance patterns (Bryk et al., 2010). No comparable systemwide studies of school workplace culture and student outcomes exist at the secondary level. However, a longitudinal mixed-methods study of 16 high schools in four metropolitan areas of California and Michigan supplies survey, interview, and observational evidence that consistently points to the influence of nested contexts (department, school, district, and sector) on teachers' professional orientation and relationships (McLaughlin and Talbert, 2001; Talbert and McLaughlin, 1994). That study was among the first in the United States to attend closely to the importance of within-school teacher groupings—especially subject departments—as significant contexts for the formation of teachers' perspectives, relationships, and practices (Siskin, 1994; Siskin and Little, 1995). Variations both within and across schools led McLaughlin and Talbert (2001) to differentiate weak from strong professional cultures, but also to observe that strong professional ties were not always associated with an improvement stance. Rather, teacher bonds might form either in support of deep questioning and the pursuit of improvement ("teacher learning community") or to protect traditional forms of instruction and a norm of privacy ("strong traditional community").

In a smaller-scale multiyear study of mathematics learning and course-taking in three comparison high schools, Boaler and Staples (2008) also attribute the superior outcomes in one school (Railside) to the strength of the department-level teacher community. An in-depth observation and interview study of department-level cultures in the same school helped to further specify the kinds of group-level perspectives and practices that could account for the measured student outcomes (Horn and Little, 2010; Nasir et al., 2014).

Findings from studies such as those described above prompted schools and districts across the country to change the structuring of time during the workday (before, during, and/or after school) so that teachers might engage in "professional learning communities," "critical friends groups,"

---

[3]Bryk and colleagues (2010) define and measure professional capacity as a combination of an improvement orientation, strong professional community, and access to high-quality PD.

"common planning time," "teacher communities," and "study groups." Teachers may meet in grade-level teams or by disciplines, and the frequency and focus of this time vary widely (Cobb et al., 2018; Curry, 2008). Results of the 2011–2012 SASS show that a large majority (81%) of teachers surveyed reported regularly scheduled collaboration with other teachers on issues of instruction, with slightly less collaboration reported by teachers with three or fewer years of experience (76%) and by teachers in high schools (76%). Teachers in elementary schools reported the highest levels of collaboration (85%) (Rotermund et al., 2017).[4]

Rotermund and colleagues (2017) caution that the SASS data show patterns of participation in collaborative activity but offer no indication of the quality of the experience or its impact on teachers' perspectives or classroom practices. In an earlier paper based on the 2000 Fast Response Survey System, Parsad and colleagues (2001, p. v) reported, "Teachers who engaged in regularly scheduled collaboration with other teachers at least once a week were more likely to believe that participation had improved their teaching a lot (45%), compared with teachers who participated two to three times a month (23%), once a month (15%), or a few times a year (7%)." Of course, it is not possible to establish causal direction in this instance; teachers who are working assiduously to improve their teaching may be more inclined to collaborate frequently.

Ronfeldt and colleagues (2015) conducted one of the few district-level, large-scale quantitative studies of the impact of teacher collaboration on student achievement. Drawing on survey and administrative data from more than 9,000 teachers in the Miami-Dade County Schools over 2 years, they found that 84 percent of all teachers reported collaborating with their colleagues on instructional issues, and nearly 90 percent of those teachers reported that the collaboration was "helpful" or "very helpful." However, there was wide variation in what teachers reported as the focus of their collaboration, namely the extent to which they focused on instructional strategies and curriculum (e.g., coordinating curriculum across classrooms, developing materials), discussing instructional strategies students (e.g., discussing the needs of specific students, reviewing student work, discussing classroom management); and/or assessment (e.g., reviewing test results, reviewing formative assessments). Consistent with a number of qualitative studies, Ronfeldt and colleagues (2015) found that "the vast majority of variation in collaboration is within, not between, schools, suggesting the need for attention to differences in collaboration even among teachers in the same school environment" (p. 479).

---

[4]The SASS results differ somewhat from those resulting from the 2018 NSSME+ survey targeted specifically to STEM teachers. In that survey, between 55–68 percent of secondary teachers, as compared to 43–53 percent of elementary teachers, indicated they participated in teacher collaborative time in the past 3 years (Banilower et al., 2018, p. 50).

Ronfeldt and colleagues found that on the whole, teachers who reported engaging in greater degrees of collaboration and who found it to be helpful, showed greater gains on value-added[5] analyses of students' achievement in reading and in mathematics, and "usually at statistically significant and meaningful levels" (p. 506). In general, they found positive effects of collaboration on student achievement, no matter the focus of the collaboration, although a focus on assessment was "most often significantly predictive of achievement in math and reading" (p. 506). However, Ronfeldt and colleagues caution against taking this finding to suggest that teacher collaboration should exclusively focus on analyzing student assessment data. They write:

> Does this mean that building collaboration around assessments is good policy? Not necessarily. It is possible, for example, that test score gains may have resulted from an excessive focus on test preparation, possibly at the expense of focusing on other educationally meaningful topics. Finding collaboration about assessments to predict better performance on assessments is not so surprising. Had our dependent variable been a different educational outcome, for example, teachers' pedagogy or students' critical thinking, it is possible that collaboration about assessment would not have been as predictive. Future research should continue to investigate whether different educational outcomes are more responsive to collaboration with different foci. (p. 509)

Qualitative research indicates that workplace conditions shape the extent to which analyzing data is used primarily to target students' performance on an assessment, and/or to fundamentally improve the quality of instruction and thus students' learning opportunities. (See Box 7-1 for a discussion of teacher collaboration and data use.)

In addition, the available research also supplies evidence that simply meeting together—even with shared aims of improvement—does not ensure that the group will constitute a PLC (Curry, 2008; Grossman, Wineburg, and Woolworth, 2001; Horn et al., 2016; Lefstein et al., 2019; McLaughlin and Talbert, 2001). Based on a synthesis of the literature on teacher collaboration in relation to ambitious goals for teacher learning, Horn, Kane, and Garner (2018) write that, "at its best, teacher collaborative time can provide teachers with opportunities to contend with school-level problems of practice and adapt the big ideas of pull-out PD to the complex daily realities of particular classrooms" (p. 96). They argue that a key marker of productive teacher collaborative time is the opportunity to discuss not only *how* to adapt an idea relative to one's context, but also *why* a particular practice or adaptation makes sense. However, this requires not only the

[5] See Chapter 4 for a brief discussion of value-added.

BOX 7-1
Teacher Collaboration and Data Use

In recent decades, education has joined other human service fields, including medicine and social work, in promoting evidence-based decision making. School and district leaders' enthusiasm for evidence-based or data-driven decision making, fueled in part by accountability demands, manifests itself in the widespread use of designated teacher collaboration time for "data use" and in practical guides developed for school and district leaders (Boudett, City, and Murnane, 2013). The data under consideration range broadly, including the results of standardized tests, periodic benchmark assessments, samples of student work, attendance reports, climate surveys, and more. In principle, teachers' opportunities to examine and interpret such evidence collaboratively should better equip them to set priorities and to identify areas in which they would benefit from professional development (PD).

Published studies of data use have multiplied in recent years, aided in part by the Spencer Foundation's research program Data Use and School Improvement (Coburn and Turner, 2012; Farley-Ripple and Buttram, 2015; Marsh, Bertran, and Huguet, 2015). Numerous studies have focused on the perspectives and practices of teachers and others (school leaders, coaches, counselors) as they work to understand and interpret multiple kinds of data. For example, Datnow, Park, and Kennedy-Lewis (2013) employed interviews with teachers and with district and school leaders to probe

> the sources and types of data that teachers had access to and used; expectations for how teachers should use data and for what purposes; structural support mechanisms such as collaboration time, training, and personnel to assist with data use; evidence of a culture of data use in the school and the teachers' own beliefs about the use of data; and how teachers used data to inform classroom instruction . . . [and] outstanding needs and areas for improvement in the use of data at the school site. (p. 349)

The researchers found that many common supports for data use, such as structured collaboration time or the availability of discussion protocols, could function in practice either as affordances for or constraints on productive interaction. A widely reported factor in exploiting their affordances was the role of "leadership

---

establishment of trust between colleagues to discuss and make sense of the deeply personal accounts of teaching, but also that individuals in the group have the expertise necessary to tackle problems of practice in ways that advance teaching and learning.

Productive collaboration is marked by teachers' openly sharing their practices and dilemmas, questioning current practice and assumptions in the face of student struggle or failure, and connecting evidence of student learning to instructional decisions. Yet qualitative studies, both large and small scale, indicate that it is rare that the focus, facilitation, and structure of teacher collaborative time in most U.S. schools support

focused on thoughtful use of data" (p. 350). Leaders framed data-driven decision making as a "collective responsibility," helped to create norms and processes for productive data discussions, and worked to cultivate a culture of trust.

In addition to research focused on data use practice, other studies have concentrated on the kinds of PD, coaching, network support, or other resources that would enable teachers to make more informed interpretations of data and more fruitful decisions about how data might inform instructional decisions. For example, Marsh, McCombs, and Martorell (2009) investigated the extent to which school-based reading coaches focused attention on teachers' capacity for data use in instructional decision making. This mixed-methods study in 113 middle schools in eight Florida school districts found that coaches engaged in a broad range of activities to support teachers, but that greater than 60 percent "reported placing a major emphasis on supporting the analysis of data to guide instructional practice" (p. 889). More experienced coaches and coaches assigned to lower performing schools were more likely than newer coaches to devote extensive time to data use activity. In another example, Supovitz (2012) reviewed and synthesized more than 100 empirical studies related to test design to specify design qualities that would make assessment instruments more useful to teachers in three respects. He argues that assessments will be useful to teachers to the extent that they "convey information about students' developmental path toward a learning goal," "provide information about students' thought processes," and reveal information about students' misconceptions within a content area" (p. 1). However, Supovitz notes that "adjusting subsequent instruction based on assessment information tends to be the most difficult task for teachers. . . . [T]his suggests that absent either external guidance or guidance embedded within the assessment system, teachers will have difficulties productively adjusting instruction to remediate deficiencies indicated by assessment data" (pp. 19–20).

Despite the large the investment in collaborative data use, few studies collect data on its effects on teachers' instructional practice or student outcomes. Marsh, McCombs, and Martorell (2009), however, note that "One of the only program features that we found significantly and positively related to better reading scores was the frequency with which reading teachers reported that the coach reviewed assessment data with them (either individually or in a group)" (p. 898).

teachers' development of perspectives and practices in ways that would allow them to productively respond to the expectations described in Chapter 3.

Findings from the Middle School Mathematics and the Institutional Study of Teaching (MIST) study are especially illustrative of the challenges districts and schools face in organizing and implementing teacher collaborative time that supports substantial teacher learning (Horn, Kane, and Garner, 2018). They conducted a qualitative study focused on understanding the learning opportunities across 24 collaborative teacher groups that were nominated by district and school instructional leaders as functioning well. Each of four districts provided substantial time for teachers to meet with their colleagues during the school day. Based on an analysis of 111 video recordings of meetings from the selected 24 groups of middle-school mathematics teachers, Horn, Kane, and Garner found that "pacing and logistics meetings accounted for more than 40 percent of the meetings in [the] sample" (p. 98). In another 24 percent of meetings, teachers primarily focused on sharing "tips and tricks," or the "how" of instruction absent a discussion of the "why." In the remaining third or so of meetings, teachers focused on both the how and why of problems of practice. Teachers likely find it useful to discuss pacing and logistics, as well as to share tips and tricks. However, Horn, Kane, and Garner argue that those kinds of meetings, on their own, are unlikely to support teachers in developing the perspectives and practices necessary for the engagement of a broad set of students—one of the high expectations for teaching (see Chapter 3). Based on these findings, Horn, Kane, and Garner concluded, "Despite [substantial investment in teacher collaborative time] . . . we found that *effective* teacher collaboration that had the potential to support teachers' development of ambitious and equitable instructional practices happened relatively infrequently in our partner districts" (p. 94).

Findings from this and other studies point to the challenge of developing a robust teacher community where it does not already exist, yet there remain few studies that trace the formation of such relationships over time. In one widely cited example, Grossman, Wineburg, and Woolworth (2001) followed a group of high school English and history teachers as they gradually came to terms with the differences and disagreements (e.g., about the nature of "evidence" in literary versus historical texts) that limited their ability to forge an interdisciplinary curriculum. The authors characterize the group's development over 2 years as a move from "pseudo-community" to "authentic" community (p. 989).

In another example, participants in a long-term department-initiated process of mathematics reform supply accounts of how the department's leaders and teachers forged agreements, developed new knowledge and practices, and tracked their progress by attending closely to evidence of student learning. Tsu, Lotan, and Cossey (2014) describe the impetus for the department's collective endeavor (an accreditation site visit that confronted the department with its record of student failure and students' expressed frustration), and the teachers' subsequent efforts to work and learn together as they made changes. A key contributor to the department's success was its partnership with the PD program Complex Instruction, based at Stanford University. Cabana, Shreve, and Woodbury (2014) supply an additional account of the same group's evolution as a teacher community, focusing on the group's decisions, routines, and practices: detracking Algebra I, doing mathematics together, building a curriculum consistent with Complex

Instruction pedagogy, developing an approach to hiring and induction, and cultivating distributed leadership.

One potential benefit of increased time to collaborate with peers is the development of teacher networks, whereby teachers increasingly turn to one another to garner new ideas or ask for advice about their practice. In the past two decades, there has been increasing research on the development and maintenance of teacher networks, especially in relation to the implementation of ambitious instructional initiatives—both within and across schools and districts (Daly, 2015; Moolenaar, 2012). Evidence indicates that networks in which teachers see one another as resources, turn to others with relevant expertise, and interact in robust as opposed to superficial ways, can serve as important supports for teachers as they implement new forms of practice, including after formal supports such as PD or coaching are phased out (Coburn, Mata, and Choi, 2013; Lieberman and Wood, 2003; Penuel et al., 2012).

However, research is less clear on why some teachers develop networks characterized by depth and support for instructional improvement whereas others do not. A study of a 3-year districtwide implementation of an ambitious elementary mathematics curriculum indicates that school and district context and policy matter in the formation of networks (Coburn, Mata, and Choi, 2013). Coburn, Mata, and Choi studied the formation of teacher networks in relationship to changes in district policy regarding the use of the new curriculum and the provision of supports. Teachers were initially provided with time to collaborate with colleagues and coaches, as well as districtwide PD; however, these supports were reduced by the third year. Teachers' social networks reflected these changes; social networks initially expanded as teachers were provided increasing time to collaborate with colleagues, including those outside their own schools, and then networks contracted as that collaboration time was removed. However, even though the district retracted supports in the third year, Coburn, Mata, and Choi also found that because of the robust nature of the supports initially provided, teachers increasingly sought out others whom they viewed as having relevant expertise over the 3 years, and that they increasingly viewed *other teachers* as having relevant expertise and sources for guidance alongside coaches. Coburn, Mata, and Choi performed their own assessment of teachers' expertise in relation to the mathematics reform initiative and found that their own assessment matched with teachers' assessment. Coburn, Mata, and Choi write, "Teachers not only developed an appetite for expertise, driving their reasons for seeking out others, but also improved in their ability to identify those in the school with expertise" (p. 322). This study indicates that it is possible to design the conditions under which teacher networks are likely to flourish and continue even when those supports are removed, and thus provide an important support to teachers.

Instructional Coaching

The model of one-on-one instructional coaching as a component of teachers' PD originated in the 1980s (Joyce and Showers, 1982; Showers, 1984) but has become a more commonplace and visible feature of the workplace over the past two decades, yielding both practical guides (West and Staub, 2003) and a body of research (Baldinger, 2018; Campbell and Malkus, 2011; Coburn and Woulfin, 2012; Gibbons and Cobb, 2017; Lockwood, McCombs, and Marsh, 2010; Woulfin, 2015). As with the other forms of PD, the frequency and focus of coaching varies. According to results of the 2015–2016 National Teacher and Principal Survey, 66 percent of all schools had specialist or coaching positions, although such roles were less common in small town and rural schools, and other evidence suggests that few teachers may experience one-on-one coaching. Banilower et al. (2018), drawing on the 2018 National Survey of Science and Mathematics Education (NSSME+), write: "Across subject areas and grade ranges, one-on-one coaching is relatively rare except in elementary school mathematics, where over 4 in 10 schools offer coaching" (p. 66). Moreover, they found that the "proportion of teachers who are coached is small," with about 10 percent of science teachers and 13–18 percent of math teachers (depending on the grade level) reporting having been provided with coaching (p. 67). Cost is a likely factor in accounting for the variable availability of instructional coaches across subject areas, in rural areas, and at the level of the individual classroom; however, the committee is not aware of studies focused on the cost structure of coaching and on related system-level decisions about resource allocation.

A recent meta-analysis demonstrates the potential of instructional coaching to yield improvements in teachers' instructional practice and in students' measured achievement. Kraft, Blazar, and Hogan (2018) combined results from 60 rigorous studies of coaching in the United States and other developed countries: the studies focus primarily on literacy coaching in pre-K and elementary settings but include a few at the high school level and a few in math and science. The authors define coaching programs as "all in-service PD programs where coaches or peers observe teachers' instruction and provide feedback to help them improve" (p. 548). In contrast to conventional PD, "coaching is intended to be individualized, time-intensive, sustained over the course of a semester or year, context specific, and focused on discrete skills" (p. 548). They note that nearly all the coaching models in the selected studies (90%) were joined to other forms of PD such as summer workshops, group PD events during the academic year, or the provision of new curricular and instructional materials.

Kraft, Blazar, and Hogan (2018) attribute their ability to conduct such a meta-analysis to substantial improvements in research design over the past decade, spurred by the Education Sciences Reform Act in 2002. With respect to effects on instruction measured in 43 studies, results show large positive effects of coaching, with a pooled effect size of 0.49 SD.[6] The meta-analysis also shows a general positive effect of coaching on student achievement. In the 31 studies that included achievement measures, they estimate that coaching raised student performance on standardized tests by 0.18 SD; however, Kraft, Blazar, and Hogan caution that their ability to gauge achievement effects across coaching models is limited by the fact that most of the achievement effect sizes relied on reading assessments as the outcome measure. In a finding that parallels other recent reviews and meta-analyses (Kennedy, 2016; Lynch et al., 2019), Kraft et al. find no evidence that dosage matters. They conclude, "The lack of evidence supporting dosage effects suggests that the quality and focus of coaching may be more important than the actual number of contact hours" (p. 565). On a sobering note, but one that invites future research, the authors indicate that the effect sizes for both instructional outcomes and achievement outcomes diminish as teacher sample size increases. Using sample size as a proxy for scale of implementation, they urge attention to what it will require to build "a corps of capable coaches whose expertise is well matched to the diverse needs of teachers in a school or district" (p. 571; on this point, see Coburn and Russell, 2008).

Each of the arrangements highlighted above—induction support and mentoring for new teachers, time and structures for teacher collaboration, and instructional coaching—may supply teachers with opportunities to meet heightened expectations for "deeper learning" and for working successfully with a diverse population of students (as described in Chapter 3). However, the effectiveness of such arrangements likely depends on the degree to which they constitute part of an integrated system of supports for teacher learning and school improvement.

BUILDING THE CAPACITY OF TEACHERS AND SCHOOLS TO RESPOND TO NEW EXPECTATIONS

Responding productively and on a large scale to new demographics and new expectations for teaching and learning will require not only a workforce of well-prepared individuals but also schools with the collective capacity for continuous improvement. The significance of a school's collective capacity forms the central argument of two major bodies of research conducted since the 1990s and published in recent volumes.

Over two decades, the Next Generation of Teachers Project at Harvard engaged in a series of studies of elementary, middle, and high schools to

---

[6] The associated standard deviation of the estimated random effect (0.33 SD) nonetheless points to considerable variability across programs.

investigate the school-level and system policies and practices related to hiring, induction, curriculum, teacher collaboration, and teacher evaluation that contributed (or not) to teachers' commitment and supported their learning. In the recent volume *Where Teachers Thrive: Organizing Schools for Success,* Johnson (2019) draws on studies conducted between 2008 and 2015 to argue that the prevailing policy logic—the notion that schools can be improved through a singular focus on *human capital,* or the knowledge and skill of individual teachers—is fundamentally flawed. Without denying the importance of teachers' knowledge, skill, and judgment, Johnson argues that relying primarily on individual teacher qualities will prove insufficient to support effective teaching, deepen teacher commitment, or stimulate and sustain school improvement. Each of the book's eight chapters illuminates the contrasts between an individualistic perspective and a collective perspective on selected levers on teacher quality (including teacher collaboration, teacher leadership, and teacher evaluation), and how those contrasts play out with respect to outcomes of interest.

A second major set of multiyear studies, situated in Chicago's elementary schools, identified "professional capacity" as one of five core elements characteristic of schools that recorded improvements in student achievement and attendance (Bryk et al., 2010). As defined by the researchers, professional capacity encompassed an improvement orientation, professional community marked by relational trust, and access to high-quality professional development. In a volume summarizing the cumulative results of the research, Bryk and colleagues (2010) argue that effective school-level leadership constitutes the most crucial of the five elements—the primary driver of a school's organizational capacity, with well substantiated consequences for teacher commitment and retention as well as for schools' measured student achievement and other outcomes.[7]

Although school-level leadership in the Chicago studies reported by Bryk and colleagues (2010) referred specifically to the elementary school principal, other studies adopt a distributed leadership perspective (Spillane, 2006) to examine the practice and perspectives of teacher (Mangin, 2007; Spillane, Hallett, and Diamond, 2003). Such studies illuminate variations in the work teacher leaders are engaged in doing and how (or whether) they are positioned to support fellow teachers in meeting new expectations. In some instances, studies point to the role of the district in supporting principals and other school-level leaders in building a productive school culture (Coburn and Russell, 2008; Honig, 2008, 2012; Johnson, 2019).

---

[7] Other key elements included parent-community ties, a student-centered learning climate, and a system of instructional guidance.

Synergies Between the Workplace and
Structured Professional Development

Studies spanning several decades suggest the potentially synergistic relationship between teachers' collective participation in PD and improvements at the classroom, department, or school level (Bryk et al., 2010; Desimone, 2009; Franke et al., 1998, 2001; Horn, 2005; Little, 1993, 2006; Nasir et al., 2014). In one widely cited study of PD implementation, teachers who had participated in the mathematics PD program Cognitively Guided Instruction (CGI) reported that collegial support was a significant factor in their implementation and sustained use of the ideas and practices introduced by the PD. "Each teacher began the project in a school where the majority of teachers were participating in the professional development program. Many teachers reported that that level of support from colleagues was critical, in that it made the reform a school endeavor rather than a single teacher's endeavor" (Franke et al., 2001, p. 679).

However, the CGI researchers also reported that the nature and intensity of teachers' collaborative interactions varied both within and across schools. In some groups, teachers "questioned each other, shared articles with each other, talked about tasks, and talked about students, all focused on learning more about children's mathematical thinking in their classrooms. The teachers in these collaborative groups felt that continuing the reform without this level of support would be difficult" (p. 679). However, "other teachers in these same schools did not develop the same level or type of collegial support" (p. 680). Teachers with the highest levels of implementation, sustained over time, tended to be those with the most intensive forms of collaboration.

Examining factors specifically at the secondary school level, intensive teacher collaboration linked to participation in PD (when found at all) appears more common at the department level than at the whole-school level, especially in large comprehensive high schools (McLaughlin and Talbert, 2001; Siskin, 1994). One compelling example is the mathematics department in an urban high school with an ethnically, linguistically, and economically diverse student population. Over the course of two decades, teachers were aided by a succession of skilled department leaders, intensive teacher collaboration focused on student learning, collective participation in Stanford's Complex Instruction program of PD, and participation in various reform-oriented mathematics teacher networks. These conditions enabled a series of progressive accomplishments, which were the focus of complementary sets of studies at Stanford and Berkeley, reported in a series of published works (among them, Boaler and Staples, 2008; Horn, 2005; Nasir et al., 2014).

In the past decade, studies employing social network theory and methods of social network analysis have provided a conceptual, methodological, and empirical bridge between what has long been rather separate lines of research on teacher learning in PD and teacher learning in the workplace (Penuel et al., 2012; Sun et al., 2013). Penuel and colleagues (2012) write, "It is a relatively recent development within studies of teacher networks to consider simultaneously the effects of formal professional development and collegial interactions" (p. 110). In a longitudinal (3-year) study conducted in 20 schools serving as local partnership sites of the National Writing Project,[8] they employ PD participation data (contact hours) and social network data to help account for variations in teachers' reported changes in writing instruction by year 3. The analysis, which controlled for prior instructional practice and for teacher background characteristics (including years of teaching experience, gender, and subject taught), was designed to estimate the direct effect of PD participation and any added indirect effects of collegial interaction on year 3 instructional practice.

Penuel and colleagues (2012) report significant positive effects of participation in PD and of informal interaction with peers who had gained expertise through their participation in the PD. However, the contribution made by participation in the PD and by interaction with colleagues varied in relationship to teachers' self-reported prior instructional practice; teachers with the lowest prior level of writing process instruction benefitted significantly from both the PD and peer interactions, while those reporting intermediate levels of prior instruction were significantly influenced by the PD and less by colleague interactions, and teachers with the highest levels of prior writing instruction were influenced primarily by peer interaction.

In a related analysis, Sun and colleagues (2013) investigate the "spillover effects" of PD "in which the provision of professional development to some teachers shapes the practices of other teachers in the school who may or may not directly participate in professional development" (p. 347). The researchers ask how the duration, focus, and strategies of writing-related PD may affect the number of colleagues whom a participating teacher subsequently helps with writing instruction, and how the teachers being helped make changes in their writing instruction. Annual schoolwide surveys in 39 schools supplied data on teachers' background, writing-related PD experience, professional networks, practices of writing instruction, and school contexts. The surveys also asked respondents to name up to five colleagues

---

[8] This large-scale NWP evaluation study entailed random assignment of 39 middle schools to a treatment (partnership) or control (delayed partnership) condition. The analysis in Penuel et al.'s (2012) paper relies on data collected in the 20 partnership schools; the related analysis reported by Sun et al. (2013) paper employs data from all 39 schools.

who had helped them with writing instruction, and to report both the frequency and type of help offered. Sun and colleagues (2013) find that:

> teachers were more likely to provide help to others with teaching writing if they had intensively participated in professional development of longer duration, with a broader range of writing-related content, and that employed a larger number of active learning strategies. . . . Moreover, we found that the expertise that teachers gained from Year 2 professional development spread to other teachers as they offered professional help. In some cases, the spillover effects on the improvement of instructional practices were almost equal to the direct effects of teachers' participation in professional development. (pp. 359–360)

Overall, the available research points to an association between teacher workgroup capacity (professional community) and effective use of PD, with demonstrated impact on classroom practice and student learning. Further, it suggests a set of propositions about the interaction of external PD and opportunities for workplace-embedded learning. First, the greater the demands on teachers for deep understanding of content, instructional planning and design, and conceptually oriented and equity-driven pedagogical practice, the more teachers are likely to need implementation support and collaborative problem-solving to make good on the promise of PD.

Second, if new ideas and practices introduced by PD are to have meaningful and measurable impact on students and schools, they must be implemented in more than isolated classrooms. And, third, the greater the collective capacity of teachers in a grade level, department, or school, the better positioned they are to judge the relevance and worth of particular PD and to exploit the benefits of PD, even if that PD may be short or episodic. Together, these research-based propositions point to the significance of the larger school systems in which individual schools are embedded.

The Significance of the System

Research indicates that the broader system in which schools are located shapes the impact of workplace-embedded learning opportunities and formal PD on teachers' perspectives and practice (Cobb et al., 2018; Coburn, 2003; Coburn and Russell, 2008). Districts emerged as both consumers and providers of PD by the 1970s, but little research focused specifically on the district role until around 1990 (Honig, 2008; Little, 1989; Spillane, 2002).[9] Two prominent examples of research conducted since 2000 center

---

[9] In recent years, school systems have come to include charter management organizations, but the available system-level research focuses principally on districts.

around efforts to promote more conceptually rich and equitable mathematics instruction.

Coburn and Russell's (2008) study of the scale-up of innovative mathematics curricula and instructional practices compares the system of instructional coaching and network formation established in two districts. The study points to the influence of district-level conceptions of teacher learning opportunity and strategies for supporting it. Both districts introduced instructional coaching to promote teachers' use of new curricula and instructional practices but contrasted in the degree to which they systematically prepared and supported coaches in doing that work. Coaches were more effective and teacher networks more firmly established where the district invested in the professional development of the coaches themselves.

A second example is the previously described MIST study (Cobb et al., 2018). Across each of four districts, the researchers found that there was no shortage of professional learning opportunities. Districts provided mandatory pull-out PD in summer and across the year. District-based or school-based coaches worked in most schools. And, across the districts, teachers were provided with consistent time to collaborate with their colleagues. However, rarely were these various forms of professional learning connected and coordinated. Jackson, Horn, and Cobb (2018) wrote:

> Most often . . . one-on-one coaching does not directly build on either the district-wide PD in which the teachers have participated or their work during teacher collaborative meetings. Additionally, what happens in teacher collaborative time remains disconnected from what happens in . . . PD. This makes for an incoherent set of supports that implicitly communicates to teachers that they should select the practices that best suit them, thereby undermining the potential of any one form of support to have any lasting impact. (pp. 68–69)

So, although teachers reported participating in a great deal of PD, they were often not provided opportunities to work consistently and deliberately on improving specific aspects of their practice. In response, researchers have argued for the importance of conceptualizing professional learning in terms of a system in which the various supports for teachers' learning (e.g., districtwide PD, coaching, teacher collaborative time) are deliberately coordinated, "so that the goals for improving classroom practice in one type of support are built on and elaborated in other types of support" (Jackson, Horn, and Cobb, 2018, p. 69). However, the field has yet to conduct research that evaluates the impact of systems of supports for teacher learning on teacher practice and student learning.

SUMMARY

Together, this chapter and the preceding chapter respond to changing student demographics and to heightened expectations for student learning by highlighting two fundamental resources for teachers' professional work and development: (1) the ideas, materials, and guidance offered through structured PD and (2) the social and material fabric of the workplace, including teachers' professional relationships and networks in and beyond the school.

Workplace opportunities for teacher learning now commonly include induction and mentoring for new teachers, time to collaborate with peers, and instructional coaching in key subject areas and for purposes of data-driven decision making. However, decades of research on the school workplace confirms that schools vary widely in the tenor of the workplace culture, the vision and skill of school leadership, the availability of high-quality PD, the norms and routines that mark teachers' professional relationships, and the systems that provide structure and guidance for teachers' work with students. Empirical research on the three specific strategic interventions of induction and mentoring, collaborative time, and instructional coaching has yielded mixed results, suggesting that a fruitful question is under what conditions each of these interventions proves effective in retaining teachers, stimulating instructional improvement, and boosting student learning.

Overall, there are a number of important players to consider when ensuring teachers are able to respond to the challenges and opportunities presented in the classroom. For practicing teachers, responding to these circumstances and meeting these expectations will require both the disposition and the opportunity for continuous learning. For schools, achieving success will require building the collective capacity for innovation and improvement. Districts and other systems in which schools are embedded (e.g., charter management organizations) play an important role in creating the conditions for schools to develop the capacity to respond productively to these changes.

REFERENCES

Baldinger, E. (2018). *Learning Together: Investigating Possibilities for Mathematics Teachers' Equity-Focused Learning Through Coaching.* Unpublished Ph.D. dissertation, University of California, Berkeley.

Ball, D.L., and Cohen, D.K. (1999). Developing practice, developing practitioners: Toward a practice-based theory of professional education. In L. Darling-Hammond and G. Sykes (Eds.), *Teaching as the Learning Profession: Handbook of Policy and Practice* (pp. 3–32). San Francisco: Jossey Bass.

Banilower, E.R., Smith, P.S., Malzahn, K.A., Plumley, C.L., Gordon, E.M., and Hayes, M.L. (2018). *Report of the 2018 NSSME+.* Chapel Hill, NC: Horizon Research, Inc.

Boaler, J., and Staples, M. (2008). Creating mathematical futures through an equitable teaching approach: The case of Railside School. *Teachers College Record, 110*(3), 608–645.

Boudett, K., City, E., and Murnane, R. (2013). *Data Wise: A Step-by-Step Guide to Using Assessment Results to Improve Teaching and Learning*. Cambridge: Harvard Education Press.

Boyd, D., Grossman, P., Ing, M., Lankford, H., Loeb, S., and Wyckoff, J. (2011). The influence of school administrators on teacher retention decisions. *American Educational Research Journal, 48,* 303–333.

Bryk, A.S., Sebring, P.B., Allensworth, E., Luppescu, S., and Easton, J.Q. (2010). *Organizing Schools for Improvement*. Chicago: University of Chicago Press.

Cabana, C., Shreve, B., and Woodbury, E. (2014) Building and sustaining professional community for teacher learning. In N. Nasir et al. (Eds), *Mathematics for Equity: A Framework for Successful Practice* (pp. 175–186). New York: Teachers College Press.

Campbell, P.F., and Malkus, N.N. (2011). The impact of elementary mathematics coaches on student achievement. *Elementary School Journal, 111,* 430–454.

Cobb, P., Jackson, K., Henrick, E., Smith, T., and MIST team. (2018). *Systems for Instructional Improvement: Creating Coherence from the Classroom to the District Office*. Cambridge, MA: Harvard Education Press.

Coburn, C.E. (2003). Rethinking scale: Moving beyond numbers to deep and lasting change. *Educational Researcher, 32*(6), 3–12.

Coburn, C.E., and Russell, J.L. (2008). District policy and teachers' social networks. *Educational Evaluation and Policy Analysis, 30*(3), 203–235.

Coburn, C.E. and Turner, E.O. (2012). The practice of data use: An introduction. *American Journal of Education 118*(2), 99–111.

Coburn, C.E., and Woulfin, S.L. (2012). Reading coaches and the relationship between policy and practice. *Reading Research Quarterly. 47*(1), 5–30.

Coburn, C.E., Mata, W., and Choi, L. (2013). The embeddedness of teachers' social networks: Evidence from a study of mathematics reform. *Sociology of Education, 86*(4), 311–342.

Curry, M.W. (2008). Critical Friends Groups: The possibilities and limitations embedded in teacher professional communities aimed at instructional improvement and school reform. *Teachers College Record, 110*(4), 733–774.

Daly, A.J. (Ed.), (2015). *Social Network Theory and Educational Change*. Cambridge, MA: Harvard Education Press.

Datnow, A., Park, V., and Kennedy-Lewis, B. (2013). Affordances and constraints in the context of teacher collaboration for the purpose of data use. *Journal of Educational Administration, 51*(3), 341–362.

Desimone, L.M. (2009). Improving impact studies of teachers' professional development: Toward better conceptualizations and measures. *Educational Researcher, 38,* 181–199.

Evertson, C.M., and Smithey, M.W. (2000). Mentoring effects on proteges' classroom practice: An experimental field study. *The Journal of Educational Research, 93*(5), 294–304.

Farley-Ripple, E. and Buttram, J. (2015). The development of capacity for data use: The role of teacher networks in an elementary school. *Teachers College Record, 117*(4), 1–34.

Fletcher, S., Strong, M., and Villars, A. (2008). An investigation of the effects of variations in mentor-based induction on the performance of students in California. *Teachers College Record, 110*(10), 2271–2289.

Franke, M.L., Carpenter, T., Fennema, E., Ansell, E., and Behrend, J. (1998). Understanding teachers' self-sustaining, generative change in the context of professional development. *Teaching and Teacher Education, 14*(1), 67–80.

Franke, M.L., Carpenter, T., Levi, L., and Fennema, E. (2001). Capturing teachers' generative change: A follow-up study of professional development in mathematics. *American Educational Research Journal, 38,* 653–690.

Friend, M., Cook, L., Hurley-Chamberlain, D., and Shamberger, C. (2010). Co-teaching: An illustration of the complexity of collaboration in special education. *Journal of Educational and Psychological Consultation, 20*(1), 9–27.

Gibbons, L.K., and Cobb, P. (2017). Focusing on teacher learning opportunity to identify potentially productive coaching activities. *Journal of Teacher Education, 68*(4), 411–425.

Glazerman, S., Isenberg, E., Dolfin, S., Bleeker, M., Johnson, A., Grider, M., and Jacobus, M. (2010). *Impacts of Comprehensive Teacher Induction: Final Results from a Randomized Controlled Study* (NCEE 2010-4027). Washington, DC: U.S. Department of Education.

Grossman, P., Wineburg, S., and Woolworth, S. (2001). Toward a theory of teacher community. *Teachers College Record, 103*(6), 942–1012.

Honig, M.I. (2008). District central offices as learning organizations: How sociocultural and organizational learning theories elaborate district central office administrators' participation in teaching and learning improvement efforts. *American Journal of Education, 114*(4), 627–664.

Honig, M.I. (2012). District central office leadership as teaching: How central office administrators support principals' development as instructional leaders. *Educational Administration Quarterly, 48*(4), 733–774.

Horn, I.S. (2005). Learning on the job: A situated account of teacher learning in high school mathematics departments. *Cognition and Instruction, 23*(2), 207–236.

Horn, I.S., and Little, J.W. (2010). Attending to problems of practice: Routines and resources for professional learning in teachers' workplace interactions. *American Educational Research Journal 47*(1), 181–217.

Horn, I.S., Garner, B., Kane, B.D., and Brasel, J. (2016). A taxonomy of instructional learning opportunities in teachers' workgroup conversations. *Journal of Teacher Education,* 1–14.

Horn, I.S., Kane, B.D., and Garner, B. (2018). Teacher collaborative time: Helping teachers make sense of ambitious teaching in the context of their schools. In P. Cobb, K. Jackson, E. Henrick, and T. Smith (Eds.), *Systems for Instructional Improvement: Creating Coherence from the Classroom to the District Office* (pp. 93–112). Cambridge, MA: Harvard Education Press.

Ingersoll, R., May, H., and Collins, G. (2019). Recruitment, employment, retention and the minority teacher shortage. *Education Policy Analysis Archives, 27*(37).

Ingersoll, R., and Strong, M. (2011). The impact of induction and mentoring programs for beginning teachers: A critical review of the research. *Review of Educational Research, 81*(2), 201–233.

Jackson, K., Horn, I.S., and Cobb, P. (2018). Chapter four: Overview of the teacher learning subsystem. In P. Cobb, K. Jackson, E. Henrick, T.M. Smith, and MIST team (Eds.), *Systems for Instructional Improvement: Creating Coherence from the Classroom to the District Office* (pp. 65–75). Cambridge, MA: Harvard Education Press.

Johnson, S.M. (2019) *Where Teachers Thrive: Organizing Schools for Success.* Cambridge: Harvard Education Press.

Johnson, S.M, Kraft, M.A., and Papay, J.P. (2012). How context matters: The effects of teachers' working conditions on their professional satisfaction and their students' achievement. *Teachers College Record, 114*(10), 1–39.

Joyce, B., and Showers, B. (1981). *Teacher Training Research: Working Hypotheses for Program Design and Directions for Further Study.* Paper presented at the annual meeting of the American Educational Research Association, Los Angeles.

Kang, S., and Berliner, D.C. (2012). Characteristics of teacher induction programs and turnover rates of beginning teachers. *The Teacher Educator, 47*(4), 268–282.

Kennedy, M.M. (2016). How does professional development improve teaching? *Review of Educational Research, 86*(4), 945–980.

Kraft, M.A., and Papay, J.P. (2014). Can professional environments in schools promote teacher development? Explaining heterogeneity in returns to teaching experience. *Educational Evaluation and Policy Analysis, 36*(4), 476–500.

Kraft, M.A., Blazar, D., and Hogan, D. (2018). The effect of teacher coaching on instruction and achievement: A meta-analysis of the causal evidence. *Review of Educational Research, 88*(4), 547–588.

Lefstein, A., Louie, N., Segal, A., and Becher, A. (2019). Taking stock of research on teacher collaborative discourse: Theory and method in a nasccent field. *Teaching and Teacher Education, 88.* doi: 10.1016/j.tate.2019.102954.

Lieberman, A., and Wood, D. (2003). *Inside the National Writing Project: Connecting Network Learning and Classroom Teaching.* New York: Teachers College Press.

Little, J.W. (1982). Norms of collegiality and experimentation: Workplace conditions of school success. *American Educational Research Journal, 19*(3), 325–340.

Little, J.W. (1984). Seductive images and organizational realities in professional development. *Teachers College Record, 86*(1), 85–102.

Little, J.W. (1989). District policy choices and local professional development opportunities. *Educational Evaluation and Policy Analysis, 11*(2), 165–179.

Little, J.W. (1993). Teachers' professional development in a climate of educational reform. *Educational Evaluation and Policy Analysis, 15*(2), 129–151.

Little, J.W. (2006). *Professional Community and Professional Development in the Learning-Centered School.* Arlington, VA: National Education Association.

Lockwood, J.R., McCombs, J.S., and Marsh, J. (2010). Linking reading coaches and student achievement: Evidence from Florida middle schools. *Educational Evaluation and Policy Analysis, 32*(3), 372–388.

Lortie, D.C. (1975). *Schoolteacher: A Sociological Study.* Chicago: University of Chicago Press.

Lynch, K., Hill, H.C., Gonzalez, K., and Pollard, C. (2019). Strengthening the research base that informs STEM instructional improvement efforts: A meta-analysis. *Educational Evaluation and Policy Analysis, 41*(3), 260–293.

Mangin, M. (2007). Facilitating elementary principals' support for instructional teacher leadership. *Educational Administration Quarterly, 43*(3), 319–357.

Marsh, J.A., Bertrand, M., and Huguet, A. (2015). Using data to alter instructional practice: The mediating role of coaches and professional learning communities. *Teachers College Record, 117*(4), 1–40.

Marsh, J.A., McCombs, J.S. and Martorell, F. (2009). How instructional coaches support data-driven decision making. *Educational Policy,* 1–36.

McLaughlin, M.W., and Talbert, J.E. (2001). *Professional Communities and the Work of High School Teaching.* Chicago: Chicago University Press.

Moolenaar, N.M. (2012). A social network perspective on teacher collaboration in schools: Theory, methodology, and applications. *American Journal of Education, 119*(1), 7–39.

Nasir, N.S., Cabana, C., Shreve, B., Woodbury, E., and Louie, N. (2014). *Mathematics for Equity: A Framework for Successful Practice.* Reston, VA: National Council of Teachers of Mathematics.

National Academies of Sciences, Engineering, and Medicine. (2015). *Science Teachers' Learning: Enhancing Opportunities, Creating Supportive Contexts.* Washington, DC: The National Academies Press.

National Center for Education Statistics. (2018). *Characteristics of Public Elementary and Secondary School Teachers in the United States: Results From the 2015–16 National Teacher and Principal Survey First Look.* Washington, DC: Author.

Parsad, B., Lewis, L., Farris, E., and Greene, B. (2001). *Teacher Preparation and Professional Development: 2000.* Washington, DC: National Center for Education Statistics.

Penuel, W.R., Sun, M., Frank, K.A., and Gallagher, H.A. (2012). Using social network analysis to study how collegial interactions can augment teacher learning from external professional development. *American Journal of Education, 119*(1), 103–136.

Ronfeldt, M., Farmer, S.O., McQueen, K., and Grissom, J. (2015). Teacher collaboration in instructional teams and student achievement. *American Educational Research Journal, 52*(3), 475–514.

Ronfeldt, M., and McQueen, K. (2017). Does new teacher induction really improve retention? *Journal of Teacher Education, 68(4), 394–410.*

Rosenholtz, S. (1989). *Teachers' Workplace*. New York: Longman.

Rotermund, S., DeRoche, J., and Ottem, R. (2017). *Teacher Professional Development by Selected Teacher and School Characteristics: 2011–2102*. Washington, DC: National Center for Education Statistics.

Schwille, S.A. (2008). The professional practice of mentoring. *American Journal of Education, 115*(1), 139–167.

Showers, B. (1984). *Peer Coaching: A Strategy for Facilitating Transfer of Training*. Eugene: Center for Educational Policy and Management, University of Oregon.

Siskin, L.S. (1994). *Realms of Knowledge: Academic Departments in Secondary Schools*. London: Falmer Press.

Siskin, L.S., and Little, J.W. (Eds.). (1995). *The Subjects in Question: Departmental Organization and the High School*. New York, Teachers College Press.

Smith, T., Desimone, L., and Porter, A. (Eds.). (2012). *Organization and Effectiveness of Induction Programs for New Teachers*, National Society for the Study of Education No. 0077-5762. New York: Teachers Colleage Press.

Spillane, J.P. (2002). Local theories of teacher change: The pedagogy of district policies and programs. *Teachers College Record, 104*(3), 377–420.

Spillane, J.P. (2006). *Distributed Leadership*. San Francisco: Jossey-Bass.

Spillane, J.P., Hallett, T., and Diamond, J.B. (2003). Forms of capital and the construction of leadership: Instructional leadership in urban elementary schools. *Sociology of Education, 76*(1), 1–17.

Stanulis, R.N., and Floden, R.E. (2009). Intensive mentoring as a way to help beginning teachers develop balanced instruction. *Journal of Teacher Education, 60*(2), 112–122.

Stigler, J.W., and Hiebert, J. (1999). *The Teaching Gap: Best Ideas from the World's Teachers for Improving Education in the Classroom*. New York: Summit Books.

Sun, M., Penuel, W.R., Frank, K.A., Gallagher, H.A., and Youngs, P. (2013). Shaping professional development to promote the diffusion of instructional expertise among teachers. *Educational Evaluation and Policy Analysis, 35*(3), 344–369.

Supovitz, J. (2012). Getting at student understanding—The key to teachers' use of test data. *Teachers College Record, 114*, 29.

Talbert, J.E., and McLaughlin, M.W. (1994). "Teacher professionalism in local school contexts." *American Journal of Education, 102*, 123–153.

Tsu, R., Lotan, R., and Cossey, R. (2014). Building a vision for equitable learning. In N. Nasir et al. (Eds), *Mathematics for Equity: A Framework for Successful Practice* (pp. 129–144). New York: Teachers College Press.

Vangrieken, K., Meredith, C., Packer, T., and Kyndt, E. (2017). Teacher communities as a context for professional development: A systematic review. *Teaching and Teacher Education, 61*, 47–59.

Vescio, V., Ross, D., and Adams, A. (2008). A review of the research on the impact of professional learning communities on teaching practice and student learning. *Teaching and Teacher Education, 24*, 80–91.

West, L., and Staub, F.C. (2003). *Content-Focused Coaching: Transforming Mathematics Lessons*. Portsmouth, NH: Heinemann.

Woulfin, S.L. (2015). Catalysts of change: An examination of coaches' leadership practices in framing a reading reform. *Journal of School Leadership, 25*(3), 526–557.

8

Conclusions, High-Priority Issues Requiring Immediate Action, and Research Agenda

Overall, the committee was tasked with answering three broad questions:

1. What do the current workforce demographics and expectations of the teacher workforce suggest about how the future workforce will change?
2. What does the changing nature of the teacher workforce mean for the way higher education and other providers address K–12 teacher preservice and inservice education?
3. In light of the current and anticipated structural changes in the teacher workforce, how can effective models, programs, and practices for teacher education (including principles of deeper learning) be sustained and expanded?

To address these questions, the committee reviewed the relevant evidence from the peer-reviewed literature as well as from ongoing programs. As noted in Chapter 1 and throughout the report, the committee did not find strong evidence to support the assumption that there have been substantial changes in the demographics of teachers. But what has become clear is that what it means to be a teacher today—that is, the expectations and demands placed upon teachers—has changed.

This chapter opens with 14 conclusions that reflect the committees' consensus understanding of the current state of evidence. The committee then turns to a discussion of four high-priority issues requiring the immediate attention of education stakeholders. What follows is the committee's consensus on the conclusions, high-priority issues requiring immediate action, and an agenda to direct future research.

CONCLUSIONS

As described in Chapters 2 and 4, given the particular timeframe examined (past 20 years), the trends in the composition of the teacher workforce remained relatively unchanged. That is, on average, there have been modest changes, at best, in race/ethnicity (although there have been some increases in Black and Hispanic teachers), gender (still majority female), average age (42 years old), and teaching experience. These relatively modest changes for the time period examined are contrary to other data that suggest more substantial changes in the makeup of teachers observed over a longer duration. As such, the committee concludes:

CONCLUSION 1: At the national level, the composition of the teacher workforce (e.g., distribution in gender, age, race and ethnicity, years of experience) has been relatively stable over the past 20 years.

Today's Classrooms and Expectations for Teachers

Despite little change in the composition of the teacher workforce as described above, there have been marked changes with respect to the expectations for teachers in the classroom (beyond things like the increasing paperwork burden). As described in Chapter 2, dramatic shifts in the U.S. education policy contexts combined with an increasingly diverse student population have altered expectations for what teachers should be able to do in their classrooms. These changes are also compounded by states that may have recently adopted and are in the process of implementing newer rigorous national content standards that move from a sole focus on demonstrating understanding of concepts to also asking students to also demonstrate proficiency in disciplinary practices that require them to use their knowledge (see Chapter 3). Moreover, there has been an increasing emphasis in technology, both in terms of how teachers use technology as a vehicle for learning, for communication with families, and as a medium for sharing ideas with other educators.

Chapter 3 highlights how teachers are increasingly charged with ensuring that classrooms serve as equitable learning communities, fostering trusting and caring relationships among students and with teachers. Moreover, with shifts in standards that require attention to deeper learning, the expectations for students' learning have increased, which in turn has raised expectations for instruction. These compounded expectations for learning, combined with the demand to create a learning environment that responds to the experiences of all students, call for innovative approaches to instruction that may differ substantially from teachers' own experiences as students or their preservice education.

The committee concludes that:

CONCLUSION 2: There are more explicit demands placed upon K–12 teachers today. There continues to be an increase in the level of content and pedagogical knowledge expected of teachers to implement curriculum and instruction aligned to newer content standards and deeper learning goals. Teachers are called on to educate an increasingly diverse student body, to enact culturally responsive pedagogies, and to have a deeper understanding of their students' socioemotional growth. Integrating these various, layered expectations places substantially new demands on teachers.

CONCLUSION 3: The adoption of state standards and accountability systems has contributed to increased expectations for what teachers need to accomplish for all students in terms of achievement and content mastery.

The Teacher Workforce

Chapter 4 provides an overview of the trends in the teacher labor market, highlighting some of the issues that arise with staffing different types of classrooms for schools in different labor markets that serve different kinds of students. Overall, it is clear that national statistics mask the dynamics of the labor markets and the ability of teacher preparation programs to respond at the state and local level. State policies determine teacher licensure, seniority, tenure, and pension rules, and they differ from one another in ways that can create barriers for cross-state teacher mobility. The strong state role in influencing teacher labor markets results in labor market conditions that vary from state to state and sometimes even from locality to locality.

The finding that labor market trends vary from state to state and even locally is seen in both staffing challenges as well as in teacher turnover. Although teachers develop a number of valuable skills during their preparation, there still remains a mismatch in terms of the preparation teacher candidates seek out and the job opportunities available. A common finding across states is that staffing challenges are generally far greater for schools serving students living in poverty, students who are low-achieving, students of color, rural schools, those geographically far from teacher education programs, and in high-needs subjects, such as science, technology, engineering, and mathematics, and special education. This is similar to what is observed for teacher turnover: there is somewhat more turnover in schools with larger numbers of students from low-income families, students who are low-achieving, and students of color as well as in the south and cities (as compared to suburbs or more rural areas).

Because higher turnover rates have been attributed to lower-quality working conditions, it is important to understand why working conditions matter for teachers' experiences. In particular, schools with higher turnover typically have teachers who are less qualified, in addition to less effective leaders, greater leadership churn, fewer resources, and less adequate facilities. These are long-standing issues with the way the teacher labor market functions (or fails to function well) and merit greater attention. The committee concludes that:

> CONCLUSION 4: Teacher labor markets are quite localized. As a result, national statistics provide a limited understanding of the trends in the K–12 teacher workforce. Local labor markets are shaped by a variety of factors including state rules and regulations regarding licensure, tenure, and pensions.

> CONCLUSION 5: There is a mismatch between the areas of certification chosen by those preparing to be teachers and the areas in which schools and school systems struggle with teacher shortages. For example, there are often many more teacher candidates that are prepared with an elementary education credential than there are slots. At the same time, school systems often struggle to fill science, technology, engineering, and mathematics and special education positions.

> CONCLUSION 6: The current racial/ethnic composition of the teacher workforce does not mirror the racial/ethnic composition of students being served in schools today. The mismatch has grown larger over the past 20 years and is an artifact of both the rapidly changing student population and historical policy decisions connected to school desegregation efforts. There is good evidence that the discrepancy has negative consequences, particularly for underrepresented minority students who often lack teacher role models.

> CONCLUSION 7: Students of color, students from low-income families, and students who are low achieving more often are served by teachers who are less qualified. These inequities have been documented across states, districts, schools within districts, and even within schools.

Teacher Education in Response to Changing Expectations

Creating classroom learning experiences that respond to more rigorous content standards while promoting the success of all students regardless of background is no easy task. Responding to these dual demands is likely to require significant shifts in what teaching looks and sounds like in most U.S. classrooms. Both preservice and inservice education are considered to play key roles in helping teachers respond to the changing conditions of K–12 education; however, the committee also notes the role of the workplace in teacher learning. Chapter 5 provides an overview of the literature on preservice teacher preparation, while Chapters 6 and 7 discuss opportunities for professional development (Chapter 6) and the role of the workplace to support teacher learning (Chapter 7).

As described in Chapter 5, the research base on what makes preservice teacher preparation effective is more limited than the nature of the evidence described in Chapters 6 and 7. This is attributed in part to the variability in the pathways and program models of teacher preparation programs, making it difficult to decipher what was "actually" taught and the accuracy with which it is subsequently measured in student learning. Whereas it is difficult to assess the causal impact of programs on teacher candidates given the wide array of programs (including increasing prevalence of online programs), factors such as coherence and integration across program components, strong mentors and field experiences, and preparation in culturally responsive pedagogy are indicators of promising changes. The difficulty of assessing the causal impact of programs on teacher candidates presents a challenge for understanding the ways in which teachers are being prepared to meet the changes in the expectations of the classroom.

Similarly, as illustrated throughout Chapter 6, inservice experiences for teachers vary widely and there is disagreement in the research community about the strength of the evidence for effective design of professional development. Furthermore, the evidence suggests that inservice experiences alone are not sufficient for shaping teachers' instructional practice. Rather, as described in Chapter 7, what teachers do in their classrooms is shaped by a variety of factors, including the nature of the social relations, material resources, and organizational conditions of the schools and districts in which teachers work. Workplace conditions (e.g., school leadership, salary, resources, mentoring, and induction supports) have also been linked with whether teachers move schools or leave the profession. Moreover, for some teachers, school-level characteristics (e.g., school size, percent of students eligible for free- or reduced-price lunch, student demographics, and teacher demographics) are a determining factor in whether they move schools.

Making substantial changes to current teachers' perspectives and practices will require significant and sustained opportunities for professional learning. Such opportunities encompass opportunities embedded in the school workplace as well as specially designed programs of professional development. Responding productively and on a large scale to new demographics and new expectations for teaching and learning will likely depend on relationships established between external professional development providers and local workplace conditions and learning opportunities. The committee concludes that:

> CONCLUSION 8: The current landscape of preservice teacher education in the United States exists as a large, varied array of programs and pathways. In this respect, it reflects the traditions of state and local control.

> CONCLUSION 9: There has been a significant growth over the past two decades in online teacher education and professional development, but very little is known about the efficacy of this increasingly prevalent mode of providing preservice and inservice education.

> CONCLUSION 10: The research base on preservice teacher preparation supplies little evidence about its impact on teacher candidates and their performance once they are in the classroom. Preservice programs in many states assess the performance of teacher candidates for purposes of licensure, but few states have developed data systems that link information about individual teachers' preservice experiences with other data about those teachers or their performance. Overall, it is difficult to assess the causal impact of teacher preparation programs.

> CONCLUSION 11: Features of the school and district context in which teachers do their work matter greatly for teacher retention, for teachers' attitudes about their work, and for how teachers' preservice and inservice experiences translate into effective classroom instruction. Characteristics of the workplace matter for ensuring that teachers are equipped to respond to the changing expectations.

> CONCLUSION 12: Induction supports for newly credentialed teachers are associated with reduced odds that teachers (a) leave the profession or (b) move schools within the first 5 years of teaching. Providing multiple supports increases the retention of teachers in the profession and reduces teacher migration in the first 5 years.

> CONCLUSION 13: Based on nationally representative surveys, teachers report that they receive minimal opportunities to engage in professional development that is explicitly focused on supporting a broad and diverse student population (e.g., English learners, students who receive special education supports). Moreover, teachers report that when they do receive professional development focused on supporting specific student populations, it tends to be disconnected from the subject matter they teach.

CONCLUSION 14: There is mixed evidence about the impact of professional development on student outcomes. There is better evidence that inservice, content-specific professional development programs with the following characteristics can have a positive impact on student learning:

- work on instructional strategies is specific to the content area;
- professional development is organized around the actual instructional materials teachers use;
- teachers participate with colleagues from their own school; and
- opportunities are built into the professional development sessions to discuss how to adapt the focus to teachers' local needs.

The amount and frequency of professional development is not necessarily related to student learning outcomes; the impact depends on the quality of the professional development.

HIGH-PRIORITY ISSUES REQUIRING IMMEDIATE ACTION

While reports from the National Academies of Sciences, Engineering, and Medicine often provide explicit recommendations to the field, here the committee declined to prescribe specific actions for specific education stakeholders to pursue due to a number of different concerns. The committee made this decision for three reasons: first, there is some disagreement in the field about what kinds of outcomes should be used for making decisions about policy and programming in teacher education and preparation. That is, should student outcomes (such as achievement and completion data) be the sole outcomes used to judge the quality or effectiveness of teacher learning experiences? Can teacher outcomes, such as improved knowledge and classroom instructional practice be used instead of student outcomes, or should a combination of student and teacher outcomes be used?

Second, there is ongoing debate in the field about sufficient evidence that is needed to clearly establish links between the characteristics or design of a program for teachers and student and teacher outcomes. That is, there is not agreement on whether there is enough evidence to date on particular programs or program models that could lead to specific and measurable outcomes (at either the student or teacher level). The committee itself could not come to consensus on what kinds of indicators should be considered as sufficient evidence upon which to make recommendations.

Third, the evidence base itself is uneven. As described throughout this report, the evidence linking preservice teacher education and programming to student outcomes is extremely limited. While the evidence linking inservice programming to student outcomes is somewhat more robust, the committee did not feel that, when taken as a whole, it was enough to warrant specific recommendations. With respect to the role of the workplace in predicting student outcomes, the variability of local contexts is so important to how students fare that it is challenging to make a recommendation about how to improve the workplace that would apply to all contexts.

However, the committee does not wish to suggest that action on the issues highlighted throughout this report is not warranted. On the contrary, the committee has identified four high-priority issues for the U.S. system of preparing and educating teachers that require immediate attention from all stakeholders. Given the variability in local context described throughout this report, the committee offers for each of these issues some considerations for policy makers to take into account as they are deciding how to act.

These are not issues that require the creation of new lines of research in order to inform immediate action: rather, the research in these fields is relatively robust, but the action that stakeholders should take is contingent upon the needs and particularities of their regional and local context. The following four high-priority issues guide the committee's thinking about future action:

1. Preparing Teachers to Meet Changing Expectations
2. Diversifying the Teacher Workforce
3. Ensuring the Equitable Distribution of Teachers
4. Mapping Teacher Preparation to Teacher and Student Outcomes

Within each of these issues, the committee offers a set of considerations that policy makers and others should attend to in order to make decisions for their specific contexts.

Preparing Teachers to Meet Changing Expectations

From the evidence presented throughout the report, it is clear that ensuring teachers have adequate preparation and learning experiences across their careers is paramount for helping teachers meet the changing expectations for them. This is a systemic issue that cannot be left solely to preservice or inservice education. This issue goes far beyond the notion that teachers get "prepared" in their credential program and are then "updated" through job-embedded professional development, and it is important that the relevant constituencies across the entire education system (e.g., preservice preparation programs, inservice professional development providers, states, districts, accrediting bodies, curriculum developers) consider the types of actions in a coordinated way that are needed to ensure that teachers have the time, resources, and learning opportunities to support student learning.

In particular, as described in Chapter 3, meeting the changing expectations that occur in response to the changes in student demographics require teachers to be attentive not only to students' academic and socioemotional learning, but also to the cultural experiences students bring to the classroom. One suggestion is for teacher candidates to have opportunities during preservice preparation to develop culturally aware pedagogy. In addition, the range and complexity of these combined expectations make it important for practicing teachers to have access to high-quality, job-embedded learning opportunities throughout their careers.

The evidence suggests that teachers show better outcomes when they have access to content-specific professional development opportunities that (1) work on instructional strategies specific to the content area, (2) are organized around the actual instructional materials teachers use, (3) allow teachers to participate with colleagues from their own school, and (4) provide opportunities for teachers to discuss how to adapt the focus to their own local needs.

Given the variability that exists at a local level, it is important to consider the types of professional development opportunities that teachers have access to and how those offerings map to the local needs of the schools. For example, if the schools have a large number of English learners, it would likely be beneficial for teachers to have access to opportunities that allow for a deeper appreciation of the students' cultures and experiences while also learning strategies that facilitate content learning and language development. In addition to professional learning that focuses on pedagogy, it may be necessary to (1) examine the instructional materials that teachers have access to, (2) assess whether the instructional materials are aligned to the deeper learning goals exhibited by state standards, and (3) provide teachers with time to work both alone and with others to implement the curriculum. (See also National Academies of Sciences, Engineering, and Medicine [2018] for a richer discussion of promising strategies for STEM subject learning for English learners.)

Diversifying the Teacher Workforce

Given the mismatch between the makeup of the student population and the teacher workforce described in Chapters 2 and 4, there has been substantial attention on how to increase the diversity of the teacher workforce. In particular, there have been efforts at multiple stages of the teacher pathway to recruit and retain teachers of color.

For example, it has been suggested that preservice preparation programs and providers identify and reduce barriers that make it challenging for underrepresented minorities to pursue a path toward a career as a teacher. Potential barriers can be found throughout preservice preparation including recruitment, retention, and placement. When looking at recruitment, it may be beneficial to consider the barriers to access (e.g., standardized testing/praxis) and the potential access teachers can have to programs. For example, some programs have sought to recruit from local, diverse communities, as these are contexts with which potential teacher candidates are familiar (e.g., grow-your-own programs). This could not only provide a greater level of comfort but also reduce the burden of getting to and from school.

A number of different considerations that need to be taken into account when ensuring the retention of teacher candidates of color in a program. One major issue requiring immediate attention is the financial burden associated with becoming a teacher, such as program costs, expectations that preservice teachers will complete unpaid clinical experiences, and other barriers. Addressing this issue may require policy makers and other stakeholders to find ways to offset the costs through fully covering or reimbursing a portion of the educational costs. Other contributing factors that might be leveraged include ongoing mentoring, tutoring, and access to job placement services as part of teacher preparation programs.

Ensuring the Equitable Distribution of Teachers

As highlighted in the evidence in Chapter 4, inequities exist in the distribution of teachers. That is, students of color, low-income students, and low-achieving students typically are served by teachers who are less qualified (Conclusion 7). To help address inequity in the distribution of teachers, state and local policy makers may need to consider ways to make teaching positions in hard-to-staff schools relatively more desirable. This could include providing teachers with higher compensation or reviewing the relationship between compensation packages and recruitment and retention to inform school funding formulas and funding allocations between districts. Moreover, to hire and retain the best teachers, it may be necessary for schools and districts to evaluate and adjust hiring policies and practices as well as consider compensation changes and offer comprehensive induction. As discussed in Chapter 7, the research suggests that being matched with a veteran mentor who can provide coaching and feedback may help with teacher retention.

A central part of ensuring that the teacher workforce is equitably distributed also has to do with ensuring that the workforce is diverse: that is, having a robust supply of teachers of color (as well as those with disabilities) so that the unique assets of these professionals can be put to use in schools. That said, in order to ensure that teachers can recognize and leverage the various assets students are bringing into the classroom, *all* teachers need to be prepared to respond to the needs of a shifting population of students. As outlined in Chapter 2, it is not enough simply to ensure that teachers of color are placed in schools with large concentrations of students of color, nor is that an end-goal that the committee sees as productive.

Mapping Teacher Preparation to Teacher and Student Outcomes

As the committee grappled with how to address the high-priority issues articulated above, it became clear that better infrastructure could help education stakeholders understand the linkages across the teacher education and preparation systems. As noted earlier, because "there is currently little definitive evidence that particular approaches to teacher preparation yield teachers whose students are more successful than others" it is challenging to distill uniform recommendations for how programs could best prepare teachers (NRC, 2010, pp. 62–63). To begin to address this basic question, the committee believes that a comprehensive data system with a feedback loop between teacher preparation programs and the school systems they serve is one potential mechanism that could help education stakeholders as they make determinations about how to address the issues raised above.

One way to achieve this goal could be through the formation of partnerships. That is, teacher preparation programs could document features of the program overall while also keeping track of the experiences each teacher candidate receives. States and districts could use this information to consider the opportunities new teachers might need to be successful in serving their students while also sharing information back to teacher preparation programs on different teacher outcomes. More specifically, the formation of such a data system could allow state departments of education to craft the requirements for individual programs and teacher preparation programs could make better informed decisions about what strategies to use during preservice education.

In particular, teacher preparation programs could collect data that would allow for examining the features of the program that are aligned with meeting the changes in the expectations for K–12 teachers. Some important features to examine might include the overall goals of the program, requirements for admission into the programs, mechanisms for retaining teacher candidates (e.g., mentoring, tutoring), the provisions for integrating coursework preparation and field experience, the timing and nature of student teaching, the courses in pedagogy and academic subjects that are required, teacher candidate evaluations, and placement of teacher candidates. Systemic collection of these data could allow for a deeper understanding of what goes on inside particular teacher preparation programs and could identify aspects of the program that are beneficial for all potential teacher candidates. Systemic collection could also allow for understanding across similar local contexts to add to our understanding of how these aspects play out across states and districts.

Such a data system need not be a comprehensive national one, including all programs, in all states. Indeed, the cost of a national system and the interstate agreements needed, might not, at present, be justified. Instead, individual states or groups of states might extend current data systems, collecting additional data on program features and strengthening connections to data from the districts and schools where program graduates are employed. With that additional data, trustworthy inferences might be made about the effects of program features on performance outcomes. Without allocating some resources for such data system expansions, policy makers will continue to lack information needed to support specific directions for change in teacher preparation.

RESEARCH AGENDA

Overall, through the consideration of research on the teacher workforce, the changing student demographics, the evolving expectations for student learning, and the contributions of teacher education and professional development, a number of different areas in which the field would benefit from more research have been identified. The existing body of research seeks to measure the impact of factors on changes in teacher candidates and teachers (first order effects), and additional research could expand understanding to how the first order effects impact student learning and outcomes (second order effects). This extension would allow providers of preservice and inservice teacher educators to adapt the range of programs, curricula, and other experiences to affect teacher candidates' and teachers' knowledge, skills, and dispositions, as well as the downstream effects of the first order effects on student learning.

The research agenda describes seven areas of potential research:

RESEARCH AREA 1: Preservice Recruitment, Selection, and Teacher Candidate Motivation

- What factors motivate individuals to or discourage individuals from choosing teaching as a profession? How, if at all, do these factors vary by the gender, racial/ethnic group, or age of the candidates? How, if at all, do these factors vary by provider, discipline, and grade level?
- How selective are preservice teacher programs, and which metrics are available to determine selectivity? How does the selectivity vary between providers, disciplines, and grade level?
- What are the factors in preservice teacher education that have the most impact on teacher shortages and diversity of teacher candidates?

RESEARCH AREA 2: Outcomes of Preservice Experiences

- How can field experiences and student teaching experiences be designed to build skills, concepts, and mindsets in teacher candidates? What are the expected learning outcomes associated with these experiences?

- How can the goals between content focus and equity focus converge?
- What are the impacts of technology-enhanced practices on preservice teacher education? This may range from research on understanding the learning opportunities created by simulations, tracing the development of a teacher candidate's practices over time, and evaluating the effects of simulations on novice teachers' perspectives and practice.
- In what ways can preservice teachers benefit from guidance on how to best communicate with students and families using newly available technologies?
- What are the factors in preservice teacher education that have the most impact on inservice teacher outcomes?

RESEARCH AREA 3: Professional Development Outcomes

- How can professional development, which may provide a deeper connection to specific concepts, practices, or issues in a discipline, provide opportunities for teachers to connect and adapt learning outcomes to align with the local curriculum in the classroom?
- How can team and network models inform the development of strong, improvement-oriented professional development community?
- What is the impact of culturally responsive professional development on teachers' practices, as opposed to existing research on shifts in teachers' beliefs and stances? In turn, how, if at all, does the shift in teachers' practices, beliefs, and stances affect student learning?
- How can systemic research across theoretical approaches, professional development designs, and data collection methods build the evidence base for definitive conclusions about the characteristics of effective professional development?
- What do teachers gain in terms of skills, knowledge, and disposition from access to informal resources, such as online repositories of curriculum resources or classroom video and other open source offerings?

RESEARCH AREA 4: Institutional Providers of Preservice and Inservice Education

- How do historically designated minority-serving institutions (historically black colleges and universities and tribal colleges and universities) contribute to preservice and inservice teacher education?
- Do newly formed organization and models, such as the "new Graduate Schools of Education," have differential outcomes for teacher candidates? If so, which factors contribute to the differential outcomes?

- What is the role of the community college sector in increasing the number of teacher candidates?
- What do we know about the efficacy of online teacher preservice education and inservice professional development, which range from programs composed mostly of online components to hybrid models with more frequent in-person components?
- How can the connections be strengthened between preservice providers and inservice teacher education?

RESEARCH AREA 5: Teacher Educator Workforce

- What are the characteristics of the teacher educator workforce, including but not limited to their demographics, personal characteristics, and professional characteristics including their education and credentials, professional experience, teaching ability, and mindsets/beliefs/worldviews?
- What do we know about the recruitment, preparation, and ongoing support of teacher educators?
- In what ways does the teacher educator workforce need to build capacity and knowledge to ensure that K–12 teachers have the knowledge, skills, and dispositions needed?

RESEARCH AREA 6: Labor Market Analysis

- Which incentives have the greatest effect on state and local teacher labor markets? How do these incentives vary based on the structure of state and teacher labor markets?
- How do district policies on the assignment of teachers within and across schools address the disproportionate placement of teachers (mismatch on hiring) and movement of teachers?
- How do different induction supports (including mentoring) impact teacher outcomes, including retention and the impact on quality of teaching in novice teachers? How do the effects vary across novice teachers by preservice education provider, gender, race and ethnicity, and other variables? Is there a relationship between the induction supports; their impact on novice teachers' knowledge, skills, and dispositions; and any secondary impacts related to students' learning outcomes?

RESEARCH AREA 7: Institutional Change

- What policies or practices will lead to significant changes in teacher professional learning, as informed by results from other research on systemic change in both higher education and K–12 settings?

REFERENCES

National Academies of Sciences, Engineering, and Medicine. (2018). *English Learners in STEM Subjects: Transforming Classrooms, Schools, and Lives.* Washington, DC: The National Academies Press.

National Research Council. (2010). *Preparing Teachers: Building Evidence for Sound Policy.* Washington, DC: The National Academies Press.

Appendix

Committee and Staff Biosketches

ROBERT FLODEN *(Chair)* is dean of the College of Education at Michigan State University and a university distinguished professor of teacher education, measurement and quantitative methods, mathematics education, educational psychology, and educational policy. He has studied teacher education and other influences on teaching and learning, including work on the cultures of teaching, teacher development, the character and effects of teacher education, and how policy is linked to classroom practice. He is a member of the National Academy of Education, for which he serves as Secretary-Treasurer. He is coeditor of the *Journal of Teacher Education* and serves on the Board of Directors for the American Association of Colleges for Teacher Education. Floden has a Ph.D. in philosophy in education with a minor in evaluation from Stanford University.

ANNE MARIE BERGEN is a science teaching specialist at Cal Poly State University in San Luis Obispo, California, where she educates the next generation of science, technology, engineering, and math (STEM) teachers using the experience she gained during a 25-year career as an environmental educator and elementary school science instructor. Bergen has contributed to the promotion and improvement of elementary science and STEM at the state and national levels to include chairing the California Teacher Advisory Council for the California Council on Science and Technology. She has won several awards for her skill in the classroom, including California Teacher of the Year, Amgen Award for Science Teaching Excellence, and Presidential Award for Excellence in Science and Math. She has an M.A. in education leadership from St. Mary's.

MALCOLM BUTLER is professor and director of the School of Teacher Education, and coordinator of the Ph.D. Program in Science Education at the University of Central Florida (UCF). Butler also has a secondary appointment with the Learning Sciences Faculty Cluster at UCF. Butler has taught mathematics and science to elementary, middle, and high school students. He has also been affiliated with the College of William and Mary, Texas A&M University-Corpus Christi, the University of Georgia, and the University of South Florida. In addition to other publications, Butler is one of the authors of the K–5 science curriculum, *National Geographic Science*. He has a Ph.D. in curriculum and instruction with an emphasis in science education from the University of Florida.

KENNE DIBNER is a senior program officer with the Board on Science Education. She served as the study director for the National Academies of Sciences, Engineering, and Medicine consensus study report *Science Literacy: Concepts, Contexts, and Consequences*, as well as the deputy director for *Indicators for Monitoring Undergraduate STEM Education*. Prior to this position, Dibner worked as a research associate at Policy Studies Associations, Inc., where she conducted evaluation of education policies and programs for government agencies, foundations, and school districts. She also served as a research consultant with the Center on Education Policy and as a legal intern for the U.S. House of Representatives' Committee on Education and the Workforce. She has a B.A. in English literature from Skidmore College and a Ph.D. in education policy from Michigan State University.

MARCY GARZA DAVIS has worked in education for more for than 20 years and has spent 13 of those years as a school administrator. She is currently the principal at John F. Kennedy Elementary School in West Oso Independent School District in Corpus Christi, Texas. Under her leadership, JFK Elementary is implementing science, technology, engineering, and math curriculum. She is the recipient of Texas A&M University's annual literacy award, which recognizes outstanding work serving students, teachers, and community. Garza Davis earned her B.A. and M.S. at Texas A&M University, Corpus Christi.

DAN GOLDHABER is the director of the Center for Analysis of Longitudinal Data in Education Research (CALDER) at the American Institutes for Research and director of the Center for Education Data & Research (CEDR) at the University of Washington. Both CALDER and CEDR use administrative data to do research that informs decisions about policy and practice. Goldhaber's work focuses on issues of educational productivity and reform at the K–12 level, including the broad array of human capital policies that influence the composition, distribution, and quality of teachers in the workforce, and connections between students' K–12 experiences and postsecondary outcomes. He has a Ph.D. in labor economics from Cornell University.

SUSAN GOMEZ-ZWIEP is professor of science education at California State University, Long Beach (CSULB). Her path into science education began with teaching middle school science in a mid-size, urban school district in Southern California. One of her research areas, science and language development, grew from her experience working with English learners as a classroom teacher, using language to provide equitable access to science learning and to accelerate language development. Gomez-Zwiep is also interested in learning that occurs across content domains, such as integration across English language arts, math, and science. In addition to working with preservice teachers at CSULB, she is heavily involved in teacher professional development and serves as a regional director for the K–12 Alliance at WestEd. She has a Ph.D. in science education from the University of Southern California.

JASON A. GRISSOM is associate professor of public policy and education and (by courtesy) of political science at Vanderbilt University's Peabody College. He serves as faculty director of the Tennessee Education Research Alliance, a research-policy-practice partnership that produces research to inform Tennessee's school improvement efforts. Grissom's research uses large-scale administrative and survey data to answer policy-relevant questions about school leadership, educator mobility, educational equity, and the intersections among the three. He received the Wilder Award for Scholarship in Social Equity and Public Policy, cosponsored by the National Academy of Public Administration and the L. Douglas Wilder School of Government and Public Affairs at Virginia Commonwealth University. Grissom holds a master's in education and a Ph.D. in political economics from Stanford University.

ANNE-LISE HALVORSEN is an associate professor in the Department of Teacher Education and Ph.D. coordinator of the Curriculum, Instruction, and Teacher Education Program at Michigan State University. Her research interests are elementary social studies education, historical inquiry, project-based learning, the history of education, the integration of social studies and literacy, and teacher preparation in the social studies. Halvorsen was awarded the Michigan Council for the Social Studies College Educator of the Year in 2017. She is a former kindergarten teacher and a former curriculum writer for the state of Michigan. Halvorsen has a Ph.D. in educational foundations and policy from the University of Michigan, Ann Arbor.

KARA JACKSON is an associate professor of mathematics education at the University of Washington, Seattle. Her research focuses on specifying forms of practice that support a broad range of learners to participate substantially in rigorous mathematical activity and to develop productive mathematical identities, and how to support teachers to develop such forms of practice at scale (e.g., the development of systems of professional learning across role groups and contexts). She is an executive editor of *Cognition and Instruction*. She taught secondary mathematics in Vanuatu as a Peace Corps volunteer and was a math specialist, supporting both youth and their families, for the Say Yes to Education Foundation in Philadelphia. She has a Ph.D. in education, culture, and society with an emphasis in math education from the University of Pennsylvania, and completed her bachelor's degree in mathematics at Bates College.

BRUCE JOHNSON is professor of environmental learning and science education and dean of the College of Education at the University of Arizona, where he holds the Paul L. Lindsey and Kathy J. Alexander chair. His research includes the teaching and learning of ecological concepts, development of environmental values/attitudes and actions, and curriculum development and evaluation. He serves as director of the Earth Education Research and Evaluation Team, which has conducted research on children's ecological understandings, environmental values/attitudes, and environmental actions worldwide. He is also international program coordinator for The Institute for Earth Education; principal investigator of the Teachers in Industry Program; and Co-Investigator of Promoting Behavioral & Value Change through Outdoor Environmental Education. Previously, he was an elementary and middle school teacher in Arizona and New Mexico and director of outdoor schools in New Mexico and Australia. Johnson has a Ph.D. in educational psychology with a minor in science education from the University of New Mexico.

DEENA KHALIL is an associate professor of curriculum and instruction at Howard University. Khalil's research explores teacher and leader praxes and other influences on teaching and learning, including the affective dimension of teaching and leading; the micro sociocultural and macro sociopolitical dynamics of learning environments; and how teacher and leader development may support their interrogation of the rampant inequities in urban education systems, including access to science, technology, engineering, and math subjects. This work spans multiple domains, including math education, leadership and policy, urban education, and teacher education. She earned her interdisciplinary joint Ph.D. in urban systems, with a focus on urban education policy and math education from Rutgers University, the New Jersey Institute of Technology, and the University of Medicine and Dentistry of New Jersey.

JUDITH WARREN LITTLE is the Carol Liu professor of education policy (emerita) and former dean of the Graduate School of Education at the University of California, Berkeley. She worked as senior program director at Far West Laboratory for Educational Research and Development (now WestEd) before joining the faculty at the University of California, Berkeley, in 1987. Little's research focuses on teachers' work and careers, the organizational and policy contexts of teaching, and teachers' professional development. In recent years, she has also pursued an interest in national and international developments in the composition, quality, distribution, and preparation of the teacher workforce, and has become involved in cross-field studies of education for the professions. She is an elected member of the National Academy of Education, an elected fellow of the American Educational Research Association, and a recipient of the Frank H. Klassen Award for leadership and scholarly contributions in teacher education from the International Council on Education for Teaching. She received her Ph.D. in sociology from the University of Colorado.

TIFFANY NEILL is the executive director of Curriculum and Instruction for the Oklahoma State Board of Education and the past-president for the Council of State Science Supervisors, an organization comprised of state leaders for science education. Neill is also the coprincipal investigator for the National Science Foundation Project, ACESSE, working directly with 13 states to promote equity and coherence in state science education systems. In her role at the Oklahoma State Department of Education, she works to support districts and educators in aligning their curriculum and instruction to standards and supports 13 curriculum directors in similar efforts with various disciplines. Neill is also completing a Ph.D. in science curriculum and instruction at the University of Oklahoma.

THOMAS RUDIN is the director of the Board on Higher Education and Workforce at the National Academies of Sciences, Engineering, and Medicine. Prior to joining the National Academies, Rudin served as senior vice president for career readiness and senior vice president for advocacy, government relations, and development at The College Board. During his tenure at The College Board, he also served as vice president for government relations and executive director of grants planning and management. Before joining The College Board, Rudin was a policy analyst at the National Institutes of Health in Bethesda, Maryland. In the early 1980s, he directed the work of the Governor's Task Force on Science and Technology for North Carolina Governor James B. Hunt, Jr., where he was involved in several new state initiatives. He received a B.A. from Purdue University, and he holds master's degrees in public administration and in social work from the University of North Carolina at Chapel Hill.

LAYNE SCHERER (*Costudy Director*) is a senior program officer with the Board on Higher Education and Workforce at the National Academies of Sciences, Engineering, and Medicine and served as the study director for the consensus report *Graduate STEM Education for the 21st Century*. Prior to joining the National Academies, Scherer was a science assistant at the National Science Foundation with the office of the Assistant Director for Education and Human Resources and served as an executive secretary under the National Science and Technology Council's Committee on STEM Education. As a part of her cross-agency work, Scherer developed an interest in performance management and completed training as a facilitator and graphic recorder with the Performance Improvement Council. She earned her B.A. with concentrations in English literature and the history of art from the University of Michigan and her master's in public policy from the Gerald R. Ford School of Public Policy at the University of Michigan.

AMY STEPHENS (*Costudy Director*) is a senior program officer for the Board on Science Education of the National Academies of Sciences, Engineering, and Medicine. She is also an adjunct professor for the Southern New Hampshire University Psychology Department, teaching graduate-level courses in cognitive psychology. She was the study director for the workshop on *Graduate Training in the Social and Behavioral Sciences* and recently released consensus study report *English Learners in STEM Subjects: Transforming Classrooms, Schools, and Lives*. She is currently the study director for *The Role of Authentic STEM Learning Experiences in Developing Interest and Competencies for Technology and Computing*. She holds a Ph.D. in cognitive neuroscience from Johns Hopkins University.

HEIDI SCHWEINGRUBER is the director for the Board on Science Education at the National Academies of Sciences, Engineering, and Medicine. She has served as study director or costudy director for a wide range of studies, including those on revising national standards for K–12 science education, learning and teaching in grades K–8, and math learning in early childhood. She also coauthored two award-winning books for practitioners that translate findings of National Academies' reports for a broader audience on using research in K–8 science classrooms and on information science education. Prior to joining the National Academies, she worked as a senior research associate at the Institute of Education Sciences in the U.S. Department of Education. She also previously served on the faculty of Rice University and as the director of research for the Rice University School Mathematics Project, and outreach program in K–12 math education. She has a Ph.D. in psychology (developmental) and anthropology and a certificate in culture and cognition, both from the University of Michigan.